# FLYING BLIND

# FLYING BLIND

### BY MICHAEL A. SMERCONISH

**FOREWORD BY SENATOR ARLEN SPECTER**

RUNNING PRESS
PHILADELPHIA · LONDON

9   8   7   6   5   4   3   2   1
Digit on the right indicates the number of this printing

Library of Congress Control Number: 2004095014

ISBN 0-7624-2376-5

Cover design by Whitney Cookman
Interior design by Amanda Richmond
Edited by Greg Jones
Typography: Goudy and Frutiger

This book may be ordered by mail from the publisher.
Please include $2.50 for postage and handling.
**But try your bookstore first!**

Running Press Book Publishers
125 South Twenty-second Street
Philadelphia, Pennsylvania 19103-4399

Visit us on the web!
www.runningpress.com

IN 1955, THE ISRAELI PHILOSOPHER Yishavayahu Leibowitz wrote a letter to David Ben-Gurion, Israel's first prime minister, in which he complained about innocent Palestinians killed during Israeli operations. Ben-Gurion replied, "I received your letter and I do not agree with you. Were all the human ideals to be given to me on the one hand and Israeli security on the other, I would choose Israeli security because while it is good that there be a world full of peace, fraternity, justice and honesty, it is even more important that we be in it."

# CONTENTS

# ✈ FOREWORD

MICHAEL A. SMERCONISH HAS TAKEN "TALK RADIO" TO A new level, using his microphone as a "bully pulpit" to advocate changes in public policy. Applying his Phi Beta Kappa intellect (Lehigh University graduate) and legal analytical skills (University of Pennsylvania Law School), he succeeded in having the U.S. Senate focus on improving U.S. airline security against terrorist attacks.

At a 9/11 hearing, Commissioner John Lehman, Secretary of the Navy under President Reagan, asked National Security Advisor Condoleezza Rice about a reported U.S. policy sanctioning airlines for engaging in secondary screening of more than two passengers of ethnic Arab/Muslim appearance. Dr. Rice responded she was unfamiliar with what policy was in effect, and the Department of Transportation (DOT) denied any such standard. Several airline officials confirmed the reported policy, and DOT records showed several consent decrees with U.S. airlines involving charges of ethnic/racial profiling.

Michael Smerconish then questioned whether "political correctness" was limiting appropriate screening, adding to the risk of terrorists becoming passengers. On his talk show, I cautioned against excluding prospective passengers solely on the bias of appearance, which would constitute racial profiling in violation of civil rights. Our law requires varying degrees of cause or probable cause for an arrest warrant, a search & seizure warrant, reduced cause for a "stop and frisk" or lesser degrees of restraint. At the same time, the law permits some consideration of suspicious appearance/behavior in a balancing act supported by other factors which would justify some restraint.

Adroitly, Michael asked me if this subject would be appropriate for a Senate hearing and would I arrange one. I said yes to both questions. A hearing could find the facts on what was U.S. governmental policy, sensitize both sides on the civil rights/law enforcement issues and perhaps lend to a more objective standard on what ethnicity/appearances should be considered on restraining or even excluding a passenger.

On June 24, 2004, the Transportation Subcommittee of the Senate Appropriations Committee held a hearing with witnesses from the U.S. Department of Transportation, Transportation Security Administration, a civil rights lawyer, an airline representative and, of course, Michael Smerconish. The Subcommittee is pursuing the issue to find a standard, with criteria as objective as possible, to balance airline security with civil rights where suspicious ethnic appearance/behavior is appropriately considered on the totality of circumstances in passenger screening.

Official consideration of this important issue by the Senate is a tribute to a brilliant, ingenious man who has taken a Lehman sound bite, and added the resources at hand (a 50,000 watt radio microphone, a friendly, interested U.S. Senator, then a U.S. Senate Subcommittee), to make a real contribution to public policy while enhancing his own burgeoning, national reputation.

—United States Senator Arlen Specter

✈

# ACKNOWLEDGMENTS

THERE ARE SO MANY TO WHOM I OWE SO MUCH FOR MY professional good fortune. With a prayer that no one is left out, I am grateful to the following individuals for their support of this project, and for the role they have played to give me a platform.

Thank you:

My mother and father, who've each had infinite support for and interest in all that I have tried to do, and my wife, who has unlimited tolerance.

Secretary John Lehman, for prompting my curiosity about the role of political correctness in airline security by having the courage to pursue his responsibilities on the 9/11 Commission with more interest in getting to the heart of our problems than mugging for the cameras.

Friends at the *Philadelphia Daily News*, namely, Zack Stalberg, Michael Days, Frank Burgos, and my editor, Michael Schefer, for enabling me to publish the initial columns on the issue that is now the subject of this book.

Management of The Big Talker 1210AM, for consistently supporting my radio program: Sil Scaglione, Grace Blazer, and Mike Baldini.

Those who do the heavy lifting day after day to make my radio program a success: TC Scornavacchi, Joan Jones, Pete Nelson, "Dr. Bart" Feroe, Frank Canale, and Dave Skalish.

My colleague Sid Mark, who isn't in management and does not play a role in the radio show, but serves as a role model of class and dignity in a brutal business.

Past and current interns who are en route to doing great things: Dr. Anthony Mazzarelli, Sean Hawkins, Elliot Avidan, and Ben Haney. Ben, an undergraduate at Notre Dame, and Elliot, a University of Pennsylvania Law student, worked tirelessly on this project, for which I am grateful.

Joel Hollander and Scott Herman, from Infinity Broadcasting, who've placed great confidence in my work as a broadcaster.

Those who gave me my start in radio: Larry Kane, Chuck Schwartz, and David Rimmer. And to the man who enabled me to get back into radio years later: Roy Shapiro!

James E. Beasley, Esquire, the best trial lawyer in America, who didn't waver when I walked into his law office early one morning and told him I thought it was time to reverse my legal and radio careers.

Michael Katz, my former colleague and trusted assistant editor.

Mary Russell, my former secretary, whose grammar, thank goodness, is far better than my own.

Buz Teacher, for friendship and the quick education about the publishing world that he provided.

Great writers whose counsel I have sought on a variety of projects: Lisa DePaulo, Larry Platt, Ralph Cipriani, Buzz Bissinger, Mike Mallowe, and Sal Paolantonio.

David Curtis Amidon, Jr., my college mentor, who took a guy with 990 on the SATs and turned him into a Phi Beta Kappa graduate.

Michele Malkin and Laurie Mylroie, for counseling me on how to take a story bigger than me to a larger audience.

Pat Croce, for, what else, inspiration!

Greg Jones, for a fine job editing this work.

Senator Arlen Specter, for our long friendship, and for his willingness to bring to the attention of the U.S. Senate the issues raised in this book.

Congressman James Gerlach, for taking an active interest in my radio program and my concerns about airline safety.

Jim Cramer, for inviting me to share these thoughts with your national audience on *Kudlow & Cramer*, and for not running for cover when the Department of Transportation came forward to denigrate what I had said.

Paul Diamond, my smartest friend, whose personal counsel I will miss now that President George W. Bush has nominated him to the federal bench.

George Hiltzik, whose counsel and friendship I value greatly, and Frank Murphy, for taking on a client on a percentage (of nothing) basis.

Glenn Beck, for telling my story to a national audience better than I could.

✈

# INTRODUCTION

I USED TO CURSE OSAMA BIN LADEN WHEN I WAS ASKED TO take my shoes off at airports. Now I blame Norman Mineta, the Secretary of the U.S. Department of Transportation (DOT). And the Transportation Security Administration (TSA). And the Administration that I so fervently support. And the Congress.

Let's be honest. Things are out of control.

We're fighting a war against young Arab male extremists, and yet our government continues to enforce politically correct "random screening" of airline passengers instead of targeting those who look like terrorists. Why? Because they don't want to hurt anyone's feelings. Essentially, they are putting more emphasis on protecting diversity than protecting our safety. In fact, when our government believes that our airlines are focusing attention on passengers who resemble the known terrorists, they fine them millions of dollars!

The nineteen hijackers responsible for 9/11 must be laughing their asses off in hell. Terrorists have engaged the United States in a street fight, and we've arrived wearing boxing gloves. While they plot their next decapitation, and determine who among their teenage followers will now strap on a homicide bomb, the U.S. has become awash in self-flagellation, rationalization, and kvetching over so-called civil rights and liberties.

And we wonder why we can't eradicate terrorism.

Just look at our response to recent events.

Take the Abu Ghraib prison abuse "scandal." We are at war, and our military is using whatever means possible—including the standard inter-rogation tactic of intimidation—to cull information that will keep our troops safe and strengthen our position. No one died or suffered severe physical torture at Abu Ghraib, though the details are unsavory, to be sure—but what about war isn't? Still, there is no moral comparison between putting a leash around a prisoner's neck and the beheadings of

Nick Berg and Paul Johnson. Nevertheless, this "scandal" dominated the news through Congressional inquiries, televised hearings, court-martials, and editorials calling for the ouster of the Secretary of Defense.

And what is the net effect? We've gone so far as to announce an overhaul of interrogation methods—during wartime! (I'm picturing quiche and a warm blanket instead of a rubber hose and a stack of phone books.) Overlooked is the fact that there is no logic or rationality to our enemy. They aren't like us. Our rules don't apply to them. And we sure can't evaluate them through eyeglasses fogged by Chevy Suburbans, flat-screen TVs, Mocha Java, and trips to The Home Depot. They're building bombs and strapping on suicide belts, while we're philosophizing about peace, love, and understanding. Enough already.

Continuing the discussion of how we treat prisoners in wartime, in June of 2004, Attorney General John Ashcroft was called before the Senate Judiciary Committee. The grilling focused on the contents of a policy memo that was written in 2002 to advise the Bush Administration on the limits of pain and suffering legally permitted during enemy interrogations of members of al Qaeda. Ashcroft, the quintessential wartime consigliere, condemned torture but stood his ground and refused to hand over the documents or reveal their contents. The usual suspects revealed themselves through their questioning of Ashcroft, which displayed more concern for the treatment of enemy prisoners than the safety of Americans. Dianne Feinstein, Ted Kennedy, Patrick Leahy, Joe Biden. You get the picture. Biden told Ashcroft that prohibitions against torture are intended to "protect my son in the military. That's why we have these treaties. So when Americans are captured, they are not tortured," referring to the Geneva Convention.[1] It was quite a comment. And it displayed the type of logic that causes me as much concern as the next plot hatched by bin Laden. We're philosophizing about legal principles. They're sitting in caves planning genocide.

Here's another one that galls me. Think about all the debate over the Librarian Act, uh, I mean the Patriot Act. (As former Attorney General Ed Meese once told me, if you want to shut up a Patriot Act critic, just ask him to give you a specific example of its abuse.) People are crying in their beer over Big Brother, claiming this is some partisan-inspired witch-hunt, yet they are unable to cite a single instance of where the Act has been used inappropriately. And forgotten is the fact that the Patriot Act legislation (HR 3162) passed the House by a vote of 357-66 and the Senate by a vote of 98-1,[2] and was immediately signed into law by President Bush on October 26, 2001. Partisan? Hardly.

And how about those derailed efforts to fight terrorism by thinking outside the box? Remember the attempts of Admiral John Poindexter to establish a Web-based futures trading market where experts could bet on the prospects of a terror attack?[3] The point here was that these experts' collective consciousness could be an effective intelligence-gathering technique. Or do you remember Poindexter's work with Total Information Awareness and his desire to expand the database we use to hunt down terrorists?[4] What happened? The plans got scrapped and he got handed his walking papers because people were more concerned about past association with Ollie North than accepting the insights of a military expert on how to get a leg up in the war on terror.

But of all the ways in which political correctness is compromising the war on terror, there is no better example than how we've gone soft in the defense of our airspace. Of all places, it is airline safety that remains most vulnerable to political correctness. Consider the fact that nineteen look-alikes hijacked four airplanes on 9/11, and yet we have a DOT and TSA completely embarrassed by the idea that they should be keeping an eye out for future terrorists who resemble the last ones. Take a look at the mug shots of those nineteen murderers and tell me what you see. Any light complexions? Any light-colored hair? See any blue eyes?

It defies logic that we don't rely upon this information. And it is intolerable that we bend over backwards to nullify it. As I like to tell my radio audience on The Big Talker 1210AM in Philadelphia, if the Philadelphia Police Department was besieged by one-armed muggers on Walnut Street, they wouldn't be spending too much time giving the hairy eyeball to those with both wings!

What is the root cause of this problem? Well, that's what this book is all about. Through a combination of happenstance, inquiry, and exposition,

I think I've come as close as anyone might to putting my finger on the problem and stating its solution. As you will see, my curiosity about the role of political correctness in airline safety was sparked by two things: my own flying experiences and a single question uttered in the 9/11 Commission hearings, which received absolutely no media attention. Little did I know, while watching the hearings on TV one April day, that I would soon start down a long path of discovery regarding who gets stopped for additional scrutiny when flying in a post-9/11 world. And how could I have known that the discovery would be so brutal?

Along the way, I've had the opportunity to get several major players to speak on the record about this issue, including 9/11 Commissioner John Lehman, Mayor Rudy Giuliani, Senator John McCain, Senator Arlen Specter, Congressman John Mica (Chairman of the House Subcommittee on Aviation), Southwest Airlines founder and chairman Herb Kelleher, and former Pentagon spokeswoman Torie Clarke. I've read countless documents about Secretary of Transportation Norman Mineta, analyzed the litigation files of several "discrimination" cases initiated by his office against major airlines after 9/11, and reviewed hundreds of stories from my radio listeners who, like me, question whether we're securing our flights in the correct manner. I've taken an investigation that began with a seemingly minor incident at the Atlantic City airport and rode it all the way to the U.S. Senate, where I testified at a subcommittee hearing called *because of* my investigation. What is the bottom line? A pretty frightening picture in which those responsible for keeping us safe are unwilling to state with clarity exactly who the enemy is, and whose direction in performing their invaluably important task is questionable at best.

It is my hope that this book will serve as the catalyst for some difficult, but necessary, dialogue about how America as a whole can get the upper hand in our battle against those who seek to destroy us and our way of life. I've done my part; I took something I heard on TV and pursued it with an intensity that resulted in a hearing before the U.S. Senate. Now I need your help. But be prepared. Because I intend to tell it like it is, and some are going to be offended.

Let's start with the following multiple-choice test. If you have a computer, I'll bet you've seen it before, but it bears repeating:

**In 1979, the U.S. embassy in Iran was taken over by:**
(a) Norwegians from Ballard
(b) Elvis
(c) A tour bus full of 80-year-old women
(d) Muslim male extremists mostly between the ages of 17 and 40

**In 1983, the U.S. Marine barracks in Beirut was blown up by:**
(a) A pizza delivery boy
(b) Crazed feminists screeching that being able to throw a grenade beyond one's own burst radius was an unfair and sexist requirement in basic training
(c) Geraldo Rivera making up for a slow news day
(d) Muslim male extremists mostly between the ages of 17 and 40

**In 1985, the cruise ship Achille Lauro was hijacked and a 70-year-old American passenger was murdered in his wheelchair and thrown overboard by:**
(a) The Smurfs
(b) Davy Jones
(c) The Little Mermaid
(d) Muslim male extremists mostly between the ages of 17 and 40

**In 1988, Pan Am Flight 103 was bombed by:**
(a) Luca Brazzi, for not being given a part in "Godfather 2"
(b) The Tooth Fairy
(c) Butch and Sundance who had a few sticks of dynamite left over from the train thing
(d) Muslim male extremists mostly between the ages of 17 and 40

The 19 murderers of September 11, 2001. (Turn to page 214 to see the FBI's current list of Most Wanted Terrorists. Notice any similarities?)

**On October 12, 2000, 17 U.S. sailors lost their lives on the USS *Cole*, and this was done by:**
(a) The purple Teletubbie
(b) Gary Condit
(c) LA Crips
(d) Muslim male extremists mostly between the ages of 17 and 40

**On 9/11/01, four airliners were hijacked and destroyed by:**
(a) Bugs Bunny
(b) The Supreme Court of Florida trying to outdo their attempted hijacking of the 2000 Presidential election
(c) Mr. Bean
(d) Muslim male extremists mostly between the ages of 17 and 40

**In December 2001, a person tries to light a shoe bomb on a commercial jetliner and this was done by:**
(a) Mother Theresa
(b) An Italian guy from New York City named "Giacomo".
(c) Hardworking Hispanic farm workers
(d) Muslim male extremists mostly between the ages of 17 and 40

**In 2002 reporter Daniel Pearl was kidnapped and murdered by:**
(a) Bonny and Clyde
(b) Captain Kangaroo
(c) Billy Graham
(d) Muslim male extremists mostly between the ages of 17 and 40

My mother always tells me there is truth in jest. Well, this is a good example. I only wish I knew who wrote it so that I could give them credit. Until then, I'll chalk it up to American ingenuity. Now, in the immortal words of Todd Beamer, "Let's roll!"

# 1: BOARDING

MY WIFE AND I ARE BAD FLIERS. IT'S A WONDER WE EVER travel. She detests flying; I hate checking in. I am not sure where it even began. I've never been bumped from a flight, and yet I get worked into a lather if I can't get a seat assignment before I have to show up at the airport.

No doubt it's largely due to the fact that we have four kids. I can't imagine what I'd do if we got split up; my nerves get frayed going from curbside to the door of the airplane. But after that I am fine. The flight itself is never a problem for me. Usually I sleep. It's the pre-boarding stuff I find distressing. The cattle-call scenario. The lines. The rudeness that is all too common. And, in a post-9/11 world, the added hassle of taking off my shoes, emptying my pockets, showing that my telephone is just that, and stopping just short of undergoing a proctologic exam before we board. It irritates me.

My wife doesn't mind any of this. The flight itself is the killer for her. Any sign of turbulence wipes her out, especially if the kids are flying with us. I always tell her she should take a Halcion and forget it. She tells me that she can't because then she'd miss the turbulence. Go figure.

In the spring of 2004, two and one-half years after 9/11, we flew to Florida for our kids' spring break. We have a place on Florida's West Coast, and were anxious to get away for a week of (mostly) R & R. Seeking refuge from the anxiety of a big airport check-in (and the generally higher-priced fares offered by US Airways in Philadelphia, where we live) we made arrangements to fly from Atlantic City, New Jersey, to Fort Myers, Florida. I had been told good things about Spirit Airlines, and callers to my radio program on The Big Talker said that traveling in and out of Atlantic City's airport was a snap compared to Philly. We were not disappointed. We walked from the curb about twenty steps to the check-in counter before heading to the security screening. A pleasant woman asked for our e-ticket information, and then wanted to know "which one is Michael, Jr.?" I pointed to my 8-year-old. "Oh, that won't work," she said. She then explained that he'd been designated for secondary screening, meaning he would be subjected to more of a search than just taking off his shoes and walking through the metal detector. I told her I would gladly take his place and she obliged.

Wait a minute. What's wrong with this picture?

First of all, why the hell should my 8-year-old be subjected to secondary screening? Was it his menacing Pokemon backpack? The ketchup on his chin? Or maybe the steely glint in his eyes as he played his Gameboy? And furthermore, what does it say about the process of secondary screening if I was so easily able to negotiate taking his place? It tells me the process is a joke!

The funny thing is, we keep clothing in Florida to spare us the need to constantly pack garments, so that day I was traveling with very little gear. I had a cloth briefcase, and the only thing inside it was Sean Hannity's new book, Deliver Us from Evil. As it turned out, the TSA (Transportation Security Administration) employee who had to search me recognized me and claimed to be a listener of my radio show. When he then asked me to empty the briefcase, he couldn't help but smile when he saw Hannity's mug. Hopefully it would have been different if I had been carrying the Koran!

I didn't complain about the added hassle. Instead, I cursed bin Laden under my breath and considered this to be my small part to play in the post-9/11 world. As you will soon see, I no longer believe that to be the case.

For one week, we enjoyed ourselves in Florida. While we were there, the very first televised hearings of the National Commission on Terrorist Attacks upon the United States (a.k.a. the "9/11 Commission") occurred, and I watched with great interest. Madeleine Albright, Colin Powell, William S. Cohen, George Tenet, Sandy Berger, and Richard Armitage all testified. I could not take my eyes off it. And then came Richard A. Clarke, the former National Coordinator for Counterterrorism. Clarke distinguished himself by throwing the Bush Administration under the bus, particularly Condoleezza Rice, and by offering an "apology" to the American people. Said Clarke: "I welcome these hearings because of the opportunity that they provide to the American people to better, to better understand why the tragedy of 9/11 happened and what we must do to prevent a reoccurrence. I also welcome the hearings because it is finally a forum where I can apologize to the loved ones of the victims of 9/11. To them who are in the room, to those of you who are watching on television, your government failed you, those entrusted with protecting you failed you, and I failed you. We tried hard, but that doesn't matter because we failed."[1] Exactly what authority entitled Clarke to be the governmental apologist escaped me, but he was the big story that week nonetheless.

Our Florida place is wired for sound, enabling me to host my radio show from there, which I did while we were on vacation. The 9/11 Commission testimony dominated those broadcasts, as well as the daily newspaper headlines at the time. There was a technical problem one day with my broadcast, and our station engineer, David Skalish, asked me to bring a piece of my sound equipment back home to Philadelphia. It's something called a Comrex Matrix, and it's about the size of a football. As a matter of fact, I call it the "football," a reference to the nuclear "football" that the president carries in case he needs to launch nuclear codes. An uninformed observer would have a tough time identifying what it is, other than to say it is something having to do with electronics. So one week after our arrival, we headed to the Fort Myers airport for a return flight to Atlantic City. This time, my cloth briefcase contained not only Sean Hannity's book, which I had read on the beach, but also the Comrex. Once again, we had electronic tickets and checked in curbside. And once again, the attendant asked me to identify "Michael, Jr." When I did, she said that he had been randomly selected for secondary screening. Incredible. As I did when we had headed southbound, I told this airline attendant that I would gladly take his place. Like the woman at the airport in Atlantic City, she said, "fine." Walking from the curb to the gate, it occurred to me that the Comrex would surely generate questions from security personnel, and to spare myself that hassle, I handed my briefcase to my wife. (Yet another indication of what a joke random screening has become—anyone with a brain knows when they have been selected because of the rudimentary "X" they put on your boarding pass, affording you the opportunity to discard your bomb, box cutter, or Comrex before you go near the TSA!) My wife walked through the metal detector with our four kids without incident, even though she had the Comrex, while I was delayed for a very short time while I was put through a more thorough inspection. "That bastard bin Laden," I still said under my breath as I finally headed to our airplane. And that was the uneventful way in which the trip ended.

Two weeks after our return home, the Bush Administration, after dragging its tail for several days, decided to make Condoleezza Rice available to the 9/11 Commission in a public setting. She testified on April 8, 2004. The eyes of the nation were upon her and I watched from my home. "What did the President know and when did he know it?" was again heard in our nation's capital.

Most media attention on her testimony focused upon the questions posed by Commissioner Richard Ben-Veniste pertaining to the President's Daily Briefing (PDB) of August 6, 2001 (about a month before 9/11).

RICE: What the August 6th PDB said, and perhaps I should read it to you . . .
BEN-VENISTE: We would be happy to have it declassified in full at this time, including its title.
RICE: I believe, Mr. Ben-Veniste, that you've had access to this PDB. But let me just . . .
BEN-VENISTE: But we have not had it declassified so that it can be shown publicly, as you know.
RICE: I believe you've had access to this PDB—exceptional access. But let me address your question.
BEN-VENISTE: Nor could we, prior to today, reveal the title of that PDB.[2]

Well, the title was indeed revealed that day: "bin Laden Determined to Strike in US." It captivated the nation. And understandably so. The full contents of the PDB were made public shortly thereafter by the Bush

Administration. But my attention was elsewhere. I was focused on what I had heard someone other than Ben-Veniste ask Dr. Rice—something that didn't get any coverage on that night's TV news, nor in the next day's newspapers. My attention was on John Lehman, another member of the 9/11 Commission.

Lehman is an interesting character who immediately impressed me. First of all, he's a Philly guy. Maybe some of his no-BS style can be traced to his Jesuit training at St. Joseph's University, or, perhaps, to his experiences flying combat missions over Vietnam as a Navy reserve officer. He's served 25 years in the naval reserve. The man has an impeccable résumé. This is an individual who was only 38-years-old when Ronald Reagan tapped him to be Secretary of the Navy, a post he held from 1981 until 1987, all the while overseeing a massive military buildup. During his tenure as Secretary of the Navy, Lehman was responsible for building up a 600-ship Navy, establishing a strategy of maritime supremacy, and reforming ship and aircraft procurement. Lehman's bona fides also include his service as a staff member to Henry Kissinger on the National Security Council. He was educated not only at St. Joe's, but also had a B.A. and M.A. from Cambridge University, and a Ph.D. from the University of Pennsylvania. In addition, Lehman is the author of numerous books, including *Command of the Seas*, *Making War*, and *On Seas of Glory*. He serves as chairman of the Princess Grace Foundation USA, a charity that provides scholarships, apprenticeships, and fellowships in the art fields to students. (Lehman's involvement in the charity stems from his family ties to Princess Grace: her father was his grandmother's brother, and his mother had been Princess Grace's babysitter.) Now retired from government service, he serves as chairman of J.F. Lehman & Company, a private equity investment firm. Unlike Ben-Veniste, Lehman didn't seem to be playing to the cameras. And he was touching on subject matter that I had never heard so candidly discussed.

His importance, and uniqueness among 9/11 commissioners, was on full display when Condoleezza Rice testified. Lehman chose to utilize his ten primetime minutes questioning Dr. Rice by reminding observers of something that was more important than the partisan bickering which had become all too common. Specifically, Lehman's focus was the transition between the Clinton and Bush Administrations. He told Dr. Rice that he was "struck by the continuity of the policies, rather than the differences," and then he proceeded to ask Dr. Rice a series of blunt questions as to what she was told during the transition. His questions were themselves loaded with facts, and in many ways were more revealing than her answers:

Q: First, during the short or long transition, were you told before the summer that there were functioning al Qaeda cells in the United States?

Q: Were you told that there were numerous young Arab males in flight training, had taken flight training, were in flight training?

Q: Were you told that the U.S. Marshal Program had been changed to drop any U.S. marshals on domestic flights?

Q: Were you told that the red team in FAA—the red teams for 10 years had reported their hard data that the U.S. airport security system never got higher than 20 percent effective and was usually down around 10 percent for 10 straight years?

Q: Were you aware that INS had been lobbying for years to get the airlines to drop the transit-without-visa loophole that enabled terrorists and illegals to simply buy a ticket through the transit-without-visa-waiver and pay the airlines extra money and come in?

Q: Were you aware that the INS had quietly, internally, halved its internal security enforcement budget?

Q: Were you aware that it was the U.S. government-established policy not to question or oppose the sanctuary policies of New York, Los Angeles, Houston, Chicago, San Diego for political reasons, which policy in those cities prohibited the local police from cooperating at all with federal immigration authorities?

Q: Were you aware—to shift a little bit to Saudi Arabia—were you aware of the program that was well established that allowed Saudi citizens to get visas without interviews?

Q: Were you aware of the activities of the Saudi ministry of religious affairs here in the United States during that transition?

Q: Were you aware of the extensive activities of the Saudi government in supporting over 300 radical teaching schools and mosques around the country, including right here in the United States?

Q: Were you aware at the time of the fact that Saudi Arabia had, and were you told that they had in their custody, the CFO and the closest confidant of al Qaeda—of Osama bin Laden, and refused direct access to the United States?

Q: Were you aware that they would not cooperate and give us access to the perpetrators of the Khobar Towers attack?[3]

Go back and read all of that again. It's some scary stuff. As individual points, we'd heard some of it before. But taken together, Lehman's line of inquiry painted the big picture, the collective failures that enabled 9/11 to happen. And not everything Lehman asked Dr. Rice had already received a public airing. There was one nugget in particular that got buried in the proceedings, but I immediately considered it to be worthy of more attention than the President's Daily Briefing. Secretary Lehman asked Dr. Rice this question:

Q: Were you aware that it was the policy . . . to fine airlines if they have more than two young Arab males in secondary questioning because that's discriminatory?[4]

Her reply—that she did not know the "kind of inside arrangements for the FAA"—was inconsequential.[5] My interest was in what Lehman was talking about. What the hell did he mean by saying you can't question more than two Arabs at a time in airport screening? Was there really such a policy and, if so, what motivated it? In the back of my mind, I was also thinking about having just flown to Florida and stepping in for my son, who had been randomly selected for heightened scrutiny before boarding an airplane—on both legs of the trip.

I needed to learn what John Lehman was talking about. Who better to ask than John Lehman?

✈

# 2: READY FOR DEPARTURE

IMMEDIATELY AFTER WATCHING SECRETARY JOHN LEHMAN ask National Security Adviser Condoleezza Rice whether airlines were prevented from questioning more than two Arab males at a time (at the risk of being charged with discrimination), I invited him to appear on my radio program. I was horrified at the thought that in the aftermath of 9/11, a date on which nineteen Arabs launched the greatest assault on American life during my forty-two years of existence, political correctness was handicapping our fight against those who still seek to kill us. Surely Lehman had misspoken, or there was some other explanation for what I'd heard. Either way, I had to have this man spell it out directly.

It didn't take long to get an answer. I caught up with him two days later, on the Saturday of Easter weekend. This was the only time his staff offered me, so instead of speaking with him live during morning drive, I came into the Big Talker studios on a holiday weekend to record our conversation for later airing. This was an important interview; I surely didn't mind. And besides, the conversation was only supposed to last five to ten minutes—the length of one of my show segments between commercials. In the end, I think the relaxed nature of a holiday weekend played to my advantage. My producer, Pete Nelson, rolled tape while I spent thirty-five minutes doing unrestricted Q & A with Lehman. He was about twenty-five miles away from me on his farm in suburban Bucks County, the county of my birth and upbringing. As a matter of fact, we have friends in common, although to my knowledge I had never interacted with him before this conversation. John Lehman was gracious, freewheeling, and direct. Maybe this was due to the fact that there were no handlers on the line, although the more I have learned about him, the less I think that would have mattered. When I asked Secretary Lehman what he was referring to when he questioned Dr. Rice about an Arab quota in airport screening, he pulled no punches.

"We [in the 9/11 Commission] had testimony a couple of months ago from the past president of United Airlines, and current president of American Airlines, that kind of shocked us all. They said under oath that, indeed, the Department of Transportation continued to fine any airline that was caught having more than two people of the same ethnic persuasion in a secondary line for questioning, including, and especially, two Arabs."[1]

This was mind-boggling to me in a post-9/11 world. All that I could think of were the similarities among the nineteen known hijackers. Was he telling me that the PC movement was handcuffing law enforcement from utilizing such information?

"That's really the source, because of this political correctness that became so entrenched in the 1990s, and continues in the current Administration. That no one approves of racial profiling, that is not the issue. But, the fact is that Norwegian women are not, and 85-year-old ladies and aluminum walkers are not, the source of the terrorist threat. The fact is, our enemy is the violent Islamic extremism, and so the overwhelming number of people that one need to worry about are young Arab males, and to ask them a couple of extra questions seems to me to be common sense. Yet if an airline does that in numbers that are more than proportionate to their number in a particular line, then they get fined and that's why you see so many blue-haired old ladies and people that are clearly not of Middle Eastern extraction being hauled out in such numbers because they have to do that, otherwise they get fined."[2]

I love this guy. His was the kind of candor which, unfortunately, is too much the rarity. While others on the 9/11 Commission seemed intent on advancing a partisan agenda, Lehman came across as a guy more interested in getting to the truth of what permitted 9/11 to transpire, and fixing that cause. That may have been due to the manner he got onto the Commission. He wasn't selected by the Bush Administration, nor the Democrats.

"I was not appointed by this Administration, I was appointed by John McCain, and some in this Administration see that as worse than the Democrats, so I have not received a single call from the White House," he reminded me with a laugh.[3]

The creation of the 9/11 Commission was controversial from Day One, and it was not until Senators Joe Lieberman and John McCain joined forces and introduced legislation to create a bipartisan commission with subpoena power to make a full inquiry into 9/11 that the investigation got moving. McCain had negotiated for himself the ability to appoint one of the members; he picked Lehman.

McCain was one of the few Republican senators who wanted this Commission. I shared his view, and despite my support for the Bush Administration (I had served in an appointed capacity in the Administration of his father, Bush 41), I was continually disappointed with the recalcitrance with which the Administration treated the Commission, particularly early on. My view has always been that the American people were entitled to know everything about the events of 9/11, and I for one wanted to hear it all, even if it jeopardized W's reelection. As one with more than a fair share of political experience, I was also continually amazed at how the Administration shot itself in the foot politically by dragging tail in dealing with the Commission. What should have been an opportunity for the Bush Administration to contrast its "get-tough" posture with the drift of the Clinton years started to become a big negative. There was the perception that the President had been hindering the investigation. (Perception, hell. It's the reality.)

First, there was the fumbling of the access to the President's daily briefings. Then the ridiculous plan that the President could be questioned for only one hour. And, finally, the idea that Condoleezza Rice would speak only in private because of the dangerous precedent that might be set. (At that rate, I was worried it was a "precedent" that would affect the Kerry administration.) I remember a particular *New York Times* story about Dr. Rice under this headline: "Panel Hasn't Heard from Official It Wants Most," giving the impression that she hadn't spoken to them, when, in fact, as noted in paragraph six of that article, she had already given them four hours on February 7, 2004.[4] But most Americans believed she was stonewalling them, which wasn't true and could be easily corrected. The bottom line: the American people can handle the truth. I thought they should have it. I know I wanted it. The events of 9/11 were the seminal event in my life outside of births, marriages, and deaths. Although I did not lose anyone close to me on that date, I think about it daily and worry about how it has impacted the world in which my children will, hopefully, raise their children. That, to me, is far more important than any Administration, or the party listed on my voter registration card.

I think the same is true for John Lehman. When we spoke, he was totally uninterested in the blame game. Despite having served in a Republican Administration, Lehman seemed unconcerned in allowing partisanship to drive his participation in the Commission.

"While it's certainly a lot more fun to be doing the 'Who struck John?' and pointing fingers at which policy was more urgent or more important, so forth, the real business of this Commission is to learn the lessons and to find the ways to fix those dysfunctions."[5]

Lehman told me he was not interested in any Clinton vs. Bush assessment. He made it clear to me that he saw everything as more of an institutional failure than any individual failure.

"The real problem that enabled this shoestring operation—it cost less than half a million dollars in total—to succeed and penetrate every single one of our defenses was because of a whole series of longstanding dysfunctions in our security systems."[6]

I pressed him with questions about the differences between the Clinton and Bush Administrations' responses to terrorism, but he didn't take the bait. John Lehman made it clear that if forced to focus on such a choice, he'd be looking in both directions.

"If you look at the blame game, if that is what people want to get into, the Democrats are far more vulnerable because the Clinton Administration was there eight years and did nothing effective against al Qaeda, while the Bush Administration, while they might not have had as much of a sense of urgency, for which they might justifiably be criticized, nevertheless, they were only there for eight months."[7]

I wondered what that meant in the context of our lack of response to the attack on the USS *Cole*, which I believed to be one of a growing list of incidents where we were victimized by terrorism at the hands of young, Arab, extremist males. Lehman again told it like it was.

"Both should have responded. I don't accept the excuses that both Administrations have put forward for not retaliating effectively against the Cole. Everybody knew al Qaeda did it the day after it happened, except the bureaucracy would not take a position on it until they'd gone through their laborious process and treated it like a law enforcement issue, as all terrorism has been, and that's been one of the problems. So you had plenty of time in the Clinton Administration to do a proper counterattack on things that would really make a difference in Afghanistan, and had even longer in the Bush Administration, and they didn't do anything, either."[8]

I told Secretary Lehman that I thought the Bush Administration was running the risk of creating a perception that it has something to hide by balking at numerous requests from the 9/11 Commission. Lehman agreed that this was a perception the Bush Administration had created, and told me that it is an indication of one of the problems that enabled 9/11. "Lawyers run every part of this government," he said.[9]

He also expressed his belief that the public side of the work of the 9/11 Commission was a bit of a distraction. He said he questioned the value of the public hearings themselves.

"Really, in a way these public hearings have been a real distraction from our mission because all of the people you have seen appear, we have already interviewed in depth. We had fifteen hours, for instance, with [former White House counterterrorism coordinator Richard] Clarke in private before he testified in public, so nobody on the Commission learned anything, but it was felt that the public needs to understand and get a view of what was going on. However, once you put the cameras on everybody, it really becomes theater, so particularly the Democrats are under extreme pressure from the Democratic leadership not to let President Bush off the hook. Unfortunately, that brought a partisan edge to the Clarke hearing and, with several of the Commissioners, to the Condi Rice hearing."[10]

Reflecting on the fact that both President Clinton and Vice President Gore had recently completed testimony in front of the Commission,

Lehman said, "All of these people feel very deeply that things are not as they should be within government, that things could have been done better, that we've got to make some . . . changes, and some have begun, but things are by no means where they need to be. So they are not playing politics in private. That is why I think the public hearings are a distraction to our work because we learn nothing. It's theater. But, we have nothing but full cooperation and seriousness in the private meetings where there are no cameras."

I also asked Secretary Lehman how he believed the American people would react to the President's Daily Briefing of August 6, 2001, which had just seen the public light of day. Secretary Lehman said, "It's alarming stuff, and the President was alarmed when he saw it.

"It is not a smoking gun. It is a pulling together of intelligence reporting of the prior, especially six months, and it makes it very clear that there is a heightened activity among terrorists, that there are terrorists in the United States, and that Osama bin Laden is determined to attack in the United States. But nowhere in that PDB will you find anything that says Osama bin Laden or al Qaeda is going to hijack airlines and use them as weapons against targets in the United States. The whole focus was the vulnerability abroad of American embassies and American officials. It was created in response to the president's questions in July. The bottom line is that, yes, there is real threat, and yes, they want to attack in the United States, but we cannot support the more extreme reports that some have sent in. Then, the bureau points out that they have 70 investigations going on in the United States."[11]

So what, then, was to be made of the President's response, or lack thereof, to the PDB, I wondered?

"The whole impression from the bureaucracy to the president was that we have a serious problem, but we're on top of it," Secretary Lehman said.[12]

If not the PDB, then, what was the most damning document regarding intelligence failures that he had seen in his work as part of the 9/11 Commission for over a year?

"We have over two million classified documents that we and our staff have pored over, for over a year. This Administration has given this

Commission more cooperation and access to sensitive documents and people than any administration in history, many times more than the Warren Commission. Everybody has been going through this and nobody had found a smoking gun. There is no smoking gun."[13]

Finally, John Lehman gave me an insight into where the work of the 9/11 Commission would end up.

"What we have is a very clear picture that we had an intelligence community that could not penetrate al Qaeda because of the post-Watergate era dismantling human intelligence and covert actions capabilities. We had a domestic intelligence community that was unable to penetrate the cells operating here in the United States and those pieces of intelligence that they did have, we had no sharing between CIA and FBI of these vital pieces of al Qaeda intelligence. We had the treating of intelligence within the FBI; most of the FBI didn't know what the rest of the FBI had because they had 'case' mindset—that anything gathered had to be sealed and protected because it might be used in a prosecution. We had a Federal Aviation Administration (FAA) that airlines kept totally toothless and ineffective and, therefore, not able to carry out its responsibilities. We had an Immigration and Naturalization Service (INS) that Congress wanted to keep weak because they desired open borders that illegals could penetrate. We had a system endorsed and supported by two Administrations that allowed cities like Los Angeles, New York, Chicago, and Houston to pass laws prohibiting their police from cooperating in any way with Immigration and Naturalization.

"People were saying, and the Clarke testimony implied, that the Bush Administration was told everything, when in fact they were told nothing about what the real problems were, and they were the things that really enabled al Qaeda to do what they did."[14]

Having John Lehman speak on the record and in such detail was an amazing "get" for me, and I was anxious to maximize the reach of the information I had obtained from him on the news of the day. In addition to hosting my daily radio program on The Big Talker, I am a columnist for the *Philadelphia Daily News*. My columns appear on Thursdays, and they usually run about 700 words. But on Easter Sunday, the day after the

Lehman interview, I sat and wrote 2,400 words about the conversation, and then called the *Daily News* editor, Zack Stalberg, at home. I told him what I had. He put me in touch with Michael Days, the managing editor, and Days told me he would gladly run my piece the following morning. That is how on Monday, April 12, 2004, I wrote a significant story for the *Daily News* about John Lehman and the 9/11 Commission. It was titled "Tough Questions from Tough Guy on 9/11 Commission."[15] The piece was given great prominence in the newspaper, and was promoted on the front cover of the tabloid. When I saw the placement, I took it as confirmation that I was onto something much bigger than me. The fact that a member of the 9/11 Commission was willing to state the role of political correctness in compromising airline security was big news, at least in some quarters.

Now fate interceded. This was to become a pattern. As I would pursue my interest in things that Lehman told me, I would benefit from many chance opportunities to question governmental and business leaders about the subject of airline security. I like to describe it as a Forrest Gumpish investigation. (Right place, right time.) And in these situations, I have tried to be a conservative Michael Moore, only with manners. Take this one particular day. The afternoon that my work appeared in the *Daily News*, the Philadelphia Phillies had their home opener and christened a new ballpark: Citizens Bank Park. I attended the game with my father, and ran into Senator Arlen Specter, who was there to enjoy the game with his son (and my close friend, Shanin Specter). I pulled Senator Specter aside for ten minutes and told him about my exchange with Secretary Lehman, all of which, I explained, was detailed in the morning newspaper. Specter hadn't seen it, so I told him how Lehman had implicated political correctness in his assessment of the problems still faced by our airlines. Specter was incredulous, and promised to look into the subject and report back on my radio show. Meanwhile, while I was at the ballpark, Lucianne Goldberg, who runs a fabulous Web site (www.Lucianne.com), posted my piece, and suddenly it was in play nationally. When I saw this, I sent the link to my *Daily News* piece to two journalists for whom I have great respect: Laurie

Mylroie, a Harvard-educated Ph.D. and internationally recognized expert on Iraq and terrorism who was also an associate professor in the Strategy Department at the U.S. Naval War College; and Michele Malkin, who, in my opinion, is the best syndicated columnist in the nation. Mylroie has appeared as a terrorism expert on my program on many occasions, and I consider Malkin a friend. Interestingly, both suggested I forward my piece to Kathryn Lopez at *National Review Online*. Ms. Lopez immediately responded that she would run it the following Thursday. And, after agreeing to run the Lehman piece, Lopez told me she had forwarded it to a friend at the *New York Post*, and that they wanted to run it that Friday. Just like that, this thing had legs!

All that week, while my initial article was disseminated in cyberspace, the issue of whether political correctness was subverting our ability to protect airspace was a source of great discussion on my radio show. My listeners heard every development as it unfolded, and I ran my interview with John Lehman all week long in short five- to eight-minute excerpts, with my commentary and analysis.

As promised, Senator Specter had his staff look into Lehman's assertions and Specter called my program to report his findings. Bottom line: the Department of Transportation denied that they ever had a quota pertaining to the number of individuals of a particular ethnic stripe who could be questioned at any one time. Specter verified that he had spoken to Lehman, and relayed that Lehman confirmed what I had written.

At that point, because of the DOT's denial, I almost let the matter drop. But fate again interceded. Two days after my *Daily News* piece hit—and the same week it was to be reprinted in *National Review Online* and the *New York Post*—I found myself in front of Herb Kelleher, the legendary founder and chairman of Southwest Airlines. The occasion was a businessperson's breakfast organized by The Big Talker to commemorate the arrival of Southwest Airlines into Philadelphia; it had nothing to do with airline security. The schedule called for me to do a live broadcast from a Philadelphia hotel, and literally during a commercial break I was supposed to walk into a ballroom filled with 400 people and introduce Kelleher. Then, immediately after concluding the introduction, I was to get back on the air.

Before the breakfast began, Kelleher was my guest on the radio. What a character. My kind of guy. No BS. Funny. Smart. And honest. My few minutes on the air with him were spent mostly talking about Southwest's discounted fares. But I was itching to get his take on the PC issue as well—if he had a take, that is. I knew from Senator Specter that the DOT was denying the existence of a quota for screening Arabs, but Secretary Lehman was not the type of guy to invent such a charge out of thin air. Moreover, I never considered the issue of political correctness compromising airline security to be limited to whether there were quotas for Arabs standing in line at the airport. The bigger picture to me has always been to what extent are we ready for a candid conversation about who it is that threatens us, and what exactly we are prepared to say and do to stop them. So, with all this in mind, I told Kelleher what Lehman had told me regarding the role of political correctness and airline security. Not only did Kelleher confirm the information, he told me when it began. Perhaps I should not have been surprised.

Kelleher said, "As a matter of fact, it goes back to the Clinton Administration when the Justice Department said they were concerned about equality of treatment with respect to screening. And my understanding is that's why the random element was put in—in other words, where you just choose people at random as opposed to picking them out for some particular reason, and that of course caused a great many more people to be screened."[16]

"So we don't offend?" I asked.

"That was the root of it, yes," he said.[17] I quickly modified my *National Review* piece to include his confirmation of what Lehman was saying, and I decided on the spot that this thing warranted further investigation.

By the way, after I gave Kelleher a brief introduction (in hurried fashion because I had only four minutes until I was due back on live radio) he approached the podium where I stood for the obligatory handshake. He greeted me and leaned over to whisper something in my ear. "Can I smoke in this place?" he wanted to know. What the hell did I care? I'm a cigar smoker. "Sure, go ahead," I told him. He then delivered thirty minutes of remarks while smoking at the podium, an uncommon sight in 2004. One day later, here is what ran in the *National Review Online*:

# LISTEN TO LEHMAN
## THE PRESS ATTENTION IS ON THE WRONG COMMISSIONERS
By Michael Smerconish

Richard Ben-Veniste and Bob Kerrey received the lion's share of media attention paid to last week's 9/11 Commission hearing with Condoleezza Rice, thanks to their generally intemperate questioning style. But while Ben-Veniste and Kerrey played to the cameras, it was their colleague, John Lehman, who was breaking new ground with the national security adviser, but few noticed. Lehman's focus was the transition between the Clinton and Bush administrations. He told Rice that he was "struck by the continuity of the policies rather than the differences," and then he proceeded to ask Rice a series of blunt questions as to what she was told during the transition.

Among Lehman's questions was this: "Were you aware that it was the policy . . . to fine airlines if they have more than two young Arab males in secondary questioning because that's discriminatory?"

Rice replied: "No, I have to say that the kind of inside arrangements for the FAA are not really in my. . . ." (Lehman quickly followed up: "Well, these are not so inside.")

Watching the hearings on television with the rest of the nation, I wondered what in the world Secretary Lehman was talking about. This, I'd never heard before. Was he saying that the security of our airlines had been sacrificed by political correctness? A few days after the klieg lights had faded, I had the chance to ask him.

"We had testimony a couple of months ago from the past president of United, and current president of American Airlines that kind of shocked us all," Lehman told me. "They said under oath that indeed the Department of Transportation continued to fine any airline that was caught having more than two people of the same ethnic persuasion in a secondary line for questioning, including and especially, two Arabs."

Wait a minute. So if airline security had three suspicious Arab guys they had "to let one go because they'd reached a quota?"

That was it, Lehman said, "because of this political correctness that became so entrenched in the 1990s, and continues in current administration. No one approves of racial profiling, that is not the issue. The fact is that Norwegian women are not, and 85-year-old women with aluminum walkers are not, the source of the terrorist threat. The fact is that our enemy is the violent Islamic extremism and the overwhelming number of people that one need to worry about are young Arab males, and to ask them a couple of extra questions seems to me to be common sense, yet if an airline does that in numbers that are more than proportionate to their number in a particular line, then they get fined and that is why you see so many blue-haired old ladies and people that are clearly not of Middle Eastern extraction being hauled out in such numbers because otherwise they get fined."

Wow. How refreshing to hear somebody tell it like it is. Too bad this critically important subject is not receiving the attention afforded to items like the PDB of August 6, 2001. Judging by Secretary Lehman's question of Dr. Rice, this ridiculous policy might still be in place by the Department of Transportation, which would mean our airlines continue to be exposed to great risk of terrorists who travel in threes!

So I ran all of this by Herb Kelleher, the legendary chairman of Southwest Airlines. Kelleher confirmed it, and that it began during the Clinton administration. The Justice Department said it was "concerned about equality of treatment with respect to screening." Kelleher said, "The random element was put in . . . where you just choose people at random as opposed to picking them out for some particular reason, and that of course caused a great many more people to be screened."

"So we don't offend?" I asked.

"That was the root of it, yes," he said.

I'm starting to understand why John McCain was insistent that Secretary Lehman be put on the commission. Like McCain, Lehman isn't beholden to the partisan Democrats, or to the administration. This former Navy reserve officer who flew combat missions over Vietnam and was named Ronald Reagan's Secretary of the Navy when he was just 38 years old, seems only to want the truth exposed, without regard for the blame game that has come to characterize the public proceedings of the 9/11 Commission. I only wish we had nine more like him, in which case I'd be much more confident that we're in the process of getting to the bottom of what went wrong and ensuring it doesn't happen again, instead of the high-stakes partisan skirmish that seems to have taken shape.[18]

As the subject of profiling young Arab males at airports was getting daily play on my radio program, some listeners sent e-mails alerting me to the fact that Ann Coulter had published a column the very day of my *National Review Online* column that hit on the same subject. I was thrilled that someone who commanded a wider platform than I was also on the case. Coulter did focus on Lehman's question about an Arab quota for airport screening, but she mistakenly said that, "In a sane world, Lehman's statement would have made headlines across the country the next day. But not one newspaper, magazine or TV show has mentioned that it is official government policy to prohibit searching more than two Arabs per flight."[19] (I sent an e-mail to her Web site saying that she was mistaken, and I had published three days earlier in the *Philadelphia Daily News*. I never got a reply.)

In addition, on the day my story appeared in the *New York Post*, nationally syndicated radio talk show host Glenn Beck did a program segment on my coverage of this issue, and played sound bites from my interview with Lehman. Glenn is a master storyteller and he spelled the thing out beautifully. This story's legs were growing, but I was about to be caught totally off guard by how the DOT would react.

# 3 : TURBULENCE

SOMEWHERE ALONG THE WAY, *INVESTOR'S BUSINESS DAILY* caught wind of the issue. David Isaac from the newspaper called me because he was interested in writing an editorial about it. Isaac told me that the DOT was denying what I was reporting, and doing so in writing. He said, "Oh, I guess you read their statement to the *Daily News*." I had no idea what he was talking about. I quickly checked with Michael Schefer at the *Philadelphia Daily News* to see if, in fact, some sort of a denial to what I had written had arrived from the DOT. No was the answer. How strange, I thought. I asked Isaac to supply me with his contact at DOT. He obliged. The fellow's name was Brian Turmail, and I quickly requested of him whatever it was that he had issued about my *Daily News* story. Here is what he sent to me:

> In a recent column, a member of the 9/11 Commission was incorrect in telling your newspaper that the Federal Aviation Administration used a quota restricting the number of foreign passengers that could be subjected to secondary screening at one time. Despite the testimony from current and former airline executives cited in your column, secondary screening of passengers is random or behavior based. It is not now, nor has ever been based on ethnicity, religion or appearance.
>
> Your readers should know that the federal government has and will continue to put in place the strongest possible security screening procedures while protecting the civil rights of all passengers in our aviation system.[1]

The DOT was hung up on the quota aspect of Lehman's questioning of Condoleezza Rice. I was already thinking bigger picture. Even if there was not a quota system to limit the number of Arab males who could be pulled out of line for secondary questioning at one time, there was still the more important issue of whether we are looking for people who resemble the 9/11 hijackers or wasting our time with ordinary Americans and others who don't have a single thing in common with the terrorists. With Herb Kelleher's confirmation of Lehman's statements fresh in my mind, I was undeterred. Thankfully, so too was *Investor's Business Daily*. A few days later, they ran this editorial:

## INVESTOR'S BUSINESS DAILY
## DEATH BY PC, Editorial
## By David Isaac

**Homeland Security:** Travelers wondered if airline security went off the deep end when it began yanking old ladies aside and ordering people to remove their shoes.

For that the airlines may be crazy indeed. But on another level, they are clearly rational, given testimony from top airline executives who said they'll be fined for scrutinizing too many young Arab males. Too many in this case is more than two.

At the heart of the story is the desire not to offend any ethnic group or, for that matter, the gods of political correctness.

The disturbing allegation, which is gradually gaining more attention, came to light during questioning of National Security Adviser Condoleezza Rice by 9/11 panel member John Lehman.

Lehman asked if she was aware of a federal policy of fining "airlines if they have more than two young Arab males in secondary questioning because that's discriminatory."

Michael Smerconish, a *Philadelphia Daily News* columnist and a talk show host, followed up with Lehman a few days later. It turns out that Lehman was referring to commission testimony from the presidents of two airlines, United and American.

Their testimony "shocked us all," Lehman said. "They said under oath that indeed the Department of Transportation continued to fine any airline that was caught having more than two people of the same ethnic persuasion in a secondary line for questioning, including and especially, two Arabs." Lehman made the observation that even the most politically correct among us could understand: The source of the terrorist threat is not "Norwegian women" or "85-year-old women with aluminum walkers."

"The overwhelming number of people that one needs to worry about," Lehman said, "are young Arab males, and to ask them a couple of extra questions seems to me to be common sense."

Lehman says the policy began under Clinton. That's understandable. What's worse is that, if true, it continues under Bush, even after 2001's horrific attack on the U.S.

The Department of Transportation denies the airline presidents' claim, saying "Despite the testimony from current and former airline executives . . . secondary screening of passengers is random or behavior based."

But this begs the question: Is the screening of passengers random or behavior based precisely because the airlines will be fined?

It's hard to know who to believe, but maybe hearings planned by Pennsylvania Republican Sen. Arlen Specter will ferret out the truth. If Lehman is right, the White House must end this absurd policy. The U.S. has enough enemies without adding itself to the list.

To put it in bumper stickerese: Political correctness kills.[2]

The subject wouldn't die. I knew from the reaction of my radio listeners that questioning the role of political correctness in airline security was something many were thinking but not saying. CNN, where I appear with regularity, called and booked me to appear on Paula Zahn's program to speak about this issue. One hour before I was to do the show, the segment was scratched and rescheduled for the next night. I didn't think much of it because I have been bumped in the past for breaking news. When it happened again the very next night, after no less than three pre-interviews, I had my suspicions as to whether CNN was willing to air the story. I wondered whether someone from CNN had called the DOT and been dissuaded from running the segment. Ultimately, CNN never called back. Meanwhile, an unsolicited invitation came from CNBC to appear on *Kudlow & Cramer*, the highly rated national cable show co-hosted by another Philly guy with whom I was acquainted, Jim Cramer. Cramer is a brilliant guy, and very un-PC. He is a Harvard grad, where he was editor-in-chief of *The Crimson*, and Harvard Law grad. We had appeared on one another's programs in the past—I on his TV show, he on my radio program.

It turns out that Cramer had just had an experience like my own in traveling to Florida. Apparently, when he got home, he had in his reading stack my column as it appeared in the *New York Post*. Needless to say, he was a receptive ear to what I had to say about the ridiculous nature of our kids being screened while those who resemble the 9/11 hijackers walk on by. I was thrilled to go on *Kudlow & Cramer* on Monday, April 26, 2004, to spell out what I was learning. Here is a transcript of that appearance:

**JIM CRAMER, co-host:** Anyway, I'm just back from vacation. Let me tell you what happened. While boarding our plane, my 11—well, my 12-year-old daughter, just turned 12—was picked out of line to be searched. Yeah, that's right. She was picked out of line, my 12-year-old. This makes no sense to me, and it apparently makes no sense to Navy Secretary John Lehman, a member of the 9/11 Commission, who asked national security advisor Condoleezza Rice about the government's policy of fining the airlines—fining the airlines!—for searching the truly suspicious types. This is Secretary Lehman on a Philadelphia radio show hosted by Michael Smerconish. (He then played the audio with Secretary Lehman.)

Michael, could you please explain to me whether political correctness got in the way of finding, perhaps even stopping, what happened on 9/11?

**MAS:** It would appear—and thank you for having me back, Jim, and hello, Donny. It would appear that yes, that's the case. And let me set this up for you. I recently flew to Florida. On the way to Florida and then on the way back, in my case, it was my eight-year-old son who got pulled out of line and went through the full interrogation, and I'm thinking to myself, 'This is nuts.'

Then we had the testimony of Condoleezza Rice in front of the 9/11 Commission, and Jim, the whole nation is like captivated by Ben-Veniste talking about the PDB [Presidential Daily Briefing]. Me, I was listening to John Lehman when he said to Condoleezza Rice, as you've just articulated, 'Were you aware of the fact that we have this policy where if the airlines pulled out of line more than two individuals of a particular ethnic stripe at once, they'd get fined?' And I say to myself—I jump out of my Barcalounger, I'm like, 'What the heck is he talking about?'

So I then interview Lehman and he offers that explanation that you've just rolled the audio. Now I should tell you, the Department of Transportation denied it. They say, 'Oh, no, you know, we don't limit the number of people you can pull out of line.' The very next day I'm with Herb Kelleher from Southwest [Airlines], and I say, 'Mr. Kelleher, I got to ask you a question,' and then I hit him with what Lehman said, and Kelleher confirmed it. He said, yeah, it dates back to the Clinton years, and we were told—we, the airlines, were told that we needed to be careful in terms of how we conducted our questioning so as not to offend anyone; I'm paraphrasing.

So the answer to your question is, it's horrific, but yes, political correctness has sacrificed the security of the airlines.

**CRAMER:** All right, Michael, who are we more afraid of? Are we more afraid of certain Arab representatives who might sue the system or are we more afraid of—I don't know—I mean, tell me who is generating this?

**MAS:** I have the whole thing figured about. Your child and my eight-year-old son are being pulled out of line—you want me to say it, I'll say it—to placate, you know, Abdul and Jugdish, so that they don't get all offended. 'Hey, why are we being pulled out of line?' Well, you're being pulled out of line because we're fighting a war against Islamic extremists, so they're pulling out the Cramer kid and the Smerconish kid just to placate the guys we're really interested in.

**DONNY DEUTSCH (filling in for Kudlow):** Michael, help me out. If in New York City, there is a murder committed by Asians, and I'm a police officer and I'm looking for the suspect and it's confirmed it's Asians, I'm stopping Asians. I'm not making judgment on Asians, but that's a fact. I'm a liberal guy. What is wrong with profiling? I mean, anybody of Middle Eastern—not just Arabs, Israelis are going to get pulled out because they have a Middle Eastern look—that's reality. That's the world we live in. What is wrong with profiling?

**MAS:** Nothing.

**DEUTSCH:** Will somebody tell me?

**MAS:** I don't know how it became such a dirty word. I mean, there's a thin line between the insidious aspects of profiling and good police work. Hey,

Donny, I've got a brother-in-law who's a cop in New York City. One of his assignments used to be Asian gangs. Why? Because Asian gangs are a problem and they needed somebody to be focused on Asian gangs. Under the logic that we're using with the airlines, somebody could say, 'Oh, that's profiling and it's offensive, and we really shouldn't focus our energies on Asian gangs.'

**DEUTSCH**: So how does this change? Is there any legislation, is there anything—because I think if you took a poll of the American public, I think this one would be a 99-percenter. So where do we go from here?

**MAS**: All right. I want to make it clear, the Department of Transportation says, you know, 'We've never had a quota. We've never said you can only pick out line one or two at a time.' I can tell you that Lehman thus far doesn't appear to be satisfied with the answers, and this is the sleeper of the 9/11 Commission. Everybody else can be focused on 'What did the August 6th PDB say?' and 'What was the president told?' and so forth. This one is where the rubber meets the road, and the 9/11 Commission, I'm told, is going to deal with this issue in their final report.

**CRAMER**: Yeah, but Michael, one of the things that I find disturbing is that, other than your column, I never read or heard about this whole debate.

**DEUTSCH**: True.

**CRAMER**: What is it about the American media that has chosen to make it so that the media refuses to bring up this issue?

**MAS**: I wrote the piece in the *Philadelphia Daily News*. It got picked up by *National Review* and then the *New York Post*, and then it stopped. And thank God you called me today, because, you know, I'm a one-armed paperhanger in Philly trying to get people to focus on this because I think that it's so God-awful. And so I can't answer that question. I don't know why it doesn't have legs. You would think it would have legs.

**CRAMER**: Well, I got to tell you, it's—people to me are so angered about this. I mean, you know, I found out—Michael, I found out from your piece just because people had mailed it to me online. It's kind of like a buzz thing.

I think that there is a tremendous contempt for your view among major media outlets. I really do, Michael. I really think that this is—somehow that people think that you and I, that your kid and my kid—yeah, well, that's the price you pay of freedom. And to me, that's not a price.

**MAS:** Jim, I used to think the logic was that if they pulled out one out of 10 people, that they were absolutely to a certainty assuring that . . . that 10 percent weren't going to cause any problem on the aircraft. Now I believe that this total randomness serves no purpose other than to placate those who they are most interested in. Come on, they're not interested in your kid. They're not interested in my eight-year-old. They know that the blue-haired old ladies with aluminum walkers—which were the words that John Lehman used with me— aren't going to cause the problem. They're worried about lawsuits, they're worried about complaints, they're worried about so-called . . .

**CRAMER:** Right.

**MAS:** . . . civil rights.

**CRAMER:** That's what they're worried . . .

**MAS:** Forget all . . .

**CRAMER:** Right. Now Michael, what I'd like to do—I'm going to call Kelleher, because he's a fabulous guy, loves CNBC. I'm just going to try to get him on the record about this. I don't want this issue to die, and you're the only guy who's leading it.

**MAS:** Listen, I not only—he's a heck of a man, and he pulled no punches, and I've got the audio—I wish I'd have brought that with me—where Kelleher said, 'Yeah, this is exactly the case, and it dates back to the mid-'80s, and we were all told, "Be careful in the way in which you go." You got to be politically correct with the way in which you interrogate at the airport.' That's essentially what he said to me.[3]

The following night, a Tuesday, I was getting out of the shower when the telephone rang. It was Jerry Cohn, who is my stepfather. Jerry is a venture capitalist who rarely misses *Kudlow & Cramer*. "Boy, did the DOT trash you," he said to me as I stood wrapped in a towel. I had no idea what he was talking about. He proceeded to tell me that he was watching *Kudlow & Cramer* and heard a statement read from the DOT which completely discredited my work.

Of course, standing there in the towel, I didn't know exactly what was said that night. All that I had to go on was what Jerry relayed in his call from Florida. But I sure as hell wanted to know what was said about me on national television. The following day, Wednesday, April 28, 2004, I sent an e-mail to Brian Turmail at the DOT and asked him to provide me with whatever he had issued to CNBC for dissemination on national television. His response was nothing short of bizarre. And all it did was further heighten my suspicion about the ways in which the DOT was compromised by political correctness.

This exchange, as you will now see, was priceless. I simply asked the DOT for a copy of the statement that they released about me and my coverage of John Lehman's questioning of Condoleezza Rice in the 9/11 Commission hearings. My intention was to write about whatever they had released to the media. Here is what ensued:

**MAS:** Please provide me whatever statements the DOT has issued concerning comments I have made or things I have written concerning the testimony presented to the 9/11 commission I have a deadline of Noon today and hope you will respond by then.
Thank you

**DOT:** What are you working on now?
If you are writing an additional column my assumption is you will provide an overview of what you plan to write and provide an opportunity for the U.S. Department of Transportation to respond specifically to what you are writing. Cheers,

**MAS:** I have been told that DOT issued some kind of statement to CNBC concerning my 9/11 work. I am asking you if that is the case, and if so, what did you give them?

**DOT:** I'm happy to provide whatever you need. But I'd like to know what you are working on. It is pretty customary to ask a reporter what they are writing and ask for the opportunity to respond completely to the story.

This is relatively common practice, and I'm sure you'll agree quite appropriate. If you would be kind enough to let me know what you are working on, and what specific questions you have, I will send you both what ran on CNBC, and whatever other answers might be appropriate. Cheers,

**MAS:** Let me get this straight. Unless I give you a peek at what I am working on, you will not give to me what you released to a cable news station?

sorry, I don't work for TASS.

I ask that you provide me with whatever you gave CNBC, and if you choose not to, I assure you I will be writing about your refusal. you are only fueling the suspicion of some that the DOT has something to hide.

**DOT:** You are asking me to share with you information sent to another news organization, without any context, without any background, without any opportunity to address some possible column you might write. All this after you have already written one incorrect column and after having been informed of those errors still repeated them on national television.

Again, I am very happy to provide you with all appropriate information needed for your reporting. I just need to know what you are working on, or what questions you have so I can be of assistance and provide you with the most accurate, timely and appropriate information possible.[4]

Thankfully, a CNBC producer was happy to oblige my request for a copy of what had been said on *Kudlow & Cramer*. Here is the exchange that was carried on national television on Tuesday, April 27, 2004:

**JIM CRAMER, co-host:** Michael Smerconish, a Philadelphia radio talk show host, appeared on K&C yesterday and criticized what he said was the government's policy of fining airlines for searching too many of the same kind of suspicious people. The US Department of Transportation sent us the following statement in reply. 'Michael Smerconish's recent column has not received much

coverage because it is wildly incorrect. The secondary screening of airline passengers has always been random or behavior based. The bottom line is the airlines, which were responsible for passenger screenings on September 11th, were never told to limit screening of passengers based on any criteria.'
Hey, that's the Department and that's what they're claiming, all right?

**DONNY DEUTSCH (co-host):** Okay. All right.

**CRAMER:** We got the Smerconish view. We got the DOT view. We present them all.

**DEUTSCH:** I just—well, I'm going to go back and say profiling. I don't know. Not such a dirty word.

**CRAMER:** Yeah, I say no free passes on *Kudlow & Cramer.*

**DEUTSCH:** Yeah. Yeah. Yeah. Right. [5]

I was also able to procure from CNBC—not the DOT—what the DOT was now saying about me. Cramer had been kind; the DOT's full statement was actually uglier than what he read on national television. Here it is:

"Michael Smerconish's recent column has not received much coverage because it is wildly incorrect. There is absolutely no ambiguity about the Federal Aviation Administration's policy on airport security screening before September 11th. The secondary screening of airline passengers has always been random or behavior based. The bottom line is the airlines, which were responsible for passenger screening on September 11th, were never told to limit screening of passengers based on any criteria.

"Even more troubling is that Mr. Smerconish himself admits he was never told such a quota ever existed. He instead has apparently misunderstood complaints expressed about civil rights violations when some air carriers denied service—not screening—to passengers based on their ethnicity. How any legitimate journalist could translate that into a mythical federal government screening quota is hard to fathom."[6]

What bastards. And wait just a minute. "Wildly incorrect"? "How any legitimate journalist. . ."? Did I deserve that slap in the face? I didn't create this story out of thin air. I was relying upon John Lehman, a former Secretary of the United States Navy and current member of the 9/11 Commission. And he was relying upon the sworn testimony of several major airlines' executives. This was the last straw. I'm a talk show host and big city newspaper columnist, not an investigative reporter, but the DOT's heavy-handedness only caused me to roll up my sleeves and try to get to the bottom of just how far off track political correctness had taken us post-9/11. Although suspicious, I had no idea of just how screwed up the situation had become, nor who was to blame. But soon those answers would be clear.

# 4: SOME NOISE FROM THE CABIN

THERE IS ANOTHER REASON I WOULDN'T LET THE MATTER rest. Not only was I angry, but I was getting incredible encouragement from the sidelines. Members of my Big Talker radio audience were now on the warpath thanks to my daily updates (including how I'd been treated by the DOT). They sent me hundreds of e-mails telling their own stories about instances similar to my 8-year-old being singled out for random screening (twice) or to Secretary Lehman's vision of airport screeners targeting "85-year-old women with aluminum walkers" instead of young Arab males.

Some of the stories are typical. Others are absolutely priceless. All present a picture of a flawed system, and reveal the emotion and concern of average Americans. Here is a sampling of what Americans are saying about their experiences with airline security:

I am a 64 year old strawberry blond, Irish/Italian woman boarding at Phila International starting out on my honeymoon to Mexico with a change over at Dallas/Fort Worth airport. After surrendering my sneakers for inspection I was pulled out of line (off to the side) to submit to a hand search by another security guard. The second person in front of me, a male wearing a turban on his head went through with no problem. (No hairy eye ball that I could see) I did not set off any bells or whistles. I was then permitted to proceed to my flight.

————

I have been listening to your fight with the DOT. If I may tell you story of what happened to me and my reserve unit.

I am a Naval Reservist who's unit was recalled for the War on Terror. Upon our return we flew a Delta flight into Atlanta to make a connecting flight to the Norfolk Naval Base in Virgina to be released from active duty.

When it was time to board our flight to Norfolk every one in my unit was pulled aside to be searched by the TSA. Please keep in mind we are traveling with military id's and under Government orders which we had in hand, plus the tickets for the flight where paid for by the Government. The TSA checked over 40 people. Needless to say the plane was 30 to 45 minutes late in leaving.

Once I was done in Norfolk, I had a US Airways flight to Philadelphia. Again, I was pulled aside by the TSA to have myself and my carry on bags searched. Again, I had my military id, orders and a Government ticket. While the TSA agent was going through my things I told the story of your return. The agent told me that TSA does not select the people to be search but it is the airlines themselves that nominate who is to be searched.

This is a short story that not only your 8 yr old and little old ladies are being pulled aside but the people who are fighting the WOT.

Best Regards

---

I have one more crazy story about airport security for you. I'm a federal agent, with an un-named agency, and I have been flying armed for the last 15 years. If you didn't know, there are numerous federal agents, not just air marshals, that fly armed on a daily basis. These agents are usually traveling to and from temporary duty assignments, this includes agents from FBI, Secret Service, DEA, etc. It is just an extra blanket of security that has been around since the 1970's. Unfortunately, the 9/11 hijackers happen to pick flights that did not have any of these agents on board.

In my current assignment, I fly armed at least once a month. When traveling, I must complete the required paperwork with each individual airline. So, I am tagged in the airlines computer as an armed federal agent. The people who check me in at the counter know that I am armed. The flight attendants and pilots are also informed that I'm flying armed. At security, TSA is notified that I am flying armed.

But here is the mind boggling part, on numerous occasions, I have been selected for additional screening at the gate. I tell the screeners who I am and show them my paperwork and my federal identification, but they still want to "wand" me. Now mind you, I have a gun on my hip and they know it, but they still insist on the additional screening. I can't figure out what their looking for? Nail clippers? Nail file? Swiss Army knife? PEOPLE I HAVE A GUN!!!!

I thought it this was just happing to me, but after talking with my colleagues, I found out they are also getting selected for additional screening. And you thought it was crazy that little old ladies were getting picked for this secondary screening.

Michael, I thought you would get a kick out of my airport experiences. Keep up the good work.

Take Care

---

Have loved listening to you since you first came to WPHT many years ago. I have to weigh in about your DOT controversy. My son has just completed his first year at the United States Coast Guard Academy, which is in Groton, CT. This summer he is assigned to a Cutter out of Alameda, CA. to do some training OPS. He flew out of Providence, RI last week, wearing full military uniform. He is blonde haired, blue eyed, was carrying a Sea Bag and military ID, and yup, you guessed it: he was randomly chosen to be searched. I guess they wanted to be sure not to offend any of the 17–40 year olds of Muslim descent. It's a moronic system that is in need of overhaul; we should not be afraid to call a spade a spade. (Oops, guess I am not allowed to say that; someone somewhere in this country could take offense) Keep telling it like it is Michael!

---

Regarding the 9/11 and the DOT, I agree with your info as it relates to standards of discrimination or "the appearance of". While going thru security at PHL this past Christmas eve, there were 5–6 obviously (my personal profiling here?) arab young men in a security line to my right. One man was asked to step aside for a full body screen and the others were allowed to pass with not much more than the standard cursory look. Each one of these men had several small bags which did pass thru the belt and were observed with not as much curiosity as my wifes carry on? I asked one of the security people why they didn't ask more of those guys to "step over here"? The response was, "we can't do that because it would create a situation which could present undue alarm among the flying public." I think that your sons being pulled out of line, for a closer look, created a bigger concern by NOT paying attention to those who could be potential threats.

———————

Recently my good friend Frank Keating, the former governor of Oklahoma, was randomly selected for a full body search by TSA agents at the Oklahoma City airport. The agents recognized Frank and conceded that it was ridiculous to search him. But orders are orders. Frank, being the good-natured fellow that he is, even went along with the agents' requests to pose with them for pictures that they could show their friends and families.

This is just another example of limited government resources being wasted—in time of war—to placate the sensibilities of the politically correct.

———————

In September, 2003, I and my wife and grown children flew to Orlando. At the airport in Philadelphia I was dismayed to see the security screeners ask a woman in her late 70's using a cane to step through the gate and remove her shoes. Your description of those being signaled out for screening to the point. This woman could hardly move the chair and had trouble sitting down let alone bending over to remove her shoes.

I believe that security should be strict but I don't believe it should be ridiculous.

I enjoy your show and look forward to your comments on the DOT and TSA reluctance to cross that Political Correctness line.

———————

Recently I have been flying quite often. I am 57 Caucasian (I hate the term white), 5'8" and bald. Up to two years ago I held a high level clearance with the department of Defense (I no longer work in that area). I have no police record, married 35 yrs to the same person with two kids. In other words, i'm one of the good guys. I get the special treatment at least 50% of my boardings. I'm so conditioned to it now that I take off half my clothes before I go through the detector. It saves time.

My conclusion. They are profiling. Short, bald, aging caucasian males. You're a target.

---

Mike, you are right on the money, keep pressing. To add to your list of examples: Medal of Honor recipient retired General Joe Foss (WWII) was pulled out of line by airport security (believe it was sometime in 2002) they made him remove his shoes, checked his baggage, and refused to let him get on the plane with his Medal of Honor, citing that it could be used as a 'weapon'. The man was 80+ years old!

My radio listeners were a terrific sanity check for me. They were hot under the collar when confronted with what I'd uncovered so far. And they were applying their own life experiences to the information that was forthcoming from my program. Secretary Lehman raised the issue of whether airport security capped the number of individuals of one ethnic stripe who were being singled out for secondary questioning at a time. That question rang true with my listeners. It was a plausible explanation to what they had seen at airports themselves. The DOT steadfastly denied this assertion. And the DOT was anxious to make clear that its screening was always random or behavior-based. But to me and to my listeners, that was an illogical way of confronting the security threat. What justification could possibly exist for "randomly" screening an 85-year-old woman with an aluminum walker, or a U.S. military person in uniform, or my 8-year-old son? It made no sense within our current state of war. The obvious answer was that these types of people were being singled out to placate those who really should be the subject of our focus.

It was time for me to dig deeper, starting with the transcripts of the 9/11 Commission. I was anxious to see exactly what had led Secretary Lehman to raise this issue. I was not to be disappointed.

# 5: REACHING MACH SPEED

THE TRANSCRIPTS OF THE 9/11 COMMISSION HEARINGS TO date were all posted online. It was past time for me to read the publicly available testimony to see where it led on the political-correctness front. I probably should have done it sooner. It didn't take a great deal of searching to find justification for John Lehman's questioning of Condoleezza Rice.

On January 27, 2004, the Commission heard from a panel of witnesses: Edmond Soliday, former security chief for United Airlines; Andrew Studdert, former COO of United; and Gerard Arpey, CEO for American. There were several panels of witnesses on this day of hearings which took place in the Hart Senate Office Building in Washington, D.C. (The testimony on the previous day concerned how the 9/11 terrorists were able to circumvent the border controls the United States had in place at the time.) On this day, the testimony looked at what confronted the terrorists in the final stage of their mission of mass murder: the American civil aviation security system as it existed in early September 2001.[1] This testimony received no media attention. Instead, the spotlight was on a stunning audiotape of the voice of Betty Ong—an attendant aboard American Flight 11. Ong was seated in the back of that Boeing 767 steadily narrating the scene while Mohammed Atta headed for the North Tower of the World Trade Center. In a very calm, professional and poised demeanor, Betty Ong relayed to American Airlines Operations Specialist Nydia Gonzalez detailed information of the events unfolding on Flight 11. With the assistance of her fellow crew members, Ong was able to provide vital information that would later prove crucial to the investigation. For approximately twenty-three minutes Ong patiently told American representatives on the ground that she thought they were being hijacked because two or three men had gained access to the cockpit and the cabin crew couldn't communicate with the pilots.[2] The audio tape was spellbinding stuff:

MALE VOICE: Sure. What is your name?

BETTY ONG: Okay, my name is Betty Ong. I'm number 3 on Flight 11.

MALE VOICE: Okay.

BETTY ONG: And the cockpit is not answering their phone. And there's somebody stabbed in business class. And there's . . . we can't breathe in business class. Somebody's got mace or something.

MALE VOICE: Can you describe the person that you said—someone is what in business class?

BETTY ONG: I'm sitting in the back. Somebody's coming back from business. If you can hold on for one second, they're coming back.

BETTY ONG: Okay. Our number 1 got stabbed. Our purser is stabbed. Nobody knows who is stabbed who, and we can't even get up to business class right now cause nobody can breathe. Our number 1 is stabbed right now. And who else is . . .

MALE VOICE: Okay, and do we . . .

BETTY ONG: And our number 5 . . . our first class passengers are . . . galley flight attendant and our purser has been stabbed. And we can't get into the cockpit, the door won't open. Hello?

MALE VOICE: Yeah, I'm taking it down. All the information. We're also, you know, of course, recording this. At this point . . .

FEMALE VOICE: This is Operations. What flight number are we talking about?

MALE VOICE: Flight 12.

FEMALE VOICE: Flight 12? Okay. I'm getting . . .

BETTY ONG: No. We're on Flight 11 right now. This is Flight 11.

MALE VOICE: It's Flight 11, I'm sorry Nydia.

BETTY ONG: Boston to Los Angeles.

MALE VOICE: Yes.

BETTY ONG: Our number 1 has been stabbed and our 5 has been stabbed. Can anybody get up to the cockpit? Can anybody get up to the cockpit? Okay. We can't even get into the cockpit. We don't know who's up there.

MALE VOICE: Well, if they were shrewd they would keep the door closed and—

BETTY ONG: I'm sorry?

MALE VOICE: Would they not maintain a sterile cockpit?

BETTY ONG: I think the guys are up there. They might have gone there—

jammed their way up there, or something. Nobody can call the cockpit. We can't even get inside. Is anybody still there?

**MALE VOICE:** Yes, we're still here.

**FEMALE VOICE:** Okay.

**BETTY ONG:** I'm staying on the line as well.

**MALE VOICE:** Okay.

**NYDIA GONZALEZ:** Hi, who is calling reservations? Is this one of the flight attendants, or who? Who are you, hun?

**MALE VOICE:** She gave her name as Betty Ong. . . .[3]

This was the first public airing of 4½ minutes of what was recorded from Betty Ong. Understandably, it dominated the news instead of the testimony of the airline executives who collectively raised the specter of political correctness as a contributing factor to our inability to prevent 9/11. And even though these executives' testimony did not win widespread airtime and column inches with the media, it was critically important to an understanding of what went wrong on 9/11 and the trouble that still plagues our security.

In his testimony, security expert Soliday told the Commission:

"Quite frankly, if you look at the record, we tested numerous things long before they were mandated. Immediately after TWA 800, we, as a company, talked with the FAA and said that we are prepared to move forward with some security measures to ramp up because we don't know what caused this. The problem is—and you can make light of it, if you like—a citizen does not have the right to search and seize. There are privacy issues and, for example, as a company who was prepared to roll CAPPS [Computer Assisted Passenger Prescreening System] out and did roll it out long before any other company, a visitor from the Justice Department who told me that if I had more than three people of the same ethnic origin in line for additional screening, our system would be shut down as discriminatory."[4]

Ah ha! That must have been the basis for Lehman's questioning of Dr. Rice on the Arab quota. So how in the hell could the DOT call me "wildly incorrect" when reporting so? By now I was beginning to picture a painful scenario: Imagine if, on 9/11, as American Airlines Flight 11 was boarding at Logan Airport in Boston, airline security believed there to be something suspicious about the passengers Satam M.A. al-Suqami, Waleed M. Alshehri, Wail M. Alshehri, Mohammed Atta, and Abdulaziz Alomari—the five hijackers. Amazingly, airport security could not have interviewed all of them, because that would have subjected the airline to a penalty.

There was more.

Arpey, the CEO of American, told the 9/11 Commission that when crew members had been uncomfortable with passengers on airplanes and asked that they be removed, the DOT sued the airline!

"But if I could share some history with you," Arpey stated, "how that law has been applied to us is that when we have tried to deny boarding— most recently after 9/11, 38 of our captains denied boarding to people they thought were a threat—those people filed complaints with the DOT, we were sued, and we were asked not to do it again."[5]

Mr. Studdert, the former COO of United, told the 9/11 Commission that he believed United had just been fined for similar behavior.[6] Pretty distressing, if you ask me. Logic dictates that airport security take a longer, harder look at individuals who have ethnic, religious, nationality, and appearance factors in common with the Islamic extremist Middle Eastern men who have initiated war against us. It's time for the DOT and federal legislators to go back and look at the mug shots of the nineteen hijackers, because none of those guys look like my 8-year-old.

Senator Bob Kerrey must have been thinking the same thing. In the midst of these executives' testimony, he said, "There's a couple of relatively simple things that could be done prior to people getting on airplanes and I think, for political reasons, we don't want to do it. And I think the American people want you to tell us what are those simple things. And if the politicians are afraid—the elected politicians, are afraid, we need to give them some room and give them permission to do it because I mean I see a lot of stuff being done here. . . . You've got to figure out how to keep people off planes that are willing to die in the act of killing passengers and killing other people on the ground, because I think—I personally feel that unless you provide us with that information, it is not likely to come from anybody else."[7]

James M. Loy, the Deputy Secretary of the Department of Homeland Security (which oversees the TSA), testified that same day—January 27—before the 9/11 Commission. Secretary Lehman told Loy that he was "surprised to hear from an earlier panel of airline officials, former and current, to learn that political correctness is still very much being enforced. . . . And I find after the experience of 9/11, that to continue that kind of political correctness, that they can't focus their attention on people that fit the profile when we're in a war against Muslim fundamentalism, that you look for Muslim fundamentalists, to be idiotic. Tell me it ain't true."

Admiral Loy proceeded to tell Secretary Lehman, "It ain't true, sir. . . ."[8]

I wasn't convinced. By now I had heard and seen too much. The listeners of The Big Talker were flooding me with e-mail confirming my suspicions. Current and former executives of airlines were citing specific incidents. And I was taking every opportunity to ask people of power what they knew of the subject. I kept U.S. Senator Arlen Specter in the loop on a weekly basis, and was grateful for his interest. At his core, Specter is the quintessential district attorney, which is how he got his start in politics. He is a tenacious interrogator and the kind of guy who will not let an issue go that interests him. I was doing my best to keep it on his radar screen, and to get it on the radar screen of anyone else I thought could impact the debate. Like his colleague, John McCain.

On April 19, 2004, I secured an interview with Senator McCain. I told him how I'd become interested in the issue when his appointee to the 9/11 Commission, John Lehman, was questioning Dr. Rice.

**MAS:** Senator McCain, what reaction do you have to John Lehman explaining to me why, uh, is that not mind-boggling?

**MCCAIN:** It's mind-boggling to a point where I can assure you, Michael, I will soon as I return—I'm in New York right now—soon as I return to Washington I . . . I will check it out and I think it's legitimate. But I would have thought it would have changed after 9/11.[9]

My next stop would be the law library, to look into the airline litigation on alleged "discrimination" post-9/11. My suspicions were about to be confirmed.

# 6: LIFT YOUR TRAY TABLES AND FASTEN YOUR SEATBELTS

THE GOOD NEWS IS THAT THE DOT HAS BEEN ACTIVE ON the litigation front since 9/11. The bad news is that this action has come in the form of a politically correct assault against airlines whose pilots were just trying to protect themselves and their passengers from a repeat of that fateful day.

This is the picture that emerges from a review of publicly available documents concerning litigation begun by the DOT and its Aviation Enforcement Office (AEO). What's worse, the DOT has included in its PC crusade the two airlines that suffered the most on 9/11: American and United. The 9/11 hijackers murdered the pilots and crew (and passengers) aboard American Airlines Flight 11, American Airlines Flight 77, United Airlines Flight 175, and United Airlines Flight 93. These two airlines lost a total of 33 personnel that day—8 pilots and 25 crew.

Thankfully, the law does not come down on the side of the DOT's crusade. But that hasn't stopped the DOT's Aviation Enforcement Office from brandishing its own little brand of terrorism. This will take a little explanation.

The pertinent legal history on airline safety has its roots in the turbulent 1960s. That's when a different breed of whackos other than the ones we are confronting today first latched onto the idea of using airplanes for their schemes. Picture Cubans wanting to return to Havana instead of Islamic extremists intent on crashing into American monuments. The Federal Aviation Act of 1958 (with relevant amendments made in 1961) placed the responsibility for passenger safety squarely on the shoulders of the airlines, requiring them to refuse passage in some instances, and empowering the airlines to make judgment calls in a broad range of other circumstances. Early court decisions that interpreted the Federal Aviation Act consistently recognized the overwhelming responsibility of the airlines for the safety of passengers and crew. Any courts forced to weigh a balance between the so-called civil rights and liberties of a single passenger against the safety interests of the other passengers had generally come down on the side of protecting the many. Which makes sense.

In a pre-9/11 world, a typical case was that which was decided in 1975 by the Honorable Robert P. Anderson of the Second Circuit Court of Appeals, based in New York. A passenger by the name of Robert Williams had sought, and been denied, passage on a TWA flight from London to Detroit. Williams was an American citizen who, years before, had fled his home in North Carolina for Canada, then Cuba, then China, to escape the FBI and charges of kidnapping. Eight years later, he decided he was ready to come home and wanted to surrender to the authorities. Williams received a visa from the U.S. Embassy in Tanzania, then flew to London for a TWA flight back home.[1] Fortunately, TWA refused to allow Williams aboard because it had been warned by the FBI that he was a fugitive for whom there was an outstanding warrant. A TWA vice president had asked for, and received, a copy of the warrant for Robert Williams, which read as follows:

**CAUTION. WILLIAMS ALLEGEDLY HAS POSSESSED A LARGE QUANTITY OF FIREARMS, INCLUDING A .45 CALIBER PISTOL WHICH HE CARRIES IN HIS CAR. HE HAS PREVIOUSLY BEEN DIAGNOSED AS SCHIZOPHRENIC AND HAS ADVOCATED AND THREATENED VIOLENCE. WILLIAMS SHOULD BE CONSIDERED ARMED AND EXTREMELY DANGEROUS.**

No wonder TWA didn't want him on the airplane. (Hey, I wouldn't either; this is usually the guy they seat next to me!)

Williams filed a lawsuit against TWA, claiming unjust discrimination and undue prejudice, but his claim just didn't have wings. Sorry. Judge Anderson noted that the law permitted an airline to refuse service to a customer "when, in the opinion of the air carrier, such transportation would or might be inimical to safety of flight." According to Judge Anderson, as long as the pilot did not act capriciously or arbitrarily, based upon what he or she knew at the time, then the airline deserved some latitude, especially in light of the law's demand that air carriers perform their services "with the highest possible degree of safety in the public interest."[2]

For decades, courts at all levels decided cases similarly, recognizing that the airlines had the difficult responsibility of deciding who gets passage, and who needs to be shown the door because of concerns for passenger safety. Strangely, this changed on 9/11. And not in the way you would think. While one would have expected the DOT to strengthen the airlines' authority at a time when our nation was under attack by terrorists using airplanes as offensive weapons, the exact opposite occurred. The discretion that had for years gone unquestioned was now called into light. The DOT sought to punish the airlines for discretionary calls made by pilots in the final moments before a scheduled takeoff where those pilots felt that the safety of the airplane and its passengers was in jeopardy because of a particular passenger. Particularly when that passenger resembled the 9/11 terrorists!

Let me be clear about this: it wasn't Congress or the courts that went awry. The statutory law hasn't changed. And the common law—meaning those cases relying upon legal precedent—continues to reflect the court's recognition that the pilot is the captain of the ship and, in the end, that judgment calls must be left to him.

Let me give another example. Consider the case of Muhammad Al-Qudhai'een and his friend Hamdan Al-Shalawi. This is an interesting case because it has pre-9/11 facts, but was decided in a post-9/11 world. And even when pre-9/11 circumstances were viewed in hindsight, the court in this matter afforded the airlines the right and responsibility to make the final boarding call.

These two men were scheduled to fly on America West Flight 90 from Phoenix to Washington, D.C. on November 19, 1999. They did not do anything to overtly threaten anyone; they did not, as court records indicate, "assault or threaten to assault a passenger or crew member; they were not hostile or disruptive but were in fact described as being 'calm' when arrested." No one, least of all America West, claimed that they made a bomb threat, threatened to hijack the plane, or possessed weapons. Nevertheless, Captain Robert Patterson chose to have these two gents removed from the flight. Why, you are wondering? Because they ignored warnings from the flight crew.[3]

Mr. Al-Qudhai'een had gotten up before takeoff and asked his friend, Mr. Al-Shalawi, who was sitting elsewhere, to come and sit by him. He also approached the first class section without permission, allegedly to use the bathroom, but the crew saw him reaching for the flight deck door. He also asked several flight attendants identical questions about the layover before Washington, D.C. and whether this particular plane would be heading for the Capitol. His persistent questions about the plane's final destination and his eagerness to sit with his friend set off all sorts of alarm bells with the crew.[4] Their gut-checks told them something was up, just in the same way that Jose Melendez-Perez didn't feel right about Mohammed Kahtani when he screened him at the Orlando International Airport on August 4, 2001 (more about him later).

Ultimately, this 2003 decision in response to the airline's motion for summary judgment supported Captain Patterson's actions in removing the two men. The judge who wrote the opinion, the Honorable George C. Smith of the Federal District Court based in Columbus, Ohio, acknowledged that the recent crash of an Egypt Air flight could have been floating around the flight crew's minds—and that this mental connection would have been understandable. It stands as yet another example of a court giving the benefit of the doubt to the people who were on the scene and responsible for the lives of others.

In fact, when dealing with charges of racial profiling, courts have confirmed that they understand the pressure on the airlines and their crews, and will still afford them sufficient latitude in the name of passenger safety. Michael Dasrath's case against Continental Airlines is one such example. In 2002, Dasrath sued Continental in Federal Court in New Jersey, alleging that the airline discriminated against him by removing him from a flight from Newark to Tampa.[5] On his way home to see his wife and children, Dasrath witnessed a passenger rather intensely observing him and two other men, one from the Philippines and one from Sri Lanka. The three men had been sitting in different sections of the plane, but one of the men was seen handing the other a cell phone and briefly talking before moving on to his seat. Dasrath did not speak to the other two men.

The observant passenger spoke with the captain, suggesting that the men were acting suspiciously. The pilot then had Dasrath and the other two men removed from the airplane. Senior judge Dickinson R. Debevoise, deciding a motion to dismiss the case, allowed it to move forward but cautioned:

"In the present case, it should not be forgotten that the decisions at issue were made in an atmosphere pervaded by the fears and [uncertainties] arising from the events of September 11th, 2001. There is no denying that, as the Court of Appeals recently observed, those events and their aftermath are 'reflected in a thousand ways in legislative and national policy, the habits of daily living, and our collective psyches.'"[6]

This decision is typical of many found in the common law, insofar as it represents the view that, in the end, it is the airlines that must determine who gets to fly, and Congress had long since enshrined in law a standard that Judge Debevoise admitted "is a very lenient one" in favor of the air crew's discretion.[7]

Meanwhile, statutory law is equally reasonable. Spelled out are those things an airline cannot do: Airlines cannot refuse passage to an individual because of that person's race, color, national origin, religion, sex, or ancestry. Nor can air carriers and foreign air carriers engage in unreasonable discrimination against individuals on flights between the U.S. and foreign points. And U.S. carriers are required to provide safe and adequate transportation, and are prohibited from engaging in unfair and deceptive practices.[8]

Also made clear is the fact that the pilot-in-command must not allow a passenger to depart on a flight if he or she believes that carriage of that passenger is or might be inimical to safety.[9] It's not just that the law *allows* the airlines to determine who, for safety reasons, gets to fly and who does not. The law *demands* that the airlines make such a call.

So, what went wrong with such a practical system after 9/11?

Norman Mineta, that's what—or who. A lifelong Democrat, a Clinton-era appointee, and a holdover in more ways than one. As Secretary of the DOT, it was he who grounded all airplanes in the hours after tragedy struck at the World Trade Center, the Pentagon, and Shanksville, Pennsylvania. (A good move, no doubt.) But when the smoke cleared, Mineta's concern that civil rights and liberties of passengers be upheld at all costs trumped his concern for airline safety. He became hell-bent on the idea that the airlines needed to be disciplined for singling out individuals who looked like the nineteen hijackers on 9/11 for heightened scrutiny. He drove home this message in DOT memoranda, public speeches, and some high-profile television interviews (which will be discussed in the next chapter).

What cannot be overlooked is the fact that Mineta brought to his work considerable biases shaped by his own family's treatment as Japanese Americans in the immediate aftermath of Pearl Harbor. So strong are his feelings, and so deeply held are his views, that I question his fitness to serve as the Secretary of Transportation in the aftermath of 9/11.

Energized by Secretary Mineta and anxious to be seen actually doing something after 9/11, the lumbering DOT bureaucracy turned its litigation guns on the airlines instead of the terrorists. Not for breaches in security, mind you, but for discrimination. And, when the government created the Transportation Security Administration, initially placing it in Norman Mineta's Department of Transportation and tasking it with protecting our airports, that entity adopted the Mineta mindset, as did the entire department.

That's where the trouble begins. And it is within the structure of the DOT that the problem escalates. The DOT, like so many government bureaucracies, lives by its own set of laws with its own set of judges to enforce them. They even have their own courts. This is traditionally where you would take your complaint that the airlines forgot to bring your aging grandmother a wheelchair. The DOT also uses this same internal resource to handle claims of all sorts of aggrieved people, including individuals who believe their civil rights have been compromised. The best part? They don't need to follow the lead of federal courts as long as they can argue that their interpretation is reasonable![10]

There were three enforcement actions initiated by the Aviation Enforcement Office in the immediate aftermath of 9/11. The crimes? Political incorrectness. On the receiving end were Continental, American, and United; the latter two lost two airplanes and a total of thirty-three employees on 9/11 at the hands of nineteen lookalikes.

Continental was accused by the DOT of "noncompliance with Federal statues prohibiting air carriers from subjecting any air traveler to discrimination on the basis of race, color, national origin, religion, sex or ancestry."[11] The DOT's AEO contended that some airline passengers were treated in a manner inconsistent with statutes prohibiting discrimination. Continental "firmly" denied the allegations, but in order to avoid protracted litigation, resolved the dispute by paying $500,000.00 toward training its pilots and cabin crewmembers in political correctness within twenty-four months of the date of the settlement. (Unbelievable. Nick Berg's head was being cut off while our airline industry—which lost four planes and thirty-three crew—was forced to undergo sensitivity training!)

Ditto for United. The consent order which marked the settlement of the United litigation read as follows:

"Shortly after the terrorist attacks of September 11, 2001, the Office of Aviation Enforcement and Proceedings (Enforcement Office) began to receive complaints against United (and other carriers) from individuals removed from flights or denied boarding on flights allegedly because those persons were, or were perceived to be, of Arab, Middle Eastern or Southeast Asian descent and/or Muslim. Because of concerns about these complaints, the Enforcement Office requested information from United regarding incidences occurring between September 1, 2001 and December 31, 2001, involving the removal or denied boarding of a passenger for safety/security reasons."[12]

It goes on to explain that United "firmly maintains that no passenger was ever removed from a flight or denied boarding under circumstances amounting to a status-based discrimination (i.e. based on a passenger's ethnic background or national origin)."[13] In its defense, United notes that it has a demonstrated longstanding commitment to nondiscrimination and has developed extensive procedures and policies that underscore that commitment. United admitted no wrongdoing and claimed that no passenger was ever removed from a flight or denied boarding based upon the passenger's ethnic background or national origin. United further contended that it was obligated by federal law to "refuse to transport a passenger or property the carrier decides is, or might be, inimical to safety."

United also emphasized that all of the allegations concerned the time period shortly after 9/11, when there were unprecedented security concerns and tension for all participants in the nation's air transportation system, especially United and American, which lost planes and employees on that fateful date.[14] Unfortunately, United was then undergoing a reorganization in an attempt to emerge from Chapter 11 bankruptcy proceedings, and the airline decided to pay the fine to make the litigation go away. How much did the DOT exact from United? One million, five hundred thousand dollars ($1,500,000.00), to be used for civil rights training for its employees. (There's a racket for you: What do you do for a living? *Oh, I am a civil rights trainer. Really? Whom, exactly, do you train? Well, I train the employees of an airline that lost many of its colleagues at the hands of young Arab extremist men, to be sure to offer a pillow and a blanket to others who look like those terrorists before takeoff.*)

American Airlines put up a fight before succumbing to the DOT. Consequently, that skirmish generated more publicly available documentation than the Continental and United cases, and is worthy of some analysis. Let me say that, before reading the file, I was suspicious that these three airlines must have done something terribly egregious to incur the wrath of the DOT after 9/11. In fact, in the case of United and American, because of the nature of the loss they experienced, I was prepared for some pretty horrific stuff. It's just not there. I also couldn't stop thinking about what the family members of the crew that died on 9/11 would say if told that those airlines were now being fined by the DOT. Did they even know?

Back to American. The DOT/AEO filed a sixty-seven-page complaint (including attachments) against American. The allegation was that eleven passengers had inappropriately been denied passage post-9/11, because, or primarily because, the passengers were or were perceived to be of Arab, Middle Eastern, or South Asian descent and/or Muslim. (As if American should have turned a blind eye to the fact that fifteen of the nineteen hijackers on 9/11 were Saudis.) American's answer to the complaint noted that, as shown in the DOT's own statistics, there were only twenty-five discrimination complaints filed by the DOT which named American Airlines in calendar year 2002, a time period in which American had 94.1 million system-wide "enplanements."[15] (I'm no math whiz, but my calculator tells me we're talking .000012 percent of the total enplanements. Hardly a sign of institutional prejudice.)

I have read about the eleven cases. In fact, the passengers who were denied passage completed declarations that were attached to the AEO complaint. Space limitations don't permit me to cover them all, and I don't want to be accused of "cherry picking" those with facts that suit an agenda, so I will briefly discuss the first three in the order listed in the complaint.

Meet Hamdy Abou-Hussesin. According to the complaint against American, he is a naturalized U.S. citizen born in Egypt. Mr. Abou-Hussesin's declaration stated that he is an engineer by trade, with a Masters of Science in Engineering from Boston University. He gives his age only as "over eighteen." His wife, whom he was going to visit in Washington, D.C. at the time of this incident, is a professor at Harvard University. On November 22, 2001, Mr. Abou-Hussesin was scheduled to depart on an American Eagle flight from Boston's Logan Airport (the airport from which Flights 11 and 175 originated on 9/11, mind you) to Reagan National Airport in Washington. The complaint said that he was issued a boarding pass and went through the security checkpoint without incident. Then, while waiting in the gate area, he was asked to come to an American counter where he was told that he had been selected for additional security screening. (In his words: ". . .

an announcement was made over the gate area loudspeaker. 'Hamdy Abou-Hussesin, Seat 12A, please come to the counter.' There were about thirty people at the gate and I was the only one that appeared to be of Middle Eastern descent. My name was the only name called over the loud speaker. I could see people shifting in their seats and staring at me as I walked to the counter at Gate B25.") According to the complaint, he was then questioned by American employees and by Massachusetts state troopers. He claimed to have heard one individual who was involved in his questioning say, "He's from Egypt." Eventually, he was told that the pilot had refused his passage. Mr. Abou-Hussesin claimed that he felt threatened by the security personnel, including once when a police officer screamed at him for asking for everyone's names. He missed his plane and was rebooked on another flight later that same day.[16]

Sounds like an ordeal for Mr. Abou-Hussesin, no doubt. So what did American have to say for itself? The following facts, among other things, were reported by American:

The American Eagle pilot-in-command never saw the passenger and was unaware of his name or national origin. The pilot-in-command was advised by one of the Federal Air Marshals that the passenger's surname was similar to several names on the federal security watch list; that his documents looked insufficient because of spelling discrepancies between his driver's license and his name as it appeared on the ticket and boarding pass; that he advised the ticket agent that he was traveling without bags but appeared at the gate with a medium-sized bag; and that he had been uncooperative. The state trooper told the pilot-in-command that he had "bad vibes about this guy." The pilot-in-command elected not to delay the flight any longer and to have these security issues resolved on the ground.[17]

Keep in mind that the legal issue here was whether the pilot acted arbitrarily or capriciously, two months after 9/11. The pilot never saw the guy and didn't know his name, and was told, according to American, that the passenger's name was similar to several on a watch list! Remember, the pilot is obligated by federal law to "refuse to transport a passenger or property the carrier decides is, or might be, inimical to safety."[18] How is he upholding that responsibility to the passengers if he allows a man to fly whose name might be on a federal security watch list? (Quick question for you. Two planes are leaving Logan in ten minutes. Pilot No. 1 will let this guy fly. Pilot No. 2 says no, because his name sounds like one on a watch list and he has been told the man has discrepancies in his luggage announcement and is uncooperative. Which plane do you now wish to board?) Moreover, there were notable disparities in the spelling of the plaintiff's name. As to the plausibility of this, we need only look at the DOT's complaint, in which the man's name is spelled two different ways, neither of which is correct: they spell the name Abou-Husesin and Abou-Huessin, even though they attached the man's affidavit, in which he spells his own name Abou-Hussesin.

Bachelor Number Two is Maneesh Agarawal, a 34-year-old software consultant who lives in California, and is a citizen of India. On October 13, 2001, about one month after 9/11, he was scheduled to fly on an American flight from Boston to San Jose, California. (Keep in mind, we're talking Logan Airport again, point of origin of two airplanes on 9/11.) He cleared security and boarded his flight, then fell asleep in seat 30A before takeoff. About twenty minutes after he boarded his flight, he was awakened by an airline employee and asked to deplane because security had additional questions for him. According to the complaint, when Mr. Agarawal asked the reason why he was being subjected to additional questioning, he was told that the flight crew was uncomfortable with him because he did not make eye contact with them. However, according to Mr. Agarawal himself, it was an INS agent who was doing most of the questioning and treating him in an "intimidating and disrespectful" manner. This additional screening caused him to miss his flight. He was rebooked on a pair of connected flights—for both of which he was upgraded to First Class by American—and arrived in San Jose five hours later than originally scheduled. American's answer offered little insight into this case, although American admitted that the flight attendants believed that this passenger, and one other who was also questioned, "were acting suspiciously." According to American, "the passenger was removed because the flight attendants reported suspicious behavior to the pilot-in-command. At his discretion, two passengers were removed for a security re-check. There was at least one passenger on the departed flight with what appears to be an Arab, Middle Eastern or South Asian surname."[19]

Arbitrary and capricious? Unreasonable on the part of American? Again, the issue here is whether the pilot exercised good judgment at the time he was scheduled to depart. Given the pilot's responsibilities, it's hard to argue that he should not put his trust in people with whom he frequently works, or with a representative of the INS who is personally speaking to the suspect; or that he should take any chances with so much at stake. Here, the pilot was told by his crew that two individuals were raising eyebrows. Both were requestioned. We know that one didn't make the flight, but was rebooked. Presumably, the other is the individual who was also subjected to additional questioning, but was permitted passage. How arbitrary and capricious does that sound? And what exactly is a pilot supposed to do as he is preparing his aircraft for departure and is told by his crew that they are uncomfortable with a particular passenger? Stop and take testimony? Interrogate a few folks himself? Maybe it would be a different case if Mr. Agarawal was one of only two Muslim men on the plane, neither of whom was permitted to fly. But American's answer suggests that is not the case. And I am stuck on the fact that after he underwent additional questioning and was rebooked, he was upgraded to First Class. The idea of his sitting in one of the first few rows of his eventual flight where everyone can see him as they walk past en route to their own seats does not seem to me like an airline determined to prevent Arabs from flying. It says something to me to the contrary.

Say hello to our next contestant, Jehad Alshrafi, a self-described "32-year-old Arab American." Mr. Alshrafi is a naturalized American citizen of Jordanian birth. According to his declaration, which accompanied the DOT/AEO's complaint, he worked for a defense contractor helping to build missiles for the military, and possessed a secret-level security clearance. On November 3, 2001, he was refused entry while trying to board a plane from Boston to Los Angeles. (So far we're three for three on planes originating in Boston's Logan Airport. Question: Was it unreasonable to have heightened scrutiny of Arab males who flew soon after 9/11 via the same city of origin as Mohammed Atta on 9/11? You know my answer.) In the complaint against American, it states that Mr. Alshrafi was denied boarding after responding to a page and reporting to an American counter. There, he was greeted by an American employee and U.S. Marshal. He was told that the pilot had denied him boarding on that flight. Mr. Alshrafi informed the American employee that he had a "secret level" security clearance from the U.S. Department of Defense. He was nevertheless told he was being denied passage. ("I was calmly contesting the pilot's decision when a state trooper arrived and asked me to move along and to deal with him. I was humiliated to be confronted by a state trooper in full view of the crowded boarding area.") Mr. Alshrafi missed his flight, but was upgraded to First Class on a later flight that day.[20]

American's answer suggests that there was more to the story in the eyes of the pilot at the time. First, American states that "at least one other passenger had reported what appeared to be his suspicious behavior to an American gate agent." Additionally, American admitted, "the Federal Air Marshal advised the pilot-in-command that the passenger had been acting suspiciously and had created some kind of disturbance and that his name was similar to a name on the federal watch list."[21]

So, imagine that you are the pilot. Here is what is known to you as you are preparing for take-off: 1) you are two months removed from the worst act of terrorism ever initiated against the United States; 2) that terrorism victimized your employer—men doing exactly what you are doing today lost their lives and the lives of others when their airplanes were used as weapons; 3) the point of origin of two of those flights was Boston's Logan Airport, where you now sit; 4) the destination for three of those flights on 9/11 was Los Angeles, which is exactly where you are headed; 6) the hijackers on 9/11 were, to a person, young Arab males; 7) there is at least one passenger who is ill at ease with another passenger who is acting in what passenger number 1 believes to be a suspicious manner; 8) the Federal Air Marshal has advised you that the passenger at issue has been acting suspiciously and has created some kind of disturbance; 9) this passenger has a name similar to one on the federal watch list; and 10) yes, let's not be afraid to say it, he is a thirtyish Arab male.

Now, you are not conducting security screenings at the airport. Instead, you are worried about the mechanics of flight. But you are obligated under federal statutory law to "refuse to transport a passenger or property the carrier decides is, or might be, inimical to safety." What are you going to do?

Even if, by chance, you believe this pilot should have flown the plane with this man on board, can you say that he acted unreasonably when he exercised his discretion to do otherwise? To think so is insanity.

I maintain that the pilot who is presented with those details and chooses to fly is derelict in his duty. However, Norman Mineta's DOT decided this conduct was worthy of legal action—legal action against a company that paid the ultimate price on 9/11. I wish I were joking.

Now let's get a few things straight before I end up suffering comparisons to the Nazis and the Ku Klux Klan. These cases are not black and white, and I have not attempted to paint them as such. Remember, I could have shopped among the eleven instances for which American was cited to cherry pick the best facts for my arguments, but instead I just dealt with the first three. Trust me, the other eight cases had the same ambiguities and could be subject to just as much Monday morning quarterbacking. The real question is, what should the pilot or the airline have done, based upon what they knew when faced with these facts? What would the reasonable pilot—who is legally charged with protecting the safety of the aircraft—have done? What would you, as a passenger seated in the airplane, have wanted the pilot to do?

Should the pilots of those flights have said to themselves, "I could get into a lot of trouble if I am wrong"? Or should their first and *only* concern have been the safety of their passengers and crew? Since 9/11, we have given the captains of U.S. flights stronger flight deck doors, the option of carrying firearms, and amazingly comprehensive boarding procedures; but we are denying them the one thing that probably makes the most difference in saving lives—discretion.

In my opinion, more heavy-handedness was evident in the DOT/AEO's throwing additional claims into the mix. In addition to alleging discriminatory behavior and racial profiling, the AEO attorneys alleged "[failure to] provide safe and adequate interstate air transportation" and "use of unfair and deceptive practices and unfair methods of competition."[22] American went bonkers over those last two charges. With respect to the first allegation, it responded: "The phrase 'adequate transportation' is not defined in §41702 [of the law] or elsewhere in Title 49, nor does the legislative history . . . provide insight into the meaning of this phrase." In plain English, this means that Congress was no help and there had never been a single suit filed in federal court where the plaintiff, let alone the judge, accepted such a bizarre definition of adequate transportation. In fact, the best that the boys in government blue could do was point to cases *in their own courts*, but even these cases referred only to airline requirements for ensuring adequate accommodations for the transporting of the handicapped.[23]

Last time I checked, Osama didn't need a wheelchair.

Ditto for the allegation of engaging in "unfair and deceptive practices, and unfair methods of competition." The AEO could only rely on a half-century-old Supreme Court decision which mentioned that what constitutes an unfair trade practice must be construed broadly, and once again was forced to turn to their self-made case law (their own legal decisions) to support their arguments. Extra points if you can figure out how they connected the dots—I sure couldn't.

I am left wondering about the reasons for including those charges in addition to racial profiling—how good a hand *did* the DOT have? They didn't need to stack the deck if they could reasonably have demonstrated that the air crews in these cases did, in fact, act in an "arbitrary and capricious" manner. Maybe they thought that if they were boldly going where no man had gone before with these charges, they were worried that people might not think they were competent to set the criteria for racial profiling. And why bother to go after the airlines for four different violations when they would have enough trouble making two of the charges stick, even in their own courts, unless they weren't completely sure about their chances? It is a kitchen-sink mentality: hit 'em with everything, including the kitchen sink.

Maybe it has something to do with the old saw about a room full of monkeys and typewriters: give them enough time and eventually one of them will write Shakespeare. As it turned out, Administrative Law Judge Burton Kolko thought all four charges made perfect sense.[24] Looking at another trip down the rabbit hole, American refused to play the role of Alice in Wonderland, and instead followed the leads of United and Continental and settled their case. In the end, American agreed to pay $1,500,000 to resolve the Complaint (once again, the money is to be used for a campfire, around which American employees are supposed to gather in Birkenstocks and sing *Kumbaya*).

The consent order that memorialized the American settlement is very insightful into the current state of the law and the way in which it was wielded against American, United, and Continental. One need not be a judge to weigh the competing articulations of the law in a post-9/11 world and render a verdict:

"Federal law is clear. An airline cannot refuse passage to an individual because of that person's race, color, national origin, religion, sex, or ancestry. 49 U.S.C. 40127(a). Similarly, 49 U.S.C. 41310 prohibits air carriers and foreign air carriers from engaging in unreasonable discrimination against individuals on flights between the U.S. and foreign points, 49 U.S.C. 41702 requires that U.S. carriers provide safe and adequate transportation, and 49 U.S.C. § 41712 prohibits unfair and deceptive practices and, therefore, prohibits invidiously discriminatory practices on the part of U.S. carriers."[25]

This is important stuff. And despite the way in which the law was articulated in the consent order, there is plenty of protection for those airlines wanting to aggressively protect their passengers by using street smarts to safeguard against a repeat of 9/11. Here are the relevant sections of the federal statutory law (the bold emphasis is all mine):

**49 USCS § 40127. Prohibitions on discrimination**

(a) Persons in air transportation. An air carrier or foreign air carrier may not subject a person in air transportation to discrimination on the basis of **race, color, national origin, religion, sex, or ancestry.**

(b) Use of private airports. Notwithstanding any other provision of law, no State or local government may prohibit the use or full enjoyment of a private airport within its jurisdiction by any person on the basis of that person's race, color, national origin, religion, sex, or ancestry.

**HISTORY:** (Added April 5, 2000, P.L. 106-181, Title VII, § 706(a), 114 Stat. 157.)

---

**49 USCS § 41310 Discriminatory practices**

(a) Prohibition. An air carrier or foreign air carrier may not subject a person, place, port, or type of traffic in foreign air transportation to **unreasonable** discrimination.

(b) Review and negotiation of discriminatory foreign charges.

(1) The Secretary of Transportation shall survey charges imposed on an air carrier by the government of a foreign country or another foreign entity for the use of airport property or airway property in foreign air transportation. If the Secretary of Transportation decides that a charge is discriminatory, the Secretary promptly shall report the decision to the Secretary of State. The Secretaries of State and Transportation promptly shall begin negotiations with the appropriate government to end the discrimination. If the discrimination is not ended in a reasonable time through negotiation, the Secretary of Transportation shall establish a compensating charge equal to the discriminatory charge. With the approval of the Secretary of State, the Secretary of the Treasury shall impose the compensating charge on a foreign air carrier of that country as a condition to accepting the general declaration of the air-

craft of the foreign air carrier when it lands or takes off.

(2) The Secretary of the Treasury shall maintain an account to credit money collected under paragraph (1) of this subsection. An air carrier shall be paid from the account an amount certified by the Secretary of Transportation to compensate the air carrier for the discriminatory charge paid to the government.

(c) Actions against discriminatory activity.

(1) The Secretary of Transportation may take actions the Secretary considers are in the public interest to eliminate an activity of a government of a foreign country or another foreign entity, including a foreign air carrier, when the Secretary, on the initiative of the Secretary or on complaint, decides that the activity—

(A) is an **unjustifiable or unreasonable discriminatory**, predatory, or anticompetitive practice against an air carrier; or

(B) imposes an unjustifiable or unreasonable restriction on access of an air carrier to a foreign market.

(2) The Secretary of Transportation may deny, amend, modify, suspend, revoke, or transfer under paragraph (1) of this subsection a foreign air carrier permit or tariff under section 41302, 41303, 41304(a), 41504(c), 41507, or 41509 of this title.

(d) Filing of, and acting on, complaints.

(1) An air carrier, computer reservations system firm, or a department, agency, or instrumentality of the United States Government may file a complaint under subsection (c) or (g) of this section with the Secretary of Transportation. The Secretary shall approve, deny, or dismiss the complaint, set the complaint for a hearing or investigation, or begin another proceeding proposing remedial action not later than 60 days after receiving the complaint. The Secretary may extend the period for acting for additional periods totaling not more than 30 days if the Secretary decides that with additional time it is likely that a complaint can be resolved satisfactorily through negotiations with the government of the foreign country or foreign entity. The Secretary must act not later than 90 days after receiving the complaint. However, the Secretary may extend this 90-day period for not more than an additional 90 days if, on the last day of the initial 90-day period, the Secretary finds that—

(A) negotiations with the government have progressed to a point that a satisfactory resolution of the complaint appears imminent;

(B) an air carrier or computer reservations system firm has not been subjected to economic injury by the government or entity as a result of filing the complaint; and

(C) the public interest requires additional time before the Secretary acts on the complaint.

(2) In carrying out paragraph (1) of this subsection and subsection (c) of this section, the Secretary of Transportation shall—

(A) solicit the views of the Secretaries of Commerce and State and the United States Trade Representative;

(B) give an affected air carrier or foreign air carrier reasonable notice and an opportunity to submit written evidence and arguments within the time limits of this subsection; and

(C) submit to the President under section 41307 or 41509(f) of this title actions proposed by the Secretary of Transportation.

(e) Review.

(1) The Secretaries of State, the Treasury, and Transportation and the heads of other departments, agencies, and instrumentalities of the Government shall keep under review, to the extent of each of their jurisdictions, each form of discrimination or unfair competitive practice to which an air carrier is subject when providing foreign air transportation or a computer reservations system firm is subject when providing services with respect to airline service. Each Secretary and head shall—

(A) take appropriate action to eliminate any discrimination or unfair competitive practice found to exist; and

(B) request Congress to enact legislation when the authority to eliminate the discrimination or unfair practice is inadequate.

(2) The Secretary of Transportation shall report to Congress annually on each action taken under paragraph (1) of this subsection and on the continuing program to eliminate discrimination and unfair competitive practices. The Secretaries of State and the Treasury each shall give the Secretary of Transportation information necessary to prepare the report.

(f) Reports. Not later than 30 days after acting on a complaint under this section, the Secretary of Transportation shall report to the Committee on Transportation and Infrastructure of the House of Representatives and the

Committee on Commerce, Science, and Transportation of the Senate on action taken under this section on the complaint.

(g) Actions against discriminatory activity by foreign CRS systems. The Secretary of Transportation may take such actions as the Secretary considers are in the public interest to eliminate an activity of a foreign air carrier that owns or markets a computer reservations system, or of a computer reservations system firm whose principal offices are located outside the United States, when the Secretary, on the initiative of the Secretary or on complaint, decides that the activity, with respect to airline service—

(1) is an unjustifiable or unreasonable discriminatory, predatory, or anti-competitive practice against a computer reservations system firm whose principal offices are located inside the United States; or

(2) imposes an unjustifiable or unreasonable restriction on access of such a computer reservations system to a foreign market.

HISTORY: (July 5, 1994, P.L. 103-272, § 1[E], 108 Stat. 1130; Oct. 11, 1996, P.L. 104-287, § 5(9), 110 Stat. 3389.)

(As amended April 5, 2000, P.L. 106-181, Title VII, § 741, 114 Stat. 174.)

---

49 USCS § 41702 Interstate air transportation

An air carrier shall provide **safe and adequate interstate air transportation**.

HISTORY: (July 5, 1994, P.L. 103-272, § 1[E], 108 Stat. 1140.)

---

49 USCS § 41712 Unfair and deceptive practices and unfair methods of competition

(a) In general. On the initiative of the Secretary of Transportation or the complaint of an air carrier, foreign air carrier, or ticket agent, and if the Secretary considers it is in the public interest, the Secretary may investigate and decide whether an air carrier, foreign air carrier, or ticket agent has been or is engaged in an unfair or deceptive practice or an unfair method of competition in air transportation or the sale of air transportation. If the Secretary, after notice and an opportunity for a hearing, finds that an air carrier, foreign air carrier, or ticket agent is engaged in an unfair or deceptive practice or unfair method of competition, the Secretary shall order the air carrier, foreign air carrier, or ticket agent to stop the practice or method.

(b) E-ticket expiration notice. It shall be an unfair or deceptive practice under subsection (a) for any air carrier, foreign air carrier, or ticket agent utilizing electronically transmitted tickets for air transportation to fail to notify the purchaser of such a ticket of its expiration date, if any.

**HISTORY:** (July 5, 1994, P.L. 103-272, § 1[E], 108 Stat. 1143.)
(As amended April 5, 2000, P.L. 106-181, Title II, Subtitle B, § 221, 114 Stat. 102.)

---

49 USCS § 44902 Refusal to transport passengers and property

(a) Mandatory refusal. The Under Secretary of Transportation for Security shall prescribe regulations requiring an air carrier, intrastate air carrier, or foreign air carrier to refuse to transport—
(1) a passenger who does not consent to a search under section 44901(a) of this title establishing whether the passenger is carrying unlawfully a dangerous weapon, explosive, or other destructive substance; or
(2) property of a passenger who does not consent to a search of the property establishing whether the property unlawfully contains a dangerous weapon, explosive, or other destructive substance.

(b) **Permissive refusal. Subject to regulations of the Under Secretary, an air carrier, intrastate air carrier, or foreign air carrier may refuse to transport a passenger or property the carrier decides is, or might be, inimical to safety.**

(c) Agreeing to consent to search. An agreement to carry passengers or property in air transportation or intrastate air transportation by an air carrier, intrastate air carrier, or foreign air carrier is deemed to include an agreement that the passenger or property will not be carried if consent to search the passenger or property for a purpose referred to in this section is not given.

**HISTORY:** (July 5, 1994, P.L. 103-272, § 1[E], 108 Stat. 1204.)

(As amended Nov. 19, 2001, P.L. 107-71, Title I, § 101(f)(7), (9), 115 Stat. 603.)

In my review of the American case, I just don't see a violation of any of these statutes. Now, here's American's defense, as similarly represented in the consent order:

"American further contends that, as a matter of law, the pilot-in-command must not allow a passenger to depart on a flight if he or she believes that carriage of that passenger is or might be inimical to safety. 49 U.S.C. 44902(b)(see above), 14 CFR 91.3 and 49 CFR 1544.2 15(c). In addition, American asserts that the pilot-in-command must make that decision based upon the facts and circumstances presented to him or her at that time, taking into account the time constraints under which the decision must be made and the general security climate in which the events unfold. According to American, the circumstances that play a part in the pilot-in-command's decision include the heightened actual dangers arising from the increased risk of terrorist acts, the catastrophic consequences in the case of air travel of any failure to detect such acts in advance, and the necessity that pilots-in-command must make safety decisions on short notice without the opportunity to make an extensive investigation. American opines that the pilot-in-command may rely without further inquiry upon the representations of other crewmembers or other responsible authorities with respect to safety and security."[26]

One more thing. As if this isn't ugly enough already. American maintained in the litigation that in some instances for which they were being held accountable by the DOT, their pilots were being advised by the very same DOT that was now bringing this enforcement action!

American admitted no fault, but agreed to pay the money because it made more sense to settle the case than to continue with costly and protracted litigation to vindicate the actions of its employees. Too bad. Me, I am left questioning how the DOT, in good conscience, could have brought enforcement actions against these three domestic carriers, two of whom suffered incalculable consequences on 9/11. This truly falls in the "How can they sleep at night?" category.

# 7: THE REAL STORY OF FLIGHT 93

HERE IS A LITTLE-KNOWN FACT: WHAT SOME WOULD label "profiling" saved the White House or U.S. Capitol Building. Let me explain.

Three of the four aircraft involved in the hijackings on 9/11 had five hijackers aboard. But United Airlines Flight 93—a Boeing 757 that departed Newark bound for San Francisco at 8:42 AM and crashed in Stony Creek Township at 10:03 AM—had only four. I'm talking about the flight that ended up slamming into a field in western Pennsylvania. Surely that was not its intended target. Presumably, it was headed for Washington, D.C., and either the White House or the Capitol. We'll probably never know for sure. But the probable explanation as to why this flight was one terrorist shy of the others, and maybe why it crashed instead of reaching its real target, suggests that we have profiling to thank.

It's time to introduce to you a great American named Jose E. Melendez-Perez. He is deserving of some recognition and analysis here. Melendez-Perez testified before the 9/11 Commission on January 26, 2004. His testimony began with his reading of a formal statement. It ended with applause from the audience. Why did this group, largely comprised of 9/11 victims' family members, offer this man their gratitude? Because he doesn't fit the mold so far described in this book. He's the antithesis of Norman Mineta.

As of the date of his testimony, Melendez-Perez was a U.S. Customs and Border Protection Inspector at Orlando International Airport in Florida. He worked previously for the U.S. Immigration and Naturalization Service (INS) from November 15, 1992, to April 30, 2003. His service to the nation also includes service in the United States Army where he served honorably for over twenty-six years. He served two tours of duty in Vietnam, 1965–1966 and 1969–1970.[1]

Consider his words:

I am a 26-year honorable veteran of the U.S. Army and am currently on my 12th year as an immigration inspector, now working for Customs and Border Protection under the Department of Homeland Security. I began my career with the Immigration and Naturalization Service in 1992 where I was first assigned to Miami International Airport and subsequently transferred to Orlando International Airport, where I currently work.

My job requires me to know the difference between legitimate travelers to the U.S., and those who are not. This includes potential terrorists. We received terrorist and other types of alerts, such as on document fraud and stolen passports, prior to September 11, but we all consider these alerts in a different light now.

The national security element of my job means that training and experience is important. In my case, training for my job as inspector has been threefold. The first was my 26 years in military service, where I learned effective listening skills, observation of body language, and determination of motives. Second, when I joined the INS, I was required to attend training at the Law Enforcement Training Center where I received approximately (16) hours of training in interview skills, sworn statements, and document fraud. Third, my experience on the job as Immigration Inspector for the past eleven years has greatly improved my skills in detecting document fraud, observing body language and understanding different cultures, including Saudi nationals, many of whom come with their families via the Orlando International Airport on their way to Disney World. Saudi nationals were held to the same legal standards as everyone else. However, service wide they were treated with more "tact". For example, in order to accommodate the Saudi culture, female Saudis unwilling to unveil were inspected by female inspectors, if available. This remains the case today.

In Orlando, as in any other port, an Immigration Inspector can only return someone foreign back home, for whatever reason under the Expedited Removal law, if the inspector is to be able to substantiate the recommendation. Supervisors for the most part support inspectors who have enough proof to substantiate removing someone. It is my belief that some supervisors in Orlando and nationwide remain intimidated by complaints from the public, and particularly by Congressional letters, about refusing admission to certain aliens. Because of these complaints, supervisors tend to be wary of supporting the inspector who recommends an adverse action against an alien.

I do not know how often people are removed from the United States, nor can I tell you before 9/11 how many Saudis entered the country or how many were refused. However, I can tell you that according to the records we have in Orlando, approximately ten Saudi nationals have been turned around for various reasons.

In regard to the incident on August 4, 2001, which I am about to talk about, I note that another inspector on duty that day made a comment that I was going to get into trouble for refusing a Saudi national. I replied that I have to do my job, and I cannot do my work with dignity if I base my recommendations on refusals/admissions on someone's nationality.[2]

Wait a minute. Stop the presses. Didn't he get the memo? Melendez-Perez has just articulated a willingness to trust his training, experience, and intuition—his street smarts—and follow those instincts even if it means offending members of a particular ethnic stripe. That puts him at odds with prevailing thought pre- and post-9/11. But he was on the right track. Just wait until you see where this leads:

> The primary inspection officer is the first official that an international traveler comes in contact with. The officer's responsibility is to verify the passenger's travel documents for validity, the purpose of their trip, and check entry/exit stamps for past travel history. In addition, inspectors query databases for passengers who maybe on a lookout list for various reasons, (i.e., terrorism, criminal records, outstanding arrest warrants, etc.). Before 9/11, some of the databases available in 2001 were: (a) TECS-Treasury Enforcement Communication System, (b) CIS-INS Central Index System, (c) NAILS-National Automated Index Lookout System.[3]

Now, brace yourself. Here it comes. This is Melendez-Perez describing events that transpired a month before 9/11. This is very important. But before you read more of his testimony, there is something you need to know that was revealed by Melendez-Perez in responding to questioning by Richard Ben-Veniste of the 9/11 Commission. It turns out that while Melendez-Perez was performing his duties at Orlando Airport on August

4, 2001, and screening a man named Mohammed Kahtani, there was someone else present at the airport. That man was Mohammed Atta, the presumed ringleader of the 9/11 terrorist operation. Coincidence? Hardly. According to Ben-Veniste, while Melendez-Perez was questioning Mohammed Kahtani, and while Kahtani was claiming that someone was upstairs to meet him, Mohammed Atta made a telephone call from that location to a telephone number associated with the 9/11 plot.[4] In other words, you are about to read how Melendez-Perez prevented the twentieth hijacker from entering the United States:

> On August 4, 2001, I was assigned as a secondary inspection officer at the Orlando International Airport. My supervisor alternates inspectors between primary and secondary inspection, and on this day I was assigned to secondary inspection. At approximately 1735 hours, I was assigned the case of a Saudi national who had arrived on Virgin Atlantic #15 from London, Gatwick Airport. As Saudis coming through Orlando to travel to Disney World are common, I had plenty of line experience with Saudis. In this particular case, the subject was referred to secondary inspection because the primary inspector could not communicate with him and his arrival/departure form (I-94) and Customs Declaration (C-6059B) were not properly completed.
>
> I first queried the subject's name, date of birth, and passport number through the above systems with negative results. Subject's documents appeared to be genuine. A search of subject and his personal belongings were also negative. Subject was enrolled in IDENT and photographed. In addition, a complete set of fingerprints was taken on form FD-249 (red). Through my INS training and military experience, my first impression of the subject was that he was a young male, well groomed, with short hair, trimmed mustache, black long sleeve shirt, black trousers, black shoes. He was about 5′6″, and in impeccable shape, with large shoulders and a thin waist. He had a military appearance. Upon establishing eye contact, he exhibited body language and facial gestures that appeared arrogant. In fact, when I first called his name in the secondary room and matched him with papers, he had a deep staring look.[5]

Hold on. Melendez-Perez was taking into account the subject's nationality (Saudi), his grooming, dress, height, and shape. He figured the man to be military. And, he thought the man was cocky. Dare I say it, he was *profiling*. And thank goodness he did. Keep in mind, this was pre-9/11. If such an assessment occurred post-9/11, you would say, "well, of course this is how it should be handled." But this was before those horrific events. And it gets even clearer.

I had the impression of the subject that he had knowledge of interview techniques and had military training. Upon my initial review of the subject's paperwork and documents, I noticed that he did not have a return airline ticket or hotel reservations. Upon learning that the subject did not speak English (or at least that is what he wanted us to believe), I contacted an Arabic interpreter from the Department of Justice's interpreter's list.

My first question to the subject (through the interpreter) was why he was not in possession of a return airline ticket. The subject became visibly upset and in an arrogant and threatening manner, which included pointing his finger at my face, stated that he did not know where he was going when he departed the United States. What first came to mind at this point was that this subject was a "hit man." When I was in the Recruiting Command, we received extensive training in questioning techniques. A "hit man" doesn't know where he is going because if he is caught, that way he doesn't have any information to bargain with.

The subject then continued, stating that a friend of his was to arrive in the United States at a later date and that his friend knew where he was going. He also stated that his friend would make all the arrangements for the subject's departure. I asked him if he knew when his friend was to arrive in the United States and he responded that he was to arrive in three or four days. I asked him what the purpose of this trip was and how long he wanted to stay. He responded that he would be vacationing and traveling through the United States for six days. At this point, I realized that his story did not seem plausible. Why would he be vacationing for only six days and spend half of his time waiting for his friend? It became apparent that the subject was being less than truthful concerning his true intentions.

At this time, I again asked him where he was going to stay. He said, "A hotel." I then told him that without knowledge of the English language or a hotel reservation he would have difficulty getting around Orlando. He answered that there was someone waiting for him upstairs. When asked the person's name, he changed his story and said no one was meeting him. He said he was to call someone from his residence that would then contact someone locally to pick him up. I then asked the subject for the person's phone number and he refused to provide it stating that it was, 'none of my business.' He stated that it was a personal matter and that he did not see any reason for me to contact that person. The subject was very hostile throughout the entire interview that took approximately 1½ hours.

Subject was in possession of $2,800.00 United States dollars and no credit cards. This amount did not appear sufficient for a six-day vacation plus a hotel room and return ticket since a one-way ticket to Dubai, where he originated from, would cost approximately $2,200.00 USD. When confronted with this fact, he responded that his friend was going to bring him some money. I then asked, "Why would he bring you some money?" He replied, "Because he is a friend." I then asked, "How long have you known this person?" He answered, "Not too long." I said to myself, I'd like to place him under oath. I wanted him to understand the consequences of making a false statement. He agreed to be placed under oath, but when I asked the first question, he said, "I won't answer." The Arabic interpreter said to me that something was not right here.

At this point, I gave my supervisor a synopsis of the case and explained my suspicions that this individual was malafide (i.e., that his true intent in coming to the United States was not clear and he appeared very evasive). After presenting the case to my supervisor, he felt that Assistant Area Port Director (AAPD) should be contacted for further instructions. Normally, second line supervisors such as AAPD are not contacted in such matters, but because of the facts that we had provided no specific grounds for removal, higher up confirmation was needed. My supervisor then proceeded to call the AAPD at home to explain the case and get concurrence for removal. After my supervisor presented the facts to the AAPD, he then asked to speak directly with me. The AAPD asked numerous questions concerning the case. I explained that apart from not having a return ticket and possibly not having sufficient funds, the subject appeared to be malafide. I further explained to the AAPD that when the subject looked at me, I felt a bone-chilling cold effect. The bottom line is, 'He gave me the creeps.' You just had to be present to understand what I am trying to explain. The AAPD then asked if I had tried to place him under oath. I replied that I had tried to place the subject under oath, but the subject refused to answer my questions. The AAPD then stated that under Section 235.1 (a) (5) of the Immigration Nationality Act an applicant could be required to state, under oath, any information sought by an Immigration Officer regarding the purpose and intentions of the applicant in seeking admission to the United States. The AAPD further stated that he was convinced from what I had stated and my beliefs about the subject that the individual was malafide and should be allowed to withdraw his application or be set up for Expedited Removal.

I then proceeded to advise the subject that he did not appear to be admissible to the United States. He was offered the opportunity to voluntarily withdraw his application for admission. Subject chose to withdraw and signed the I-275. Along with another immigration inspector, I escorted subject to his departing gate for his removal. Before boarding the aircraft, the subject turned to other inspector and myself and said, in English, something to the effect of, "I'll be back". On August 4, 2001, subject departed foreign via Virgin Atlantic flight 16 to London with connecting flight to Dubai.

On September 11, 2001 while attending a meeting with the Warden at the Central Florida Processing Center (Department of Corrections) concerning the use of their range, a corrections officer came in and advised the Warden of the incident that had just occurred in New York City. As I watched the television, I could not help but think of the two cases I had processed in August concerning Saudi Nationals. I immediately contacted the Orlando Airport (I do not remember which officer I spoke with) but I asked them to look up the cases and contact the FBI agent assigned to the airport.

To the best of my knowledge, immigration officers made copies of this August 4, 2001 incident and provided that paperwork to the FBI. The FBI has never interviewed me. I do not recall ever speaking with GITMO [U.S. Naval Base at Guantanamo Bay, Cuba] officials. INS headquarters contacted me once. I have had no other contact with intelligence or law enforcement officials. Outside of legacy INS, the only government contact I have had about this incident came from the September 11 Commission this past fall, from your border team investigating the incident.[6]

Wow. No wonder they cheered in the hearing room for this guy. A street-smart cop in a sea of political correctness. And, as even Richard

Ben-Veniste told him: ". . . taking into account that the only plane commandeered by four hijackers, rather than five, crashed before reaching its target, it is entirely plausible to suggest that your actions in doing your job efficiently and competently may well have contributed to saving the Capitol or the White House, and all the people who were in those buildings, those monuments to our democracy, from being included in the catastrophe of 9/11, and for that we all owe you a debt of thanks and gratitude."[7]

What is the basis for my belief, and apparently that of Ben-Veniste, that the absence of a fifth hijacker may have spared a high-profile target and countless more lives? Consider this: In December 2002, the House-Senate Joint Inquiry Report on 9/11 (not to be confused with the 9/11 Commission) was issued, and not long after its release, the Associated Press published a story that sullied the memory of the heroic passengers of Flight 93 by blowing out of proportion one paragraph in the 900-page report. Perhaps desperate to find a new angle, the AP misconstrued seven sentences and promoted the idea that the plane crashed because the hijackers ditched it rather than be overtaken by the passengers. The heroes of Flight 93 and their families deserved better.

Here is what the Congressional report says on page 143:

"Telephone calls from passengers and crew to family and friends described attempts by passengers and crew to retake the plane prior to the crash. One call described three hijackers wearing bandanas and armed with knives, with one hijacker claiming to have a bomb strapped to his waist. Two hijackers entered the cockpit and closed the door behind them.

"The passengers were herded to the back of the plane. The captain and co-pilot were seen lying on the floor of the First Class section, possibly dead. At the words 'Let's roll,' passengers rushed forward. As described by the FBI Director, the cockpit tape-recorder indicates that a hijacker, minutes before Flight 93 hit the ground, 'advised Jarrah to crash the plane and end the passengers' attempt to retake the airplane.'"[8]

It was the last sentence that AP writer Ted Bridis twisted into a nationwide front-page story with this lead sentence:

"U.S. investigators now believe that a hijacker in the cockpit aboard United Airlines Flight 93 instructed terrorist-pilot Ziad Samir Jarrah to crash the jet into a Pennsylvania field because of a passenger uprising in the cabin.

"This theory, based on the government's analysis of cockpit recordings, discounts the popular perception of insurgent passengers grappling with terrorists to seize the plane's controls."[9]

No wonder the *Washington Post* gave the story this headline: "Gov't.: Hijacker Crashed Flight 93 on 9/11."[10] What a stretch. Truth is, the report did not say that Jarrah crashed the plane to thwart the passengers' rebellion. It simply said that another terrorist had advised him to do so. The report is entirely in sync with the view that the passengers fought back and that their struggle itself resulted in the crash.

Alice Hoglan is the mother of Mark Bingham, who died in the crash. With other family members of Flight 93 victims, she attended an April 2002 playing of the cockpit recorder in Princeton, N.J. They were requested to keep the bulk of what they'd heard private so as not to jeopardize the prosecution of Zacarias Moussaoui, at whose trial the tape may be played. But Mrs. Hoglan was fairly forthcoming with me when I interviewed her shortly after the House/Senate joint inquiry report on 9/11 came out.

She told me that the tape was 31 minutes long and picked up right after the murder of the pilots. She said the first 25 minutes were "routine" but the last five to six were "chilling." She said it was badly recorded, that the sound of wind rushing over wings created a roar, and that voices shouting in Arabic and English could be heard. It was "very dramatic."[11]

What did she conclude?

"Any reasonable person would come to the conclusion that I did, and the other family members, that there was indeed a successful breach of the cockpit door by the passengers."

In other words, the jet crashed because the passengers reached the controls, not because the terrorists crashed before they got there.

"They definitely got into the cockpit," she said. Her opinion was "confirmed by the voices she heard, by the things being said and by the things being done that were recorded violently."[12]

Based upon what she had heard, she told me that she believes "the terrorists were themselves terrorized." I sure hope so. She explained that the FBI told her that the terrorists dropped the cruising altitude from 28,000 feet to 1,500 at full cruise speed of 575 mph and that any "little tweak" by the controls could easily have put the airplane in the ground.

The two pilot hijackers "were agonized, they knew two of their crew were killed by passengers. That is my opinion and conclusion based on what I heard."

She knew that the terrorists did indeed discuss the prospect of intentionally crashing the airplane, but that they never did.

"There was frantic dialogue between the two pilots, one asking the other, 'Should we put it in ground now, what are we going to do, we are not going to make it to Washington . . . should we put it in the ground?'"[13]

"The answer consisted of two words and meant 'we should wait.' The question was asked again after the sound of a crashing of a food cart against door. It got the same answer."[14]

She took issue not with the congressional report, but with the AP interpretation.

"I was not surprised to hear that report because it does corroborate what we heard on the flight cockpit voice recording, however the interpretation that is being put on it is creating the apparent inconsistency."[15]

In light of the 9/11 Commission Report findings that the hijackers remained at the controls when Flight 93 crashed, here is the bottom line: Two terrorists managed to get themselves behind the controls of Flight 93. Two more terrorists were in the cabin, almost certainly violently killed by the heroes who fought back. Regardless of whose fingers gripped the controls, the airplane crashed because Americans confronted the terrorists, not because the terrorists decided to ditch the craft. "I am very sorry that this misunderstanding has occurred," said Mark Bingham's mom. Me too.

The real story of Flight 93 lends credence to the view that, but for Melendez-Perez's good work on August 4, 2001, the hijackers on that flight would have had one more man on their side and, perhaps, could have overpowered the passengers and completed their mission. Had Melendez-Perez not "profiled," perhaps the passengers aboard Flight 93 would not have been successful in thwarting a crash into a high-profile Washington target like the White House or Capitol.

Guess who agrees with this analysis? Our old friend, John Lehman, that's who. Lehman spoke at the U.S. Naval Institute 130th Annual Meeting and Annapolis Naval History Symposium on March 31, 2004, and said this:

"Actions have consequences, and people must be held accountable. Customs officer Jose Melendez-Perez stopped the 20th terrorist, who was supposed to be on Flight 93 that crashed in Pennsylvania. Probably because of the shorthanded muscle on that team, the passengers were able to overcome the terrorists. Melendez-Perez did this at great personal risk, because his colleagues and his supervisors told him, 'You can't do this. This guy is an Arab ethnic. You're racially profiling. You're going to get in real trouble, because it's against Department of Transportation policy to racially profile.' He said, 'I don't care. This guy's a bad guy. I can see it in his eyes.' As he sent this guy back out of the United States, the guy turned around to him and said, 'I'll be back.' You know, he is back. He's in Guantanamo. We captured him in Afghanistan. Do you think Melendez-Perez got a promotion? Do you think he got any recognition? Do you think he is doing any better than the nineteen of his time-serving, unaccountable colleagues? Don't think any bit of it. We have no accountability, but we're going to restore it."[16]

Here is the lesson from Melendez-Perez. We need to take a page from the Israeli national airline and look not only for bombs, but for bombers.

In the fall of 2003, I flew to Israel against a backdrop of bad news. A Palestinian gunman had just shot and killed five people, including two children, at a kibbutz. Just hours before that, two Palestinians were killed in a car explosion in what police said was a failed terror attack. It was the latest in a string of suicidal acts that have wreaked havoc in that country for two years running. Yet en route to the Holy Land, I slept like a baby.

Why so relaxed?

Because I traveled on El Al, the Israeli-owned airline, and I felt as safe in the air as I do in my bed at home. At Newark International Airport, I was subjected to a courteous yet thorough interrogation. The questioning is best described as a more extensive version of the "who packed your bag and has it been out of your eyesight" routine to which we Americans are accustomed. I didn't mind a bit—in fact, I welcomed the scrutiny, and it occurred to me that this is why El Al has such an impeccable safety record despite the conflict in the Middle East.

I kept thinking that Americans who rejected the Bush Administration plan called "Operation Tips"—which solicited the support of service personnel to drop a dime in the war on terror—wouldn't sit still for this on a flight from, say, Philadelphia to Los Angeles. Too bad. I think there is a great deal to learn from the Israelis. They do things differently. Our domestic airlines look for bombs and weapons. El Al looks for terrorists. And they make no apologies in the process. Moreover, no one seems to complain.

Here at home, I can just imagine some ACLU lawyer taking umbrage when asked, as I was, about the purpose of my visit and whom I would meet on arrival. In fact, I went to Israel to do a week of radio shows. My program director, Grace Blazer, traveled with me. She was asked who made the selection of the tape recorder we brought with us, and why it was selected ("the one that works best" seemed to suffice).

She also had a new passport. That drew additional questions. "When did you decide to visit Israel?" Answer: a month ago. "Why, if you planned to visit Israel a month ago, did you only get your passport this week?" And so on.

This all occurred before we reached the ticket counter. And when ten minutes of Q&A ended, our questioner did not wave us through. Instead, she brought over a supervisor who repeated many of the questions. I got the impression that he was as interested in eye contact and body language as he was in our responses.

Profiling? Yes, the psychological kind.

"Why, if you are a radio host, does your luggage tag identify a law firm?" he wanted to know. (I am still "of counsel" to a major Philadelphia law firm.)

The questioning didn't cross the line. I wasn't offended. This is how El Al earned its reputation as the safest airline flying. Presumably, this is how El Al was able to thwart a Jordanian who in the mid-'80s tried to bring explosives aboard on the person of his unsuspecting pregnant girlfriend. And this is only the security that we see from El Al. There is more to their defense than meets the eye. On entering the aircraft, there is no opportunity to look into the cockpit and greet the pilot. The cockpit is behind double doors, which I only got to inspect privately on our arrival at Ben Gurion Airport in Tel Aviv.

U.S. airlines should take a page from the El Al playbook. I think there is market share to be gained by any airline that implements these procedures and promotes itself as the safest domestic carrier. I know I would pay extra for the peace of mind. I'll bet you would, too.

# 8: CAPTAIN GIULIANI

WHAT A LONG STRANGE TRIP THIS WAS TURNING OUT TO be. Here's a brief recap:

My 8-year-old son was designated for secondary screening on a trip to Florida, which I thought was utterly ridiculous, but I chalked it up to being a necessary part of life in a post-9/11 world. Shortly thereafter, I watched the 9/11 Commission testimony on television, and was stunned when Secretary John Lehman asked Dr. Condoleezza Rice a question that implied that there was a quota system in place at airports pre- and post-9/11 that limited the number of young Arab males who could be pulled out of line for questioning at any one time. This was a shock, and so too was the fact that nobody wrote about this revelation. So, I interviewed Lehman and found his candor refreshing, but also found his assessment of how political correctness impacted airline security very distressing. I printed what he told me in the *Philadelphia Daily News*, and brought it to the attention of Senator Arlen Specter, who promised to look into it. The DOT told Specter's office that what I had written was inaccurate. I almost let the matter drop, until I found myself in the company of Herb Kelleher, the founder and chairman of Southwest Airlines. Kelleher was the airline version of Lehman. No BS. "Tell me what you want to know," he seemed to say. He confirmed that political correctness was alive and well in airline security. So, I wrote about the subject again. This time, *National Review Online* and the *New York Post* printed what I had uncovered. *Investor's Business Daily* got into the act too. And an invitation from CNBC's *Kudlow & Cramer* arrived. That appearance went over like a lead balloon at the DOT, which then issued a statement trashing me. The DOT's heavy-handedness with me—epitomized by their refusal *to* give to me a statement they had issued *about* me, and which had been read on national television, unless I shared future columns with them pre-publication—only emboldened my efforts to see what was driving the PC effort at the DOT. I then turned my attention to the 9/11 transcripts, which proved that John Lehman was justified in asking Dr. Rice what he had asked about PC screening methods at airports. I kept going. Next, it was a look at the litigation initiated by the DOT post-9/11, which painted a horrifying picture of a federal bureaucracy going after the very airlines that suffered enormous losses on 9/11 for their efforts intended to prevent it from happening again. Why, I wondered? Where does this come from? Next up for my review, Norman Mineta, the Secretary of Transportation and head of the DOT. What I found was a man with a scarred past who was allowing his experience to cloud his current role. Thank God for The Big Talker, and the *Philadelphia Daily News*. Both my radio station and newspaper were affording me the opportunity to put a microphone in front of individuals the average American does not get access to, and I was seizing every opportunity to get answers from people in the know. John Lehman. Senator Specter. Senator John McCain. Herb Kelleher. Torie Clarke. Norman Mineta wouldn't speak to me, but his speeches on the issue spoke for him. I was far from finished. I intended to get somebody from the TSA on the record, as well as someone from the U.S. House of Representatives who held a position of authority over commercial airlines. And next would be America's Mayor. My access to him would be much like my access to some of the others—a combination of timing and my willingness to ask. As someone close to me commented while these events were unfolding, my role in trying to ferret out the role of political correctness in airline security was a combination of a conservative Michael Moore (they meant it in a good way) and Forrest Gump.

I also had the opportunity to speak with one of Mayor Giuliani's predecessors. Democrat Ed Koch is but another public official to whom I have sounded out over my concern that political correctness is compromising airline security. Mayor Koch gets it. After I gave him my take, we had the following exchange:

**MAS:** I'm pleased to be able to welcome back to the city of Philadelphia, the former mayor of the city of New York, that of course: Ed Koch. Good morning Mr. Mayor.

KOCH: Good morning. Uh, I agree with what you have said as it relates to examining people on line. It's nutty that we should worry about uh, gee, are we pulling out too many Arabs if in fact the people who are committing terrorism happen to be Arabs. That doesn't mean that the vast majority of Arabs are peaceful, but I would bet that whether you're Arab or non Arab, when you are on a plane you want to be sure that people who fit a profile of terrorism to a greater extent than others are given special attention. They shouldn't be brutalized. . . .

MAS: Course not.

KOCH: When I go through a line, I take off my shoes and I say hurrah. I want everybody to take off their shoes, including me.

MAS: But Mayor, and by the way God bless Ed Koch for expressing those sentiments because I wasn't going to ask you to wade into these waters but I'm proud to hear you just lay it on the line. Can I tell you 30 seconds of background on this issue, because I think you'll be interested.

KOCH: Yeah.

MAS: When John—when Condoleezza Rice testified in front of the 9/11 commission—John Lehman who is sort of flying under the radar screen not like Ben-Veniste and some of the others getting a lot of attention. He posed a question to Condoleezza Rice, he said were you aware of the fact when you came into office that it was the policy of the government not to question more than 2 individuals of Arab descent at a time for fear of being fined by the government. And it didn't get any attention. And I thought, what in the heck is he talking about? So I interviewed him and my listeners have heard the whole interview and he said: yeah, political correctness is wreaking havoc—I'm paraphrasing—on the airlines.

KOCH: I'm glad you picked it up.

**MAS:** And so, bottom line is now Senator Specter is . . . sufficiently interested in it to conduct a Senate hearing on the issue and now you'll follow it—Ed Koch will follow it in New York.

**KOCH:** Sure.[1]

Next up would be Rudy Giuliani. To appreciate our exchange on the issue, I think it is important to give you the background of how I was in a position to question him about the subject of this book.

Rudy Giuliani and I had something very dear in common: our friendship with the Honorable Jay C. Waldman, a federal judge who sat on the United States District Court for the Eastern District of Pennsylvania. Jay left this earth on May 30, 2003, and his death affected the two of us deeply. Jay had been counsel to Pennsylvania Governor Dick Thornburgh. At the time of his death, he and his wife Roberta were two of the closest friends to my wife and me. We ate together on a weekly basis for the last fifteen years of his life, and vacationed together as well. Not only was he Dick Thornburgh's right hand, including during the Three Mile Island scare, but he was also Rudy Giuliani's longstanding confidant. The two knew each other since they served as young prosecutors in the Justice Department, and I think we can credit Jay for Rudy's run for Mayor as a Republican. I don't rely on Jay in saying this; I rely on Rudy's recollection as presented in his book, *Leadership*.[2] At the time of his death, Jay was a United States District Court Judge (having been appointed by Ronald Reagan) who had been appointed to the Third Circuit Court of Appeals (by President George W. Bush) but not yet confirmed by the U.S. Senate.

I can't claim to be close to Rudy, but as a result of having Jay in common, I have had the privilege of being in his company on several occasions. Unfortunately, some of those were related to Jay's tragic passing at age 58. The post-funeral reception for Jay, for example, was hosted by my wife and me at our home for Jay's closest friends, and Rudy came to the house with his wife, Judith. Like the rest of America, I am a very big supporter of Mayor Giuliani. I co-hosted a fundraiser in Philadelphia for his run against Hillary for the U.S. Senate, which he had to abandon due to his cancer diagnosis. (I have always believed I had a great campaign slogan for that race. The night of the reception, I said, "Mayor, break her broomstick." He seemed to like it, but I never saw it on a bumper sticker. That's okay, there's time.)

Well, right in the middle of this airline inquiry that I was doing my best to conduct from Philadelphia, a group of Judge Waldman's friends gathered to celebrate the unveiling of his official court portrait. There was a public ceremony and then a private dinner where a group of his close friends, including Senator Specter and Mayor Giuliani, got together to raise our glasses to our deceased friend. After dinner, and while we both enjoyed cigars at a Philadelphia Italian restaurant, I shared with Mayor Giuliani the short history of my flying experience, John Lehman's questioning of Condoleezza Rice, and the events that I have described which followed. I was particularly mindful of praising Secretary Lehman because I wanted Mayor Giuliani to appreciate Lehman's level of courage in addressing these issues. Frankly, I viewed these two men as having many similar qualities—smart, engaged, not cowed by the winds of political correctness. Mayor Giuliani appeared impressed with what I told him about Lehman. Senator Specter was present for part of the discussion, and we talked about Specter's interest to get to the bottom of it by holding a hearing. He was a bit perplexed because, on the one hand, he had spoken to Secretary Lehman who had confirmed the things I had been saying, and yet, Specter knew the DOT had issued denials of things I had printed and said. Senator Specter is a frequent guest on my radio program and he knew well that this issue had captivated my radio audience and that people wanted answers. As for me, I was anxious to get Rudy's take on the whole matter.

Too bad I didn't take notes. I walked him through the chronology of how I got interested in this subject, who I had spoken with on the matter and what they had to say. The man who presided over New York City in its darkest hour was understandably interested in what I had to tell him. He also shared with me an anecdote or two about a situation where his police department had been accused of profiling. Rudy Giuliani had been on my radio program in the past. As a matter of fact, when my airtime slot moved from afternoon drive to morning drive, he was my very first guest and the subject was 9/11-related. I asked him to come back on the program and address the subject, and he agreed. He said he was about to appear in front of the 9/11 Commission and that he preferred to appear right after that testimony. I said fine. He was sufficiently interested in my issue that he told Senator Specter he would consider appearing at any hearing the Senator might schedule to pursue the issue of political correctness in airline security. Given what Giuliani had witnessed, it is understandable that he would wish to be engaged in this process. His interest was great news to me. You can call me Forrest Gump, but I was steadily enlisting some big guns for change.

Unfortunately, the next ten days would find Giuliani and Lehman somewhat at odds. Fast-forward to May 18, 2004—the eleventh public hearing of the 9/11 Commission. This hearing took place in the Big Apple, in front of a crowd of 9/11 victims' family members, and focused on the emergency response capabilities of New York City on 9/11/01.

On the first of two days of hearings, Thomas Von Essen, the former NYFD Commissioner; Bernard Kerik, the former NYPD Commissioner; and Richard Sheirer, the former Director of the New York City Office of Emergency Management, appeared. Secretary Lehman, displeased with the emergency response of New York City on September 11, had this exchange with Commissioner Von Essen:

Lehman: "I think that the command and control of and communications of this city's public service is a scandal. . . . It's a scandal that after laboring for eight years, the city comes up with a plan for incident management that puts into concrete a clearly dysfunctional system. . . . It's not worthy of the Boy Scouts, let alone this great city."

Clearly offended, Commissioner Von Essen emphatically rejected Secretary Lehman's assertions by firing back at the panel of 9/11 commissioners.

Von Essen: "I couldn't disagree with you more strongly. . . . You make it sound like everything was wrong about Sept. 11 or the way we function. I think it's outrageous that you make a statement like that."[3]

Outside the hearing, Von Essen went even further and called the questioning by Lehman "despicable."[4]

Needless to say, the newscasts that night and the newspapers the next day focused solely on this exchange. The front cover of the *New York Post* read: "Insult, Memo to 9/11 Commission: This Man Is New York Hero, He Is Not a 'Boy Scout.'" It had a large arrow pointing to a picture of a kneeling firefighter on the day of the 9/11 terrorist attacks. The paper represented a common feeling among all New Yorkers who felt that Lehman's comments were out of line and that they diminished the great and ultimate sacrifice that so many of New York's "Bravest" and "Finest" made that Tuesday in September. Most notably irritated by the comments was New Yorker in Chief, former Mayor Rudy Giuliani. Thus the stage was set for Mayor Giuliani's appearance the following day in front of the 9/11 Commission. He took the opportunity to address the heroics of the emergency personnel in the context of speaking about the President's Daily Intelligence Briefing of August 6, 2001, which mentioned New York and the World Trade Center three times. In doing so, Mayor Giuliani managed to rebuke Lehman's claim that the city was unprepared and reminded the panel of what he felt the purpose of The Commission should be:

"If that information had been given to us, or more warnings had been given in the summer of 2001, I can't honestly tell you we'd do anything differently.... We were doing at the time everything we could think of ... to protect the city.... I do think the interpretation would have been more in the direction of suicide bombings than aerial attacks.... Our enemy is not each other, but the terrorists who attacked us." The mayor acknowledged there were "terrible mistakes" made on September 11, but attributed the cause to the unprecedented circumstances. "The blame should clearly be directed at one source and one source alone—the terrorists who killed our loved ones."[5]

At this time, many family members of 9/11 victims broke into applause.

John Lehman took the opportunity to explain his comments in an op-ed published in the *New York Times* on May 26, 2004:

By their incredible bravery and selflessness, New York's firefighters and police officers saved far more civilian lives on Sept. 11 than anyone could have expected. Their leaders were also heroic, rushing to the scene and providing calm and decisive command and control under unbelievable conditions of pressure and peril. Commissioners Bernard Kerik of the Police Department, Thomas Von Essen of the Fire Department and Richard Sheirer of the Office of Emergency Management were part of this leadership team.

I regret that during last week's commission hearings, my assessment of the city's command control and communications systems within and among the agencies that responded to the Sept. 11 attacks was taken by some as a criticism of their leaders. That was not my intention.

It has long been military practice to do a thorough study after every battle to find the lessons to be learned. This does not dishonor the heroes of that battle. In addition to recognizing the magnificent heroes of 9/11, the commission must learn lessons and recommend actions to fix problems. Some will deride this as Monday morning quarterbacking, but it is a necessary duty.[6]

Sitting back in Philadelphia, I was particularly interested in the back and forth because I had Giuliani booked on the radio program to talk about political correctness and airport screening, but I had clearly credited Lehman when I first told Giuliani about the issue. I wondered if Rudy would remember that part of our conversation, and if he would be more guarded when he appeared on my radio show. After all, but for Lehman's willingness to pose certain questions to Dr. Condoleezza Rice, I would be none the wiser about what was going on here.

True to his word, Mayor Giuliani came on my program. Here is our exchange on the matter of most concern to me. He didn't disappoint. He gets it.

**MAS:** But is there a problem, Mayor, with saying that you know those 19 hijackers, they did look the same, they all had olive complexions, they all had dark hair, they all were from the Middle East, and they all represent radical Islam? Why can't law enforcement take that into account?

**RUDY:** Well it has to take into account the identifying characteristics of the suspects. Think of it as a criminal investigation for a minute, right. You have information that you're searching for a certain person who's six-foot-two and looks a certain way. Well, those are the people that are going to get more scrutiny fortunately or unfortunately, the people who look . . . who are six-foot-two and look a certain way are going to be the ones that the police are going to have a picture of, as far as the FBI are going to be looking for. Here . . . you are trying to apply that against a criteria that is much more complicated. But the fact is that those are the kinds of things you have . . . to build into the system and sometimes that is going to maybe offend one group or another, but.

**MAS:** But you can blame Osama bin Laden for that?

**RUDY:** Yeah, you can, not just Osama bin Laden, but then the intelligence that you're getting over a period of time, right. I mean, the intelligence gathering networks develop information about who's threatening us, who might threaten us, that has to all be figured into the equation.[7]

Mayor Giuliani was a bit of a sanity check for me. I wanted to know if my views were out of step with the one American that many of us will most closely recall in association with the events of 9/11. Now I had my answer. So I wasn't the aberration. What did that say about Norman Mineta?

# 9: AIRPORT
# (NOT JUST THE MOVIE, I'M AFRAID)

AN E-MAIL FROM A RADIO LISTENER REMINDED ME OF THIS pre-9/11 movie classic:

"In the movie *Airplane*, there is a scene in which a group of Arabs are ushered through security even though they are carrying machine guns and bazookas. But, when a hapless white-bread suburban type calls out to a friend, "Hi, Jack!" he is clubbed to the ground and taken away. Who knew when *Airplane* was first released that it would one day become a training film for the DOT?"

Where does this mindset come from? Clearly, from the top. I'm talking the Secretary of Transportation and head of the DOT, Norman Mineta. It didn't take any super sleuthing on my part to document Mineta's mindset on the profiling issue. He's got a long and not-so-distinguished record in this regard.

By way of quick bio, Norman Y. Mineta is our fourteenth Secretary of Transportation, having been appointed by George W. Bush. Mineta represented San Jose, California, in the Congress from 1975 to 1995, spending several years as a vice president of Lockheed Martin before returning to Washington. President Clinton chose him to be Secretary of Commerce in 2000. He was appointed Secretary of Transportation by President George W. Bush in 2001.

Of most significance, however, is his heritage. Mineta and his family were among the 120,000 Japanese Americans forced into internment camps during WWII. After graduating from UC Berkeley (now there's a surprise), Mineta joined the U.S. Army and was an intelligence officer in Japan and Korea. Mineta was the driving force behind the passage of H.R. 442, the Civil Liberties Act of 1988, which apologized for and redressed the injustices endured by Japanese Americans during WWII. No doubt this background clouded his ability to be an impartial arbiter of appropriate airport screening in a post-9/11 world. And he makes no bones about it. The P-word—"profiling"—is unmentionable in the presence of Norman Mineta. Which is understandable. But just as Michael Corleone one day had to tell Tom Hagen, "You're out, Tom" because the Godfather needed a stronger wartime consigliere, so too is the need to make some change at the helm at the DOT.

Want proof? Consider this: On December 2, 2001, three months post-9/11, Mineta was interviewed by CBS's Steve Kroft on 60 Minutes. The segment was called "That Dirty Little Word 'Profiling'." The exchanges are priceless—and disturbing.

> **MINETA:** You can't say that a person, just because he is an Arab-American and a Muslim, that he should be a suspect and be considered someone who might be a terrorist.

> **KROFT:** Are you saying, at security screening desks, that a 70-year-old white woman from Vero Beach, Florida, would receive the same level of scrutiny as a-a-a Muslim young man from Jersey City?

> **MINETA:** Basically, I would hope so.[1]

There was more, plenty more. Kroft proceeded to present the details of Mineta's background—how the government knocked on his door in 1942 and hauled his family off to an internment camp because it couldn't tell the difference between loyal Japanese-Americans and the people who bombed Pearl Harbor. While footage of Japanese internment camps rolled, Mineta said:

"I remember, on the 29th of May, 1942, when we boarded the train in San Jose under armed guard, the military guard. I was in my Cub Scout uniform carrying a baseball, baseball glove, and a baseball bat. And as I boarded the train, the MPs confiscated the bat on the basis that it could be used as a lethal weapon."[2]

To the credit of 60 Minutes, Floyd Abrams, the famous First Amendment lawyer, was brought on for balance. Abrams spoke for me when he said, "It would be crazy not to consider what people look like when we're looking for people who may be involved with hijacking."

Steve Kroft had begun the interview by stating that, at the time, all twenty-two people on the FBI's Most Wanted Terrorist List are Muslims! (As of this writing, there are still twenty-two profiles posted on the FBI's Most Wanted Terrorist List. One of those—Khalid Shaikh Mohammed—has already been located by authorities. Of the remaining twenty-one, seven have the name Mohammed as part of their names. All have Islamic names. Twenty terrorists appear to have an olive complexion. None are Caucasian. Seven are pictured wearing some sort of religious headwear [turban, etc.]. Ten are pictured wearing a beard. Seven are pictured wearing a mustache. And all are scary as hell. But, according to the prevailing mindset in our government post-9/11, we are to consider none of this as we safeguard our airports. I must be dreaming.)

Kroft asked Mineta about this fact as follows:

**KROFT:** All but one of them has complexion listed as olive. They all have dark hair and brown eyes. And more than half of them have the name Mohammed. Now if you're working for an airline or you're a security screener and you see somebody's name coming through and you see the name Mohammed, should that person be subjected to more security?

**MINETA:** No. Not just on that basis alone.

**KROFT:** Just going down a manifest list: Bob, Paul, John, Frank, Steven, Mohammed?

**MINETA:** No. But why-why should Mohammed be singled out?[3]

From my Barcalounger, I am now shouting at the TV: "Are you shitting me, Mr. Mineta?"

The *60 Minutes* speech was no aberration. On October 12, 2001, Secretary Mineta issued a statement to the U.S. Commission on Civil Rights where he said much the same thing:

I understand that of particular concern to the Commission is the potential racial, ethnic, or religious profiling of individuals as a result of revised or proposed procedures to strengthen security measures at airline checkpoints and passenger screening locations in response to the terrorist hijackings and tragic events of September 11. As a result, this statement, while describing actions taken throughout the Department, will focus primarily on steps taken to ensure that DOT's efforts to secure our air transportation system do not unlawfully discriminate. . . .

As one of the 120,000 Americans of Japanese ancestry interned by the United States Government during World War II, I know firsthand the dangers with which we are presented in the current crisis. All of us will face heightened security in the aftermath of September 11, but the security and scrutiny must never become pretexts for unlawful discrimination. . . .

In light of the terrorist hijackings and tragic events of September 11, security measures at airports and airlines have been greatly heightened. The additional security measures include more thorough carry-on baggage screening and allowing only ticketed passengers beyond security checkpoints, except for those with specific medical or parental needs. We are confident that these new security procedures are nondiscriminatory and do not abridge the rights of citizens to be free of discrimination on the basis of race, color, nationality, ethnicity, or religion. We will continue to do everything in our power to ensure that remains the case. . . .

Since September 11, the Department has received seven complaints from persons alleging that that they were removed from flights or denied permission to board because they are, or were perceived to be, of Arab, Middle Eastern, or South Asian descent and/or Muslim. The Department has also received three complaints alleging discrimination prior to boarding at security checkpoints. Each of these complaints have been reviewed, are being acknowledged, and will be investigated. We take all these cases very seriously. . . .[4]

As mentioned by Secretary Mineta in his statement, he couldn't be there to personally deliver it because he was giving a speech in Rochester, New York. I wondered what he said in Rochester that day. By now, I shouldn't have been surprised. Once again, his reaction to the events of 9/11 was clouded by his own experience in WWII:

As you know, more than a few journalists and historians have taken to describing September 11th as the new Pearl Harbor. The analogy is a good one—once again, the United States has been attacked without warning and without mercy. The attack has awakened us to a danger our Nation sometimes felt we would not have to face. And it has strengthened our resolve to face that danger—and remove it.

I think that all of you will understand that, as an American of Japanese ancestry, I find the analogy of Pearl Harbor to be particularly important. It highlights one of the greatest dangers we will face as a country during this crisis—the danger that in looking for the enemy we may strike out against our own friends and neighbors.

On Sunday morning, December 7, 1941, my family and I attended church at the Wesley United Methodist Church in my hometown of San Jose, California. And as we returned home, we heard the news that our naval base at Pearl Harbor had been bombed by the Empire of Japan.

As Americans, we were outraged by that attack. And we were fearful, as all Americans were fearful, of when the next attack might come and where it might fall.

But we had an additional cause for fear—because we knew that many of our fellow Americans would not distinguish between us and the pilots flying the Zeroes that day in the Pacific.

Sadly, that fear turned out to be very, very real.

That same afternoon, agents of the Federal Bureau of Investigation began rounding up leaders in our community. And in the weeks and months that followed, we saw our status as Americans slowly but surely called into question.

After months of racial scapegoating and fear-mongering on the West Coast and across the country, President Franklin Roosevelt signed Executive Order 9066. That Executive Order authorized the United States Army to exclude all persons of Japanese ancestry from the West Coast of the United States. . . .[5]

Speaking, then, of life in America in a post-9/11 world, he said this:

Every act of violence and discrimination has been countered by multiple acts of friendship and respect—and a commitment that these terrorist acts will not be allowed to tear apart the American community.

That commitment has been echoed almost unanimously throughout the political leadership of this country—embraced by the leadership in the Congress, and in states and local governments across the Nation.

But there is one moment that will always stand out in my mind—when the President of the United States walked through the door of a mosque in Washington, D.C. to meet with Arab American and Muslim American leaders. He told them that he understood who our enemy truly is—an isolated group of violent extremists.

And he told them who our enemy most emphatically is not—the millions of loyal and honorable Arab and Muslim Americans who call this Nation home, and the hundreds of millions of true followers of the Islamic faith around the world.

As a Japanese American, and as someone who lived through the terrible events of 1941 and 1942, I could not help but wonder whether history might have been different—whether this Nation could have avoided the tragedy of the internment if President Roosevelt had taken a similar step. We can never know the answer to that question.

But we can resolve today, as Americans, that the tremendous progress we have made toward our goal of equal justice and equal opportunity for all Americans will not be sacrificed to fear.[6]

Question: Is it fair of Secretary Mineta to compare his own horrific experience in WWII to the present plight of Arabs seeking to fly in a post-9/11 world? I think not. No one is advocating the rounding up of those who resemble the 9/11 hijackers—least of all, me.

Although some may seek to dismiss my argument as an expression of xenophobia or racism, the reality is that I am attempting to make the case for added scrutiny of those who have similarities with the enemy that has engaged us. Nothing more, nothing less. Were I advocating that we "round up" the Arabs in America for internment, that charge would have merit. But I am advocating nothing of the kind. I am suggesting that it is appropriate for law enforcement in this country in a post-9/11 world—be they protecting our borders, our airports, our chemical refineries, our nuclear plants, our stadiums, and our overall infrastructure—to be attentive to signs of suspicious activity on the part of all individuals, most notably young Arab males.

Let me give you an example. This past July 4 weekend (2004), there was a news report in Camden, New Jersey that caught my eye. First, let me give you the context. The FBI warned police of potential July 4 attacks by al Qaeda using tactics like assault teams, car bombs, and suicide bombs. In fact, an FBI bulletin on suicide bombers said that Americans needed to be on the lookout for individuals wearing irregular, loose-fitting clothing not appropriate for warm weather; sweating; mumbling prayers (somehow I don't think the Lord's Prayer was what had the FBI concerned); wearing disguises; and carrying heavy baggage not appropriate for a particular location—like a big duffel bag in a restaurant.[7] Well, against this backdrop, I saw a news report that said authorities in Camden County had put out an all-points bulletin for three men who appeared to be of Middle Eastern descent, seen taking pictures of the Benjamin Franklin Bridge that links the city of Camden with Philadelphia. The bulletin said that investigators would like to locate and question the three who were seen about 10 AM one day snapping photos of the bridge from a white Chrysler Concorde with British Columbia license plates. Anyone with information was to contact local police.[8] Now, let's spend a moment and look at the circumstances giving rise to the APB. Three guys who look like the 9/11 hijackers taking pictures of a prominent landmark out of a car with foreign plates. Hell yes I'd like somebody to ask a few questions! No phone books. No rubber hoses. Just a question or two as to what they are up to. But would I be so concerned if this were a car of elderly nuns? Or a family from the suburbs of Vancouver? Of course not. And nor, I am sure, would the authorities in Camden County. So why can't that sort of common sense apply to our airports? It makes no sense.

It makes perfect sense, however, to consider Secretary Mineta's reference to his own experience as a Japanese American a red herring, designed to suppress dialogue on appropriate safety measures by embarrassing anyone who would choose to confront his message. I will not cower in the face of such debate.

You have to give Secretary Mineta credit for one thing. He hasn't just talked the talk; he has also walked the walk. He has initiated DOT actions predicated on his viewpoints. His statement to the U.S. Civil Rights Commission made reference to a variety of written directives issued by the DOT to the airlines telling them how to operate in a post-

9/11 world. I decided that needed to be my next area of inquiry.

It turns out that the DOT issued several written memoranda post-9/11 on this issue. Taken together, they are mind-boggling. To appreciate their significance, we need to analyze them in the context of what was occurring in our nation at that time.

**SEPTEMBER 11, 2001:** 2,976 innocent people (mostly Americans) die at the hands of young, Arab, male, Muslim extremists.

**SEPTEMBER 21, 2001:** The DOT e-mailed a memorandum to major airlines (Alaska, America West, American, American Trans Air, Continental, Delta, Northwest, Southwest, Trans World, United, and US Airways) and aviation associations. We're talking ten days after 9/11. Here is what the DOT stated:

> Since the terrorist hijackings and events of September 11, we have seen several reports of airlines apparently removing passengers from flights because the passengers appeared to be Middle Eastern and/or Muslim. We caution airlines not to target or otherwise discriminate against passengers based on their race, color, national or ethnic origin, religion, or based on passengers' names or modes of dress that could be indicative of such classification. Various Federal statutes prohibit air carriers from subjecting a person in air transportation to discrimination on the basis of race, color, national origin, religion, sex, or ancestry. At DOT, we are and will continue to be vigilant in ensuring that the airport security procedures, mandated by FAA and implemented by the airlines, are not unlawfully discriminatory.
>
> We strongly encourage each airline to take steps to ensure that its employees understand that, not only is it wrong, but it is also illegal to discriminate against people based on their race, ethnicity, or religion.[9]

(*"We caution airlines not to target or otherwise discriminate. . . ."* What exactly does that mean?)

This DOT Memo incorporated a letter that had been sent by the COO of Delta Airlines to all of its employees worldwide. (What a difference two and a half years make. Here, in the immediate aftermath of

9/11, the DOT was singling out Delta as a model of how an airline should behave post-9/11, but in June of 2004, as will be discussed, it was Delta that would be on the receiving end of a DOT "enforcement action" alleging discrimination, which would be resolved only when Delta agreed to pay $900,000 towards civil rights training.) The Delta memo read, in part:

> Delta's *Code of Ethics and Business Conduct* states that, 'Delta has an uncompromising policy never to discriminate against customers on the basis of race, gender, age, national origin, disability, sexual orientation or similar classifications. The law mandates this policy—discrimination is not only illegal, it is wrong and will not be tolerated.'
> Please continue to be observant and vigilant when enforcing security that protects our passengers and our people. But don't let last Tuesday's events change you into someone suspicious of people just because of the way they look—if you do that, then the terrorists will have won.[10]

("*Please continue to be observant. . . .*" Again, what does this mean?)

**OCTOBER 11, 2001:** The U.S. government issued a warning that further terrorist attacks are imminent. It said, "Certain information, while not specific as to target, gives the government reason to believe that there may be additional terrorist attacks within the United States and against U.S. interests overseas over the next several days. The FBI has again alerted all local law enforcement to be on the highest alert and we call on all people to immediately notify the FBI and local law enforcement of any unusual or suspicious activity."[11]

**OCTOBER 12, 2001:** The DOT issued another memo. And what exactly did the DOT want to tell the airlines one day after the nation was warned of the threat of a possible imminent terrorist attack? Well, this one was titled, "Carrying Out Transportation Inspection and Safety Responsibilities in a Nondiscriminatory Manner." It read, in part (bold emphasis is all mine):

This is a reminder to Department of Transportation (DOT) employees and those carrying out transportation inspection and enforcement responsibilities with DOT financial support of longstanding DOT policy prohibiting unlawful discrimination against individuals because of their race, color, religion, ethnicity, or national origin. The terrorist attacks of September 11, 2001, have raised concerns about intimidation and harassment directed at individuals who are, or are perceived to be, of Arab, Middle Eastern, or South Asian descent and/or Muslim. Federal civil rights laws prohibit discrimination on the basis of a person's race, color, national or ethnic origin, religion, sex, ancestry, or disability. DOT applauds the professionalism and dedication of its safety inspectors and law enforcement investigators and recognizes the enormous challenges we face in ensuring the security of our Nation's transportation system. However, it is important to reemphasize that in performing our critical duties, we may not rely on generalized stereotypes or attitudes **or beliefs about the propensity of members of any racial, ethnic, religious, or national origin group to engage in unlawful activity.** . . .

—Do not subject persons or their property to inspection, search and/or detention solely because they appear to be Arab, Middle Eastern, Asian, and/or Muslim; or solely because they speak Arabic, Farsi, or another foreign language; or solely because they speak with an accent that may lead you to believe they are Arab, Middle Eastern, Asian, and/or Muslim. . . .

—**Use the "but/for" test to help determine the justification for your actions. Ask yourself, But for this person's perceived race, ethnic heritage or religious orientation, would I have subjected this individual to additional security scrutiny? If the answer is "no," then the action may violate civil rights laws.**[12]

Now let's parse some of those words. First, "propensity." It means tendency. Do young Arab males have a tendency to commit terrorist acts? No. But as compared to any other section of society in the world, is there a tendency for terrorists committing acts against the United States to be comprised of young Arab males? Absolutely. And how about that but/for test? That's the stunner. And there is no better way to pick it apart than to reflect on the example set by Jose Melendez-Perez, the INS border officer who stopped the presumed twentieth 9/11 hijacker, Mohammed

Kahtani, from entering the United States on August 4, 2001, at the Orlando International Airport (as 9/11 ringleader Mohammed Atta waited there to pick him up). But for Mr. Kahtani's Saudi roots, would Mr. Perez have conducted his interview with the man at the level of scrutiny that he did? I dare say not. Arguably, it was Mr. Kahtani's heritage that first caused Melendez-Perez's heightened scrutiny. Had Kahtani been an 85-year-old African American man from Philadelphia, I dare say he would not have been subjected to secondary screening. Why can't we just say so?

**OCTOBER 29, 2001:** The U.S. government issued another warning that further terrorist attacks were imminent. Here is how CNN reported it:

> In a quickly called news conference, Ashcroft said intelligence sources had found 'credible' information the nation could be the focus for some sort of terrorist attack within the week. He called on law enforcement agencies, citizens, and U.S. interests abroad to be on 'highest alert.'
>
> As if to underscore his warning, an American Airlines Boeing 757 en route from New York to Dallas, Texas, Monday evening was diverted to Washington's Dulles International Airport after a threatening note was found on the plane, CNN learned.
>
> Flight 785 had taken off carrying 141 passengers and a crew of eight when the note was found, a source told CNN. The FAA ordered the flight to Dulles, where the passengers exited via emergency chutes as officials closed off the western side of the airport.
>
> Ashcroft took Monday's information seriously enough to cancel a planned trip Monday night to Toronto, Canada, where he was scheduled to speak Tuesday to a meeting of the International Association of Police Chiefs.[13]

**NOVEMBER 16, 2001:** The DOT issued written guidance for screeners and other security personnel. The introductory paragraph set the tone, and the but/for test was again referenced:

> Background: In the aftermath of the September 11, 2001 tragedies, concerns have been raised about intimidation and harassment directed at

individuals who are, or are perceived to be, of Arab, Middle Eastern, or South Asian descent and/or Muslim. It is important to reemphasize that in performing critical duties, personnel may not rely on generalized stereotypes or attitudes or beliefs about the propensity of members of any racial, ethnic, religious, or national origin group to engage in unlawful activity. Specifically, there appears to have been a rash of improper and insensitive searches and other improper treatment of Sikh and Arab Americans by airport and air carrier security personnel. Exercising our role under U.S. law to carry out security activities for the safety of the traveling public should not conflict with our obligation to protect the Constitution and civil rights of our citizens. It is illegal under federal law for an air carrier or its employees to discriminate on the basis of race, color, national origin, religion, sex, or ancestry. . . .

Although actions may, at times, offend the person involved, security personnel in certain circumstances may be justified in conducting additional questioning, inspections or searches for safety or security reasons as noted below. The security personnel should use the "but for" test to help determine the justification for their actions: 'But for a person's perceived race, ethnic heritage or religious orientation, would I have subjected this individual to additional safety or security scrutiny?' If the answer is 'no' then the action is likely to be unjustified and violate civil rights laws.[14]

This memo went as far as to offer specific examples of proper conduct:

. . . Event #2: A woman is selected for an inspection solely because her hair is covered or she is wearing a veil; or a man is selected for inspection solely because he has a long beard or is wearing a hair covering.

Action: Discriminating on the basis of national origin or religion includes discriminating against someone based solely on an appearance or dress that is associated with a particular national origin or religion. Likewise, selection must not be based solely because a person speaks Arabic, Farsi, or another foreign language, or solely because they speak with an accent that may lead one to believe they are Arab, Middle Eastern, South Asian, and/or Muslim. Accordingly, these practices must not take place.[15]

I agree with this as far as it goes—just so long as the presence of a veil, a long beard, or a hair covering is something that causes an airport screener to be attentive. Sorry, I happen to believe that an elderly woman with an aluminum walker and a young Arab male with a long beard or hair covering are entitled to different levels of scrutiny.

NOVEMBER 19, 2001: The DOT issued Answers to Frequently Asked Questions Concerning the Air Travel of People Who Are or May Appear to Be of Arab, Middle Eastern or South Asian Descent and/or Muslim or Sikh. Here are two particular questions, with answers, from that FAQ:

**Question: What are my rights when I fly on a commercial airliner?**

Individuals may not be selected for additional screening based solely on appearance or mode of dress that is associated with a particular national origin or religion. For example, selecting a woman for additional screening solely because her hair is covered or she is wearing a veil, as some Muslim women do, is unlawful discrimination. Selecting a man for additional screening solely because he is wearing a long beard or hair covering, as some Muslim men do, is unlawful discrimination. Likewise, selecting a man for additional screening solely because he is wearing a turban, as some Sikh men and women do, is unlawful discrimination.

**Question: How do screeners determine when additional security screening is appropriate?**

All available facts and circumstances must be taken into account in identifying persons or property that may be a safety or security risk. Although the screeners' actions could, at times, appear to be offensive to the person involved, screeners would continue to be justified in conducting additional questioning, inspections or searches, for safety or security reasons, in certain situations; for example: a person wearing a turban or head dress, while being searched at an airport security checkpoint, triggers the handheld metal detector when it is near his or her head; or a veiled woman shows photo identification to prove her identity but it is difficult to conclude that this woman is the same person as the woman in the photo without checking her face. When it is necessary to verify the identity of a veiled woman, whenever possible, her face should be checked by female safety or security personnel in private or only in the presence of other women so as not to violate her religious tenets.[16]

This is actually what I am saying, so long as "all available facts and circumstances" include those attributes that the 9/11 hijackers had in common, namely, religion, origin, and appearance. Then there was the good ol' but/for test again:

"Airline and airport personnel must use the 'but/for' test to help determine the justification for their actions. *But for this person's perceived race, ethnic heritage or religious orientation, would I have subjected this individual to additional safety or security scrutiny?* If the answer is 'no,' then the action may violate civil rights laws."[17]

**DECEMBER 3, 2001:** Secretary of Homeland Security Tom Ridge made the following announcement at the White House:

I've just completed a conference call with the nation's governors to let them know what I'm here to share with the American people. I might add, I also wanted to commend them for their work in improving and strengthening homeland security since September 11th. We've been in frequent communication either with the organizations or with individual governors, and I think their work to date has reflected the kind of relationship between the federal and the state and local government that we need to make a permanent part of our homeland security defense.

Over the last several days our intelligence in law enforcement agencies have seen an increased volume in level of activity involving threats of terrorist attacks. The information we have does not point to any specific target either in America or abroad. And it does not outline any specific type of attack.

However, the analysts who review this information believe the quantity and level of threats are above the norm and have reached a threshold where we should once again place the public on general alert, just as we have done on two previous occasions since September 11th.

During his address on homeland security in Atlanta, President Bush promised the American people that when we have evidence of credible threats we will issue appropriate alerts. That is exactly what we're doing here today.[18]

You get the picture, I'm sure. The nation is on pins and needles and Norman Mineta is papering the airline industry with warnings about political correctness. Here's the bottom line: Norman Mineta carries with him the emotional scars of his internment as a Japanese-American boy during World War II. He has decided views on the issue of airport screening that are opposed to the weighing of ethnicity and appearance when it comes to determining who should be subject to secondary screening at airports, despite the fact that the nineteen hijackers from 9/11 have ethnicity and appearance in common. Unfortunately, Mineta's view has become the mindset of the DOT in the midst of the war on terror. (And as the TSA has supplanted the DOT under the direction of the Department of Homeland Security, that mantra has continued.) In the process, I believe Mineta, and this liberal thinking, is jeopardizing our security.

However, to be fair to Norman Mineta, it should be understood that the foundation for the intrusion of political correctness on airline security was laid a few years before 9/11. And one of the excavators was none other than Al Gore. Here's how that happened.

On a Wednesday night in late July 1996, a Boeing 747 took off from New York's John F. Kennedy Airport bound for Paris. On board were a cross-section of travelers: a contingent of high school kids from Pennsylvania off to France for a field trip; an 11-year-old exchange student returning home after collecting loads of Chicago Bulls and New York Knicks basketball memorabilia; a Connecticut engineering manager planning a romantic interlude for the woman he hoped would agree to become his fiancé; and a mother who overcame her fear of flying so she could tour medieval castles in a bonding trip with her daughter.[19] The Boeing airframe number was N93119; but for many of us, it will forever be known as TWA Flight 800. Thirty-one minutes into its scheduled six-hour flight, the airplane exploded over the Atlantic Ocean, leaving no survivors. Two hundred and thirty perished. This catastrophe was to become instant fodder for conspiracy buffs who were quick to use the Internet to fuel speculation that the airplane had been shot out of the sky by terrorists. What was to become a long and labor-intensive investigation was initiated against the backdrop of the soon-to-begin Olympic games in Atlanta.

Within a month, President Bill Clinton tasked Vice President Al Gore to chair a commission "to study matters involving aviation safety and security, including air traffic control, and to develop a strategy to improve aviation safety and security, both domestically and internationally."[20]

The Commission on Aviation Safety and Security, or "Gore Commission" as it came to be known, was born. It had a broad mandate to address airline security in the wake of TWA Flight 800. Unfortunately, that opportunity was squandered.

When Vice President Gore turned in his report on February 12, 1997, some six months after the TWA 800 disaster, it included Recommendation 3.19, which advocated that the government "Complement technology with automated passenger profiling," especially since "such systems are employed successfully by other agencies, including the Customs Service."[21]

Sounds good, right? Unfortunately, something called the Civil Liberties Advisory Board got in the way. Charged with reviewing the Gore Commission's findings and providing their own two cents (somehow, the value seems appropriate), they began their own findings by noting their objection to any system of profiling whatsoever. "In light of the serious civil liberties issues raised by any profiling system, we urge the Commission and the President to consider carefully **whether any profiling system is appropriate** [bold emphasis added]."[22]

Thus, the Gore Commission's call for an automated passenger profiling system included this not-so-insignificant passage: "No profile should contain or be based on material of a constitutionally suspect nature—e.g. race, religion, national origin of U.S. citizens. . . . [Furthermore] profiling should last only until explosive detection systems are reliable and fully deployed."[23]

In other words, go ahead and profile, just don't use those key factors that would enable you to apprehend terrorists, and when we have better explosive detection systems, we will end even that limited form of profiling.

Even before TWA Flight 800 and the Gore Commission, there had been debate within the airline industry as to the role of passenger profiling. Just four months before the TWA Flight 800 tragedy, the General Accounting Office (GAO), a nonpartisan watchdog chartered by Congress, noted the frustration of staff at the Federal Aviation Administration (FAA) in pushing for greater airport security. Working with the aviation industry, the FAA developed a plan including various procedures to be introduced "depending on the nature and degree of the threat. Among these procedures are passenger bag match and passenger profiling."[24] You'd think the TWA crash would have ensured, not hindered, the FAA's plans. But no, that wasn't to be the case. What did it in? Not only political correctness, but money, too. Because of the estimated cost of implementing such measures ($2 billion at that time), the FAA found that "standard cost-benefit analyses would likely reject these measures, and consequently, they believe a consensus is needed among industry, Congress, and the Executive branch . . . without [which] the rulemaking would fail."[25] Too bad.

Al Gore has been known to take credit for the expanded use of computer technology in airline security, but like the Internet, there is a bit more to the story. Credit for what is known as CAPPS—Computer Assisted Passenger Prescreening System—is owed to Northwest Airlines, which, in 1994, had begun developing a customer screening system with the financial assistance of the federal government, courtesy of the FAA.[26] While the Gore Commission is often credited with getting the software more recognition and spurring its dissemination (though not its mandatory adoption) throughout the airline industry, the CAPPS program actually began at Northwest.[27]

CAPPS promised a dramatic improvement in security, selecting potentially unsafe passengers for additional screening through the objective analysis of various factors in that passenger's profile. Sounds good, but it is actually a continuation of the refusal to take into account race, ethnicity, religion, and physical appearance. CAPPS ignores those common traits of the nineteen hijackers on 9/11. Facing public charges of racism and general political incorrectness from Arab-American and civil rights groups, the Department of Transportation submitted the elements comprising its profiling system to the Department of Justice for review. In October of 1997, the Justice folks announced to the world at large that CAPPS does not record race, color, national or ethnic origin, religion, or gender.[28] Wonderful news, no doubt, for both civil libertarians AND bin Laden.

Then the FAA strove throughout the late nineties to reach ever higher levels of political correctness, at one point discouraging hand searches of suspicious passengers. "Manual screening has been criticized by persons who perceived it as discriminating against citizens on the basis of race, color, or ethnic origin and gender."[29]

Recently on the drawing board was CAPPS II. Congress provided for CAPPS II in the Aviation and Transportation Security Act of 2001, the same act directing the creation of the Transportation Security Administration. The TSA would, among other things, oversee the new system.[30] Here's how they see CAPPS II:

"Under the proposed CAPPS II system, the TSA will obtain electronically, either from airlines or from Global Distribution Systems, a passenger's Passenger Name Record (PNR) as collected from the passenger by a reservation system. PNR includes the routine information collected at the time a passenger makes a flight reservation. A PNR may include each passenger's full name, home address, home telephone number, and date of birth, as well as some information about that passenger's itinerary. No additional information beyond this data is required to be collected from passengers for the operation of CAPPS II.

"The CAPPS II system will access PNRs prior to the departure of the passenger's flight. Selected information will be securely transmitted to commercial data providers, for the sole purpose of authenticating passenger identity."[31]

But of course, "CAPPS II *will absolutely not profile based on race, ethnic-*

*ity, religion, or physical appearance.*"[32] So, not only are we kneecapping ourselves before the big game, we are telegraphing all our pitches for our opponents, the terrorists, to get some wood on the ball. Meanwhile, the airlines are balking at implementing CAPPS II due to concerns over passengers' reaction to the release of their personal data. The Congressional Research Service, another nonpartisan research organization chartered by Congress, recently noted the following:

"The TSA's efforts to launch the test phase of CAPPS II have been delayed by the airline's reluctance to voluntarily provide passenger records for testing the system. The airlines' reluctance stems from recent incidents in which public criticism and legal actions resulted from airlines' voluntarily providing passenger data to government agencies. In the first instance, Jet Blue Airways supplied passenger data to an Army contractor that used the data to test a data mining system for security at Army bases. Delta Airlines was originally slated to participate in the initial test phase for CAPPS II but declined to provide the data after a privacy advocacy group launched a web site urging a boycott of Delta Airlines for their role in the program. More recently, it was disclosed that Northwest Airlines provided passenger records in the months following September 11th, 2001, to NASA researchers who were reportedly unsuccessful in using that data to develop a data-mining tool for security analysis. A class action lawsuit has been filed against Northwest Airlines on behalf of all passengers whose information was allegedly divulged. As a result of these concerns, the implementation of CAPPS II may depend on legislative or regulatory mechanisms to resolve the airline's legal concerns as well as the concerns raised regarding privacy protections. Despite these setbacks, the TSA anticipates testing CAPPS II in the Spring of 2004 and implementing the system by summer of 2004."[33]

Due "in large part to delays in obtaining needed passenger data"[34] the CAPPS II program is like the proverbial ship without a port: lost at sea. In fact, as of June 2004, the TSA seems to have abandoned the program. With each attempt to move forward hounded by the PC Brigade, we can expect little progress before the 2004 presidential election. The best the government can manage for the moment is the Registered Traveler program. Initiated in June of 2004, the Registered Traveler will enable some frequent fliers to receive expedited security clearance. Participants in the program must provide biometric data, including fingerprints, retinal scan, and a digital photo. This data will be associated with the passenger's profile and easily accessible when they fly.[35] That may help alleviate lines for business travelers at the airports, but what about the occasional flier? And another thing. Unless the TSA will change positions and take into account race, ethnicity, and religion in determining who receives the expedited clearance, it'll be just another new program failing to correct the underlying problem.

Speaking of underlying problems, I think it's only fair at this point to let Mr. Norman Mineta take the floor and defend his position.

# 10: NORMAN AND ME

THAT'S RIGHT. I AM BORROWING THIS CHAPTER TITLE from that crumb Michael Moore. (You could say I am *Joe Bidening* the chapter title.)

I want to be fair. Having watched the 60 *Minutes* segment with Norman Mineta and studied the transcript, as well as reviewing a variety of other public pronouncements from the man, I desperately wanted to interview the Secretary myself on the issues raised in this book. As a matter of fact, not only did my radio producer extend the invitation, but so too did Congressman James Gerlach (R-PA). No dice. That's okay. I am in a position to have dialogue with him right now because his views on the issue of how we screen at the airports in a post-9/11 world are about to be fully presented. What follows is the complete text of a key speech that Mineta delivered in the spring of 2002. And, in lieu of having an actual dialogue with Mr. Mineta, I have taken the liberty to add my responses and editorial remarks, in italics.

**REMARKS FOR**
**THE HONORABLE NORMAN Y. MINETA**
**U.S. SECRETARY OF TRANSPORTATION**
**ARAB COMMUNITY CENTER FOR ECONOMIC AND SOCIAL SERVICES**
**GALA DINNER**
**COBO HALL CONFERENCE CENTER**
**DETROIT, MICHIGAN**
**APRIL 20, 2002**

Good evening, and thank you for that very warm introduction. It's wonderful to be here with all of you this evening, and I am proud to bring you greetings from President Bush and Vice President Cheney, along with their best wishes for the event this evening.

Under the leadership of Ish Ahmed, the Board of Directors and the staff of the ACCESS have built this organization into a pre-eminent social service agency for the Arab American community, one that serves as a model for similar agencies around the country.

The Arab American community, along with the entire nation, has been faced with an unbelievable challenge in recent months. Thankfully, with commitment from our citizens, from the Congress, and from the Administration, the nation is rising to meet that challenge.

Tonight, I would like to tell you about some of the things that we are doing to fight terrorism, and specifically the steps we are taking to provide Americans with a secure transportation system that both ensures mobility, and helps achieve economic growth.

It has been just over seven months since that fateful day on the 11th of September. And I will always be proud of the way that our nation responded to those attacks.

On September 11, I took the unprecedented step of ordering the Federal Aviation Administration to shut down the civil and commercial aviation system—and to land every aircraft at the nearest airport as soon as possible.

With that single call, air traffic controllers, pilots, and flight attendants worked together—and in an amazing achievement—safely landed thousands of aircraft and saved other tragedies from occurring.

*(So far, so good. Didn't want you to think there was no commentary coming. Norm is doin' just fine.)*

Since that day of decision and heroism, every person on President Bush's team has been focused on fighting this war abroad and here at home.

At the Department of Transportation our mission has included bringing the air system back up and literally working day and night to develop a security system that prevents terrorists and other criminals from using our aviation system again to kill or injure Americans.

In less than six months, we have made airplanes safer, increased our federal air marshal force, restricted flights over high-risk areas, and improved the screening of passengers and baggage at 429 commercial aviation airports in this country.

*(Improved the screening of passengers? I am not so sure. I believe we've increased the time it takes to get from the curb to your gate, and that we*

*created window dressing for a more secure system, but whether it has truly improved our safety, and is as strong as it might be, is questionable at best, and not something I can concede.)*

The President has worked with a bipartisan force in Congress to create the Transportation Security Agency, and we have hired the former Director of the Secret Service—a renowned counter terrorism expert—to head it.

In an effort not seen since World War II's "dollar-a-year men," we have brought volunteers from American industry to help design an aviation security system that provides world-class security with world-class customer service.

Across the Nation, we are now swearing-in the first Federal Security Directors—each of whom will run security operations at major airports. So far, these individuals include big-city police chiefs, a retired admiral who commanded an aircraft carrier, a Marine Corps general, a Coast Guard admiral, and career Secret Service agents—all of whom have answered the call to build the safe and secure aviation system that the country deserves.

*(Sounds great. We need to beef up law enforcement. Now, tell the people what these experts will be doing and who they will be looking for.)*

Within fourteen months of the September 11th attack, we will have a security network of trained law enforcement officers, new detection technologies, and an unprecedented number of federal air marshals flying in planes that have been made safer.

In addition to these advances we are developing security procedures that are designed with three goals in mind—to keep Americans safe and secure, to keep them mobile, and to help keep our economy growing.

All Americans have a stake in our success. And as a nation, we are continuing to debate what steps must be taken to ensure that success.

I would like to spend some time tonight talking about one such step that some have proposed—large-scale profiling based solely on race—and why I believe it falls short of the mark in guaranteeing our national security.

*(Whooaaa. Attention, class. Lesson about to begin. And beware of the red herring. No one reasonable is saying we need to profile solely on race.*

*Fifteen of nineteen hijackers were Saudis. Elderly Saudi women and young Saudi children do not warrant added scrutiny at airports. But young Saudi men do indeed. Does that mean they get the rubber hose and phone-book treatment? Heck no. It just means that when someone who looks like one of the nineteen comes to an airport, the personnel with whom he interacts need to be alert.)*

There are times when race and ethnicity are relevant to law enforcement—for instance, when we have information that a crime is being planned or has been committed and among the specifics we know about the suspects are their race.

*(Stop right there. A crime of unimaginable inhumanity was committed on 9/11, and "among the specifics we know about the suspects" IS their race and ethnicity. To a man, they were young, Arab, Muslim, and with olive complexion. Fifteen of the nineteen were Saudis. Now you are making my point. And as for the planning, correct me if I am wrong, but doesn't the same hold true for virtually every individual we are seeking to pursue threats of future terrorism against the United States?*

*I went looking for support for some of my arguments in academia, and think I hit paydirt at no less than Harvard. Frederick Schauer is the Stanton Professor of the First Amendment at the Kennedy School of Government and has written a book called* Profiles, Probabilities and Stereotypes.[1] *In it, he explains the background behind the bad rap given the word "profiling," and why it shouldn't be so. When I got the chance to talk to the professor, I started by asking him to confirm that profiling does indeed occur in everyday life. He replied, "Everywhere, we all profile, it's how we think, we think in categories, we make predictions based on generalizations. The IRS profiles in determining who to audit. The customs service—even apart from the issues of race and ethnicity— Customs profiles in determining who to look at closely and so on, it's part of how we think."[2]*

*So then I took this thought a step further. I asked him outright if it would be fair to say that the P-word was not such a dirty word. His answer?*

"*Right, I mean there's good profiling, there's bad profiling, but it's hard to imagine what the world would be like with no profiling.*"

So if I am someone charged with the responsibility for airport security, and if I take into account one's country of origin, is that good or bad profiling? According to Professor Schauer, "*In almost all cases it provides some information we otherwise wouldn't have. It comes with a risk and we can't ignore that risk. There is some risk that certain profiles, certain generalizations that might actually tell us good, important, useful information will be treated by people as more reliable than they are and they'll crowd out a number of other factors.*"

I have no problem with that. I'm not trying to ignore that risk. I'm not asking that we take ONLY race and ethnicity into consideration. I'm saying you MUST take them into consideration, along with everything else you can think of to keep our airplanes safe. And I'm saying that race and ethnicity shouldn't be ignored for fear of offending someone else waiting in line.

As far as what should be taken into consideration in an airport security profile, in his book, Professor Schauer lists many factors: "*gender (male), ethnicity (Middle Eastern), demeanor (nervous), frequent flyer membership (no), date ticket purchased (last-minute), time of check-in (late), form of purchase (cash), use of travel agent (no), type of luggage (carry-on). . . .*" [Profiles, Probabilities and Stereotypes, p. 186]

My point? If you've got any of these other things going on, and you're male, and you're Middle Eastern, then you'd better be getting the hairy eyeball, and a big one at that. But we need to stop the practice of having our screeners look for a list of characteristics that leaves out the obvious.

Professor Schauer believes there is more risk when you look the other way and rely on "*folk wisdom, street wisdom and hunches, much of which turns out to be wrong.*" He says, "*I would much rather have a carefully worked out list of, say, 47 different attributes—including some of the ones you just mentioned—make a careful profile for numerous different purposes, using all of them arrayed in the proper relation to each other, rather then just saying to someone, 'Use your hunch, use your instinct.' Or something of that nature.*"

*To which I respond, on that list we need to have Muslim, Young, and Male at the very top in bold. Right now, those factors are absolutely disallowed by our government. But the professor and I agree where it is most important. Stop ignoring the obvious. "Profiling" is not a bad word; it is a powerful and useful tool and could save us again and again and again.*

*We also agree on the issue of Norman Mineta and his belief that the screening system needs to be race-blind. The professor commented, "What troubles me about what he and others say is they're not clear about why they're saying it. They're not clear about whether they believe, probably inaccurately, that it's irrelevant, statistically irrelevant or spurious, as the statisticians would say. . . . I agree with you that the way in which it is framed, whether it be by Mineta or by the first Gore Commission which came up with the passenger screening system, is troubling and avoids difficult questions."*

*So there it is. We both think it is time to ask those difficult questions. First among them, what valid justification exists for disregarding those characteristics held in common by our enemy?)*

But there is a firm distinction between that situation, and one where a law enforcement officer is willing to assume, based on no reason other than race alone, that a particular person is likely to be a criminal—or a terrorist.

*(Wait a minute. Let's have the blunt talk. When exactly should race be a factor? How about a circumstance that may or may not be suspicious, in combination with race as a factor? Race should then tip the balance in favor of more scrutiny, should it not? And if so, then what Mineta just said is at odds with the but/for test, as stated in DOT memos to the airlines post-9/11. Let's review. According to the test, the airline and airport personnel must use this standard: But for this person's perceived race, ethnic heritage or religious orientation, would I have subjected this individual to additional safety or security scrutiny? If the answer is "no," then the action may violate civil rights laws.*

*Consider the following hypothetical. Two men in their twenties arrive at an American airport from a foreign destination. Man No. 1 comes from*

*Heathrow, UK. He is a British citizen. He claims he is traveling to America on business. He arrived with a one-way ticket. Man No. 2 arrives from Dubai. He is a Saudi citizen. He, too, has a one-way ticket. Stop right there. Should the Saudi be asked a few more questions than the Brit? I say yes. Why? Because like fifteen of the 9/11 hijackers, he is a young Arab male, and a one-way ticket is an unusual way to travel. But for the man's perceived ethnic heritage, would he have been subjected to more questions than the Brit? No. If he were Scandinavian, he would get the same scrutiny as the Brit. But he's not. He has similarities to the people seeking to wreak havoc on our way of life. Now, is my proposed means of dealing with these two individuals a violation of the but/for test? Yes, insofar as his race or ethnicity has tipped the balance in favor of more scrutiny. But, to do otherwise would be a violation of common sense. Is the airport screener in my hypothetical assuming the man is a terrorist? No. He is simply applying an added level of scrutiny to the man because he shares characteristics with those who have posed a particular threat in the past. No one is saying anything about internment here.)*

As you are so very well aware, some commentators have been critical that the Administration has not engaged in large-scale racial profiling at airports in the wake of September 11. The criticisms they have raised are often based on misperceptions of the steps we *are* taking. Unfortunately, one of the problems I face in correcting these misperceptions is that, for security reasons, there are some details we cannot publicly discuss or disclose.

*(Well, you have the attention of one of those "commentators" right now, so let's get to it.)*

But there *are* some responses that can be made, and I would like to take the opportunity tonight to do so.

Those who have advocated a policy of routine profiling based exclusively on race generally raise three arguments:

First, they argue that because the September 11th terrorists were all young men of Arab ancestry, a system that singles out young men who look like

Arabs is an effective way to stop the next attack.

(*Indeed. But let's be clear about what we mean when we say "singles out." I am not advocating that every single individual who looks Arab be given a pre-boarding proctologic exam by the DOT or the TSA. But I AM absolutely saying that the antennae of the airport screeners need to be raised when someone approaches an aircraft and has similarities to the known 9/11 hijackers. I like to use the expression, "give the hairy eyeball," and I think most people know what that means. It suggests that a person receive a once-over. Let's take a lesson from Jose Melendez-Perez, who, you will recall from Chapter 7, was successful in turning away Mohammed Kahtani, the presumed twentieth 9/11 hijacker, at the Orlando International Airport on August 4, 2001. How did Melendez-Perez do it? He took into account the man's nationality (Saudi), as well as the appearance of the man—everything from his youth to his grooming, his dress, his height, and his physical shape. He noted that the man lacked a return ticket and a hotel reservation. He sized the guy up with some street smarts and concluded that he might be military. He thought the man seeking entry into the United States was cocky, and he factored that in. Cover your ears, Secretary Mineta, but Mr. Melendez-Perez was profiling. And this was pre-9/11. Does this mean that one of these factors alone warrants secondary screening? No. That's not what I am saying.*

*Let me try another example. If you are dealing with someone who looks like the 9/11 hijackers, and he is traveling alone, but on a plane with four others who look the same and are also alone, then the antenna needs to go up. Conversely, if you have someone who looks like the 9/11 hijackers who is traveling with a wife and three kids straight out of a Laura Ashley catalogue, then the antenna can be retracted. Really, is this so complicated?*)

Secondly, they argue that time spent searching people in other population groups is a waste of time. For example, they ask, how could a baby or a grandmother be a security risk?

(*Absolutely, lay off the 85-year-old grandmothers with aluminum walkers. Use some street smarts.*)

And thirdly, they argue that random searches should be eliminated because they are indiscriminate and a waste of time. Those who make this point apparently believe that most or all of our searches are random. In fact, only a small proportion fall into that category.

*(Yes indeed, so long as the random searches are—as I suspect—simply window dressing so that our real targets can't say they are being profiled. That is what I took away from my conversation with Herb Kelleher, the founder and chairman of Southwest Airlines. Litigation worries are driving this bus. The fear of being sued because somebody who looks like the hijackers objects and says, "Hey, you're questioning me more than Thurston Howell III because I look like the hijackers." Well, yeah. We'd be derelict in our duty if we did not.*

*I had a conversation about precisely this subject with Torie Clarke, the former Assistant Secretary of Defense for Public Affairs. You remember Torie, she was truly the "face" of the Iraqi war in its early stages with her live updates from the Pentagon. Well, she was a radio guest of mine on The Big Talker as these events were unfolding, and I think our conversation was directly on point, and that she gave me an honest answer. Here is the exchange:*

**MAS**: *Oh I don't have a quarrel with soliciting the help of the public. The concern I have is there seems to be a disconnect between John Ashcroft and Bob Mueller on one hand soliciting the support of the public and seeing the face of the government through, for example, the TSA at the airport, on the other hand focusing on my kids flying to Florida getting pulled out of line for, you know, an exam, or the 85-year-old lady with the aluminum walker. It seems like we're so afraid of offending people who might look like these hijackers when in fact we ought to say, hey, we're sorry, blame bin Laden, don't blame Bush, this is what we need to do.*

**CLARKE**: *I agree completely with the last part of your sentence. But let's go back to it about why do they take the 85-year-old lady.*

**MAS**: *Tell me.*

**CLARKE**: *They don't want lawsuits impeding the good work they're trying to do, so when somebody who may possibly look like a terrorist gets pulled out of line and gets a tough, tough scrutiny and that person says, 'You know, I'm offended by that, they're profiling me,' and wants to sue the TSA and whomever, then the TSA and all those people can say, 'Look, we don't discriminate against or for anybody, and we take old people and young people and people of all sizes and shapes, colors . . .' and they can show with numbers that they are trying to do this in a very even-handed fashion.*[3]

*Now back to Stormin' Norman.)*

The aviation security system in place today is a multi-layered one that incorporates examination of every single airline passenger, and then extra scrutiny for some.

It requires searches of every person and every carry-on bag passing through an airport security checkpoint.

It includes additional searches triggered by a classified computer-assisted passenger pre-screening system, by suspicious behavior observed by security personnel, and by some random selections.

*(Wait a minute. That classified Computer-Assisted Passenger Pre-Screening program has some holes in it. In your statement to the U.S. Civil Rights Commission on October 12, 2001, you stated that the CAPPS was founded by the Department of Justice in 1997 to be non-discriminatory on their face.*[4] *I took from that statement that CAPPS doesn't factor in ethnicity, and because it doesn't, it is flawed.)*

The critical question is what criteria should we use in making selections for these additional searches.

*(Agreed. I say we draw up a list of the criteria exhibited by those who attacked the World Trade Center in 1993, the USS Cole in 2000, the World Trade Center, Pentagon, etc. on 9/11, and so on. You get the pic-*

*ture. I mean, this is getting a bit ridiculous.)*

The criteria we use are undergoing constant revision to meet current threat conditions, and current intelligence and law enforcement information. There may be times when that information gives us knowledge concerning a possible crime or a threat to our national security.

But we are very clear on one point—routinely pulling passengers out of line and subjecting them to searches need not, and should not, be done on the basis of race. Establishing such a policy would be counterproductive to our efforts to build a solid basis for aviation security.

*(And I am not saying that you pull every Arab-looking individual out of line. I am saying that, unlike the giant Nord who comes to check in, the antennae are going up with the Arab. But guess what? If and when the Norwegians start to hijack planes, they will get the same treatment.)*

This is not a knee-jerk response. It is based on the nature of the national security threat we face, and on the realities of managing a security screening system in aviation facilities across the Nation.

It is very tempting to take false comfort in the belief that we can spot the bad guy based on appearance alone. Some are yielding to that temptation in their arguments for racial profiling, but false comfort is a luxury we cannot afford.

It is true that each of the hijackers involved in the September 11th hijackings had some characteristics in common—they were all young men of Arab ancestry.

*(Some characteristics? They were all male. All Arab. All had dark hair. All had dark eyes. All had olive skin. All were of Middle Eastern descent. All were followers of Islam. And the same can be said for those who have instigated the attack on the USS Cole, the World Trade Center in 1993, the bombing of our embassies in Kenya and Tanzania, etc., etc. Moreover, they share the same characteristics as those who are continually sought in connection with current terrorism investigations in the U.S.)*

But we cannot, we must not, and we will not assume that all future terrorists will fit that particular profile. Without more information, we simply cannot tell—and it certainly has not been true in the past.

Let me give you some examples:

In 1986, a 32-year-old Irish woman, pregnant at the time, was about to board an El Al flight from London to Tel Aviv when El Al security agents discovered an explosive device hidden in the false bottom of her bag. The woman's boyfriend—the father of her unborn child—had hidden the bomb.

In 1987, a 70-year-old man and a 25-year-old woman—neither of whom were Middle Eastern—posed as father and daughter and brought a bomb aboard a Korean Air flight from Baghdad to Thailand. En route to Bangkok, the bomb exploded, killing all on board.

In 1999, men dressed as businessmen (and one dressed as a Catholic priest) turned out to be terrorist hijackers, who forced an Avianca flight to divert to an airstrip in Colombia, where some passengers were held as hostages for more than a year-and-half.

Time permits me to cite only these few examples; there are many more.

*(All red herrings. Of course, overlooked by Secretary Mineta is the fact that the El Al security agents caught the Irish woman's bomb in the extensive pre-flight screening. This is an invalid example because it actually proves that by profiling and taking into account all things—Arab boyfriend, etc.—and asking the tough questions and observing a person's mannerisms, airline security can work. Also notable is the fact that none of these incidents were acts of terrorism against the United States, and all precede the current war against terrorism. The history of the world as we know it was rewritten on 9/11. We have an enemy. The enemy consists of suicidal, young Arab males. The sooner we focus on that fact, the sooner we will win this war.)*

So, how do we stop the terrorist—say one recruited from Chechnya—who is disguised as a priest if we are wasting our time on an unworkable profile of thousands of travelers who look a certain way?

*(Everyone needs to be screened. What we are debating here is a question of degree.)*

There is no universal racial, age or gender profile for terrorism—and we cannot pretend that there is. As President Bush has already noted, more than 60 nations are hostile to the United States.

*(That's just not true. Please take another look at the mug shots of the 9/11 terrorists on page 17. Enough said.)*

We must be alert for threats to our national security—from whatever population group they might emerge.

Even if we were to assume that all young Arab men—or all young men who practiced Islam—were potential terrorists, a directive to our security personnel to focus solely on people with those characteristics would inevitably fail.

First, it would assume that persons of Arab ancestry could be identified simply by their facial features. In fact, the diversity of the Arab world makes this impossible. Ultimately, anyone of Mediterranean or African ancestry would have to be separated out.

*(That's an unfair statement, and a clear play to enlist African Americans on his side. Nobody responsible for the death of 3,000 Americans on 9/11 was black.)*

Second, it would send a signal to our security personnel that their efforts should be concentrated on people with certain physical features. Such an operation would generate so many "false positives" that it would seriously hamper screeners in making the behavioral observations they need to make.

*(Concentrated? No. Heightened? Yes.)*

Most importantly, it would tell our enemies that extra security could be avoided simply by sending people who don't look like the stereotype that our security system was using.

*(You assume they have recruited such individuals. Name some.)*

Look at Timothy McVeigh, Richard Colvin Reid and John Walker Lindh—as law enforcement agencies around the globe gain greater success in identifying and detaining potential terrorists, using the *least* likely suspect becomes the *most* likely tactic for future attacks.

*(Not a good enough argument. Timothy McVeigh and Terry Nichols are not related to al Qaeda. They were two, domestically bred bad seeds. You may as well throw in the Columbine killers if all you are saying is that Americans sometimes turn on their own. We're talking war on terrorism here. As for Richard Reid, the infamous shoe bomber, we have alert American Airlines crew to thank for thwarting his attack. You know them; they are the folks who work for the company that lost two airplanes and more than a dozen personnel on 9/11, which didn't stop you from initiating an enforcement action against them post-9/11 which resulted in their paying $1.5 million toward touchy-feely training. As for Johnnie Walker, like McVeigh and Nichols, he is the aberration, not the norm, Norm. You've got to play the odds. And the odds at present favor terrorists who look like the nineteen. Foolproof? Hardly. That's why security in a post-9/11 world demands something of all of us, but something more from those with similarities to known al Qaeda criminals.)*

Racial profiling, or as it might be called, "facial profiling," cannot provide us with the security that we need.

*(I don't like "profiling" and/or "facial profiling," either. But I do support CRIMINAL PROFILING. That's what we're talking about here. Just like when a serial killer is on the loose and the local law enforcement agency brings in the guys from the FBI who do the same thing Jodie Foster's character did in* The Silence of the Lambs. *Let's figure out what the enemy looks like so we can catch them.)*

Some advocates of racial profiling have also focused their attention on what they consider unnecessary searches of people who appear to be innocent—elderly women, pregnant women, people traveling with children, priests, or even politicians.

Why subject a gray-haired grandmother to extra security screening? Because terrorists do not always look like today's prevailing stereotype. And, because one does not have to *look* like a stereotypical terrorist to be *used* by terrorists.

If a grandmother has been pulled aside by airport security, it is almost certainly because she has been selected for a random search.

*(Which is a waste of time, and is intended only to placate the young Arab male standing in line so he gets to say to himself, well, they pulled her out, so I guess it's not just me. Get over it. Let him blame bin Laden instead of Bush if he doesn't understand. I promise that if and when Yugoslavian [that's me] extremists pose a threat to the U.S., I won't blame the government for my getting asked additional questions.)*

For security reasons, I can't tell you what percentage of our searches are random, but I can tell you those random searches are essential. No matter what aviation security system we use, we always add a layer of random searches and we always will.

We do this first because introducing a random element into our security pre-screening system makes it more difficult to figure out how that system operates.

*(Not really. The random thing is such a joke because one can negotiate away one's selection for random screening, as I did twice in the spring of 2004. As I clarified earlier in this book, airport personnel knew it was a joke to search my 8-year-old son, so they allowed me to take his place.)*

And, along with the possibility of a random search at a security checkpoint, it sends a signal that—even if you think you've beaten the system—this still does not guarantee you won't be pulled aside.

*(Sorry. The only signal being sent through your interview on 60 Minutes, your statement to the U.S. Commission on Civil Rights, your speech at the University of Rochester, and your DOT memoranda to the airlines, is to al Qaeda, and it is this: We haven't learned our lesson.)*

I know it is an inconvenience, but taking any group of people and leaving them out would—by definition—remove the random element from the system. Along with the security benefits it brings.

*(I am not saying we leave out anyone. I am simply saying we stop kidding ourselves, and give heightened attention to those who resemble our enemy. This is starting to make me picture a basketball coach who sends his team onto the court and says, Don't just guard the guys in the other jerseys.)*

Equally importantly, it would make that protected group of people, like somebody's grandparents, a prime target for anyone trying to smuggle an item on board in someone else's carry on luggage.

*(If they could've, they would've.)*

We are hard at work on security tools that will significantly diminish—but not eliminate—the current amount of random wanding at departure gates.

In addressing the range and the scope of the threats we face, we cannot rely exclusively on race or age or gender. We need other, credible, current information. We know this from cold, hard experience.

Terrorism has a chameleon's face. And it will use people in whatever way it can to achieve its goals.

My good friend, Congressman Jim Oberstar of Minnesota, a 29-year veteran of Congress and a long-time advocate for our nation's transportation system, summed it up best when he said, "Now we know that terrorists are capable of anything. They will use old women and children as bomb carriers if we let them. Our vigilance has to match their ruthlessness." And our vigilance will match them.

*(So one of your former colleagues gave you a sound bite. It doesn't change the fact that on 9/11, there were no women and no children involved in causing terror.)*

Make no mistake, our aviation security system does regularly profile passengers—it examines every single one. But it conducts that examination on the basis of many relevant factors, including what a person *does*, what we know about that person, and what information we know about a potential crime or threat to national security.

The details of the computer assisted passenger pre-screening system we use to identify possible security risks are not publicly disclosed—and *cannot* be publicly disclosed if those factors are still to be useful.

*(Here's hoping your computer isn't a "PC"!)*

What I can say is that we focus mainly on behavior. We look at travel patterns. We look at a person's citizenship. We look at how much information we have on a particular passenger and information we have about particular national security threats—an extensive list of other factors. Our aviation security system is now in the hands of the new Transportation Security Administration, led by Under Secretary John Magaw. Our overall security system will always ensure that there are several lines of defense against a threat—never just one.

The computer pre-screening selection system will continue to undergo constant refinement.

The TSA will train new federal screeners to identify threats, to respond to current threat alerts, and to engage other elements of the security system whenever needed.

And we will constantly work to ensure that every possible threat is met—and countered—across all modes of transportation.

Will this system be perfect? No. No system operated by human beings can ever achieve perfection.

Focusing solely on race might give some Americans a false sense of security. But make no mistake about it, that sense of security would be false. It would simultaneously cast so wide a net as to ensnare far too many innocent people, and so narrow a net as to miss the mark.

*(No rational person is saying you should focus solely on race.)*

A policy based on the belief that terrorists can be identified by their race or religion without more information would be utterly flawed. An unflinching security analysis shows that it would not only be useless, but actively counterproductive.

*(But what happens when you have a situation that is in a gray area, with a racial similarity to the 9/11 hijackers? A young Arab male with a one-way ticket? A young Arab male with no luggage? A young Arab male [fill in the blank]. In that circumstance, can we agree that his ethnicity tips the balancing scale in favor of an added look-see?)*

To assume that skin color and character can be equated would be wrong. It would not only violate our most basic principles, it would send our transportation security system down a blind alley—and away from the real threats which it must face and overcome.

*(Stop already. No one is saying that.)*

Our fellow Americans know that we live in a dangerous world, and that we are confronted by an unprecedented threat. They expect us to take every step possible to meet that threat, and ensure their safety and security. And I assure you that we will.

Today, our aviation security system is better than it was yesterday. And, tomorrow it will be better than today.

President Bush has given us a clear mission. He has asked outstanding individuals like John Magaw to join in fulfilling the mission. American industry has stepped forward with their talent and resources. And polls show that the majority of Americans know that when it comes to air travel—patience is patriotism.

In all my time of public service—over thirty years—the dangers to our homeland have never been more clear and present.

I am honored that President Bush has given me the opportunity to help in the fight against these threats—and I will always be grateful for the leadership he has shown in this crisis.

When a Sikh American was murdered in a violent crime of hate, he called Sikh leaders together at the White House to condemn that act and promise a swift response.

And just six days after the September 11 attacks, the President visited the Islamic Center in Washington, D.C. where he sent a clear message to the Nation and to the world:

We know who our enemies are—a violent band of extremists who would twist the Islamic faith into a justification for terror.

And we know who our enemies are *not*—the millions of Arab Americans of all faiths who call this country home, and the hundreds of millions of true followers of Islam around the world.

*(Unfortunately, one is a subset of the other.)*

The President's message is a clear one: we will not allow this crisis to divide us as Americans.

From my own life I can tell you—it has not always been this way.

I am honored to be part of an Administration that understands the fundamental truth that all of us, regardless of race or religion, are equally entitled to call ourselves Americans.

Again, on behalf of the President and the Vice President, congratulations on thirty-one years of outstanding service to your community.

Thank you for inviting me here this evening. It's good to be with you all, God bless ACCESS, and God bless America.

*(And God bless you, Norman Mineta.)*

# 11: TSA: TROUBLE SECURING AIRLINES

WHATEVER WE WERE DOING ON 9/11 TO SECURE OUR airports didn't cut it. Airport security was made the responsibility of the federal authorities after 9/11. Under the direction of the Department of Homeland Security, the key player is now the Transportation Security Administration. Unfortunately, they're not getting the job done either. Don't let the lack of an attack since 9/11 fool you. There was similar false comfort for the decade leading up to 9/11—the lack of a hijacking or bombing was taken as accepted proof that we had a working system, even though several studies by the General Accounting Office and the DOT's Office of Inspector General documented "chronic weaknesses in the systems deployed to screen passengers and baggage for weapons and bombs. Shortcomings with the screening process had also been identified internally by the FAA's assessment process."[1]

Let's start with what went wrong on 9/11. The 9/11 Commission issued a Staff Statement (No. 3) which provided a brief overview of those civil aviation security defenses that were in existence on 9/11. Here are the several layers:

1) intelligence
2) passenger pre-screeening
3) airport access control
4) passenger checkpoint screening
5) passenger checked baggage screening
6) cargo screening
7) on-board security

The reality is that the screening process presented no defense to the hijackers, who were 19 for 19 in getting themselves where they wanted to be. Key to their success is the fact that they represented a brand of terror not contemplated by our security defenses, which were designed to stop bombings and hijackings, not terrorists trained as pilots willing to hijack and then die in the process of using airplanes as airborne missiles. Think about our component parts: 1) Intelligence: we had no intelligence that specifically indicated that bin Laden, al Qaeda, or its affiliates were actually plotting to hijack commercial planes in the U.S. and use them as weapons of mass destruction (if you think the PDB on 8/6/01 said otherwise, go read it again—don't take somebody else's word for it); 2) Passenger pre-screening: this starts with the ticketing process and concludes with passenger check-in, and none of the names of the 9/11 hijackers were identified by the FAA and provided to the airlines in order to bar them from flying or subject them to extra security measures; 3) Airport access control: this really didn't play a role on 9/11; 4) Passenger checkpoint screening: in a pre-9/11 world, this screening referred simply to efforts to prevent passengers from carrying explosive devices and other dangerous weapons on board airplanes, e.g., the use of metal detectors calibrated to detect guns and knives. What happened at the checkpoints on 9/11? The 9/11 Commission staff report offered this summary:

"Of the checkpoints used to screen the passengers of Flights 11, 77, 93 and 175 on 9/11 only Washington Dulles International Airport had videotaping equipment in place. Therefore the most specific information that exists about the processing of the 9/11 hijackers is information about American Airlines Flight 77, which crashed into the Pentagon. The staff has also reviewed testing results for all the checkpoints in question, scores of interviews with checkpoint screeners and supervisors who might have processed the hijackers and the FAA and FBI evaluations of the available information. There is no reason to believe that the screening on 9/11 was fundamentally different at any of the relevant airports. . . .

". . . at 7:18 AM Eastern Daylight Time on the morning of September 11, 2001, Majed Moqed and Khalid al Mihdhar entered one of the security screening checkpoints at Dulles International Airport. They placed their carry-on bags on the x-ray machine belt and proceeded through the first magnetometer. Both set off the alarm and were subsequently directed to a second magnetometer. While al Mihdhar did not alarm the second magnetometer and was permitted through the checkpoint, Moqed failed once more and was then subjected to a personal screening with a metal detection hand wand. He passed this inspection and then was permitted to pass through the checkpoint.

"At 7:35 AM Hani Hanjour placed two carry-on bags on the x-ray belt in the Main Terminal checkpoint, and proceeded, without alarm through the magnetometer. He picked up his carry-on bags and passed through the checkpoint. One minute later, Nawaf al Hazmi set off the alarms for both the first and second magnetometers and was then hand-wanded before being passed. In addition, his shoulder-strap carry-on bag was swiped by an explosive trace detector and then passed.

"Our best working hypothesis is that a number of the hijackers were carrying permissible utility knives or pocket knives. One example of such a utility knife is [the] Leatherman item. . . . It is very sharp."[2]

As for the other lines of security defense (5, 6, and 7 as referenced above): passenger checked baggage screening was of no consequence; nor was cargo screening; and the failings of on-board security were obvious (i.e. cockpit access, lack of armed pilots) but are not my focus.

So, what can be said of the failings in the checkpoint process on 9/11? Quite obviously, they lacked a human element. It was a purely mechanical process. "What does the magnetometer tell us?" takes the place of "What does this person's demeanor tell us?" and "What are the circumstances surrounding this person's travel?" and, yes, "What do they look like?" In short, all those things that Jose Melendez-Perez took into account on August 4, 2001, when he turned away Mohammed Kahtani at the Orlando International Airport.

My purpose is not to be critical of that which failed on 9/11. The scheme was unprecedented and beyond the most fervent of imaginations. My concern is whether we've done what we can to prevent it from happening again, and the answer is a clear no. Instead of factoring in the human elements of the enemy, we are approaching those who seek to kill us with blinders on. And for what? So that we don't offend as we attempt to protect our way of life? Ridiculous. Our Secretary of DOT led the charge in sending a message to the airlines post-9/11—it is more important to protect the so-called civil liberties of a few, even if it means jeopardizing the safety of the many. And even though the front line at the airport is now the TSA, and not the DOT, my own experience and those reported to me by my radio listeners at The Big Talker suggest that the Norman Mineta mindset prevails at the newly minted TSA.

What did the TSA have to say on these issues? Well, I was able to find out without lifting a finger.

Imagine my delight when an e-mail was shown to me soon after its arrival at The Big Talker on May 25, 2004. Here is what it said, in part:

TO: Morning Drive Producers, News Producers

Radio Interview Opportunity

Friday May 28, 2004/6:00 a.m. to 10 a.m. EDT

WHAT: SUMMER AIR TRAVEL – TRANSPORTATION SECURITY ADMINISTRA-TION ANNOUNCES A NEW PROGRAM "PREPARE FOR THE SUMMER TAKEOFF" THAT PROVIDES TIPS TO SMOOTH TRAVELERS PATHS THROUGH THE NATION'S AIRPORTS **JUST IN TIME FOR MEMORIAL DAY WEEKEND**

WHO: NICO MELENDEZ OF THE TRANSPORTATION SECURITY ADMINISTRATION.

The TSA protects the nation's transportation systems to ensure freedom of movement for people and commerce. Along with the new security measures taking place across the country, TSA continues to improve and refine air travel in the United States. Nico Melendez will offer listeners some very important travel advice: . . .

-Security awareness—Learn what to look for. what do to

Here are some specific question Nico Melendez can addess:

-What should I expect at the Security Checkpoint? [3]

This was too good to be true. Just as my inquiry was ready to focus on the TSA, here comes an invitation out of left field to interview its spokesman on airport security. Are you kidding me? Book 'em, Danno!

The on-air interview offered a pretty good oversight into the basics of the TSA and how the TSA reacts to my perspective. Here is a transcript of that interview. (My additional comments are set in italics and parentheses.)

**MAS**: I wanna ask you a preliminary question or two just to understand or appreciate the TSA. I've been referring to the TSA I think incorrectly as a part of the DOT, the Department of Transportation. But, I guess I'd be more accurate saying you come under the umbrella of Homeland Security.

**TSA**: That, that's correct. It's a—it could be a little bit confusing but as of March of last year we were originally a part of the Department of Transportation. When they created the Deptartment of Homeland Security we moved over and became one of the agencies of that department.

**MAS**: And the TSA employees—are therefore employees of the federal government?

**TSA**: That's correct.

**MAS**: Working for Homeland Security?

**TSA**: That's correct.

**MAS**: And are they—is TSA funded through the airlines or funded through, you know, the government, through tax dollars?

**TSA**: It's funded through tax dollars.

**MAS**: Okay. Because I think there are also some misconceptions out there as they relate to airport screening that this is all a process being funded by airlines, but truth be told it is not—it's a taxpayer-subsidized kind of an operation.

**TSA**: That's exactly correct.

**MAS**: What is—what is the mission of TSA?

**TSA**: Well you said it—you said it perfectly right in your open. Our job is to provide for the freedom of movement for passengers and commerce in the most safe and secure manner possible. We uh—the most visible part of our job is obviously in the airports when passengers go through our security checkpoints.

**MAS**: Uh, the security checkpoints are maintained by the TSA at how many airports?

**TSA**: Uh, about 445 give or take; it fluctuates when seasonal airports—like for instance up in Alaska—close at certain times, but, and some airports close and open, but it's in the neighborhood of 445.

**MAS**: How do you refer to the people who are the front line at the airport? Do you call them a screener? Or?

**TSA**: They are our screener workforce.

**MAS**: How many of those folks do you employ?

**TSA**: 45,000.

**MAS**: And—uh—who is it that gives them their instructions as to how they are to handle the exchange with passengers who come through those checkpoints?

**TSA**: Well our . . . our screeners come into . . . the workforce and they go through 100 hours of training—they have 40 hours of classroom training and about 60 hours of on-the-job training. And the procedures that they employ at the security checkpoints are based on the standard operating procedures that are developed through our headquarters based on intelligence . . . uh . . . of what we need to look for and what we need to do at those security checkpoints. And . . . uh . . . those processes are . . . put through to the federal security directors in our airports and then put down into two training regiments that our screeners go through.

**MAS:** What . . . what are you able to tell us as to what they are told to look for in terms of . . . of who it is that not only walks through the metal detector but goes through that . . . I guess you call it secondary screening?

**TSA:** Well, the job . . . at the security checkpoint is to ensure that no prohibited items enter into the sterile area and onto the aircraft. So they're looking for a significant number of prohibited items. A list . . . a list of those items are available to the traveling public because they're very simple things like knives and scissors or guns and brass knuckles.

**MAS:** Understood. And none of us want any of that kinda stuff on any airplane in which we're flying.

**TSA:** I wouldn't think so.

*(Okay, enough of the prelims. Let's get into it.)*

**MAS:** But how do they determine . . . because you know unless you're . . . unless you have brass knuckles sort of strapped to your chest as you walk through they don't know whether I'm carrying or whether somebody behind me is carrying them. So how are they told to . . . to determine whether I'm the guy getting pulled out of the line or whether somebody else is getting pulled out of the line for secondary checking?

**TSA:** Well the . . . secondary screening process is, is based on a couple of different things. If an alarm goes off when an individual goes through the security checkpoint, they could be selected for secondary screening to, to be able to resolve the alarm. Um . . . for instance in many cases we've heard people talking about shoes. A lot of people don't want to take their shoes off—understandably—but a lot of shoes have metal in them. So when they go through, walk through the metal detector and the alarm goes off we have to resolve that alarm to find out what the metallic object is that is setting off our alarms. So people like that can be subject to secondary screening. There is a separate group of people who are selected for secondary screening based on other things . . . uh . . . such as, when did they buy their ticket, did they buy it right before the flight or did they pay cash for their ticket, or was it a one-way ticket, so there are a couple of different things that come into play in secondary screening.

**MAS:** We're talking to Nico Melendez. Mr. Melendez, how do I properly identify you as a spokesman for the TSA?

**TSA:** That's correct, that's correct.

**MAS:** What about factoring in the appearance of the traveler himself or herself?

**TSA:** Appearance doesn't come into play. That would get into the whole profiling issue—we don't profile. Our job is to find prohibited items. It doesn't matter size, shape, color, or what you're wearing, we . . . we just want to make sure that the traveling public remains secure.

*(See what I mean? The Mineta mindset has taken hold at the TSA. Go look at the mug shots of the 9/11 hijackers again. Then tell me what you think of the TSA saying "appearance doesn't come into play.")*

**MAS:** In other words, you don't care whether a person appears to be of Middle-Eastern distract . . . extraction . . . versus someone who appears to be, you know, Norwegian?

**TSA:** No, no, it doesn't come into play. That's not our job. Our job is to look for prohibited items at the security checkpoint. To ensure those things are not introduced to the sterile area.

*(Well, whose job is it? Who is looking for bombers and not just bombs? And, in your effort to look for prohibited items at the security checkpoint, why not take into account the demographics of those who successfully got past security checkpoints on 9/11 with something that allowed them to take control of the four airplanes? Truly, not rocket science.)*

**MAS:** Well I understand that, but Mr. Melendez, I had an experience recently and I don't think that it's an unusual experience my . . . because of what I've heard from listeners. My 8 year old son—flying Atlantic City to Florida, Fort Myers, and then in return on both legs of the trip—as we left the ticketing counter had a red X put on his boarding pass, and therefore as we approached the TSA he was selected for secondary screening. So there's a random element to this that I'm trying to understand—and my listeners I know want to understand—as to how the decision is made as to who will be selected for that secondary screening?

*(You've heard the story. Let's see how the TSA responds.)*

**TSA:** Well that process is, uh, something that comes out of, um, out of a system that is employed by the airlines to develop a random secondary screening process and that is something called the Computer Assisted Passenger Pre Screening. And again it is employed by the airline right now. We are working to develop a new passenger pre-screening system that would allow for us to cut down on the number of people that are selected for . . . this secondary screening. Because right now we are in the neighborhood of 10 percent of passengers are selected on that random process and we'd like to see that cut down to 4 percent, so we're in the process of developing a new passenger pre-screening, um, system to, um, help alleviate some of those concerns.

**MAS:** Two days ago, the Attorney General of the United States, John Ashcroft, and the FBI head, Bob Mueller, stood up and they published the photographs of 7 suspected al Qaeda terrorists that they fear are in the United States, and they solicited the help of the public in finding these individuals. Uh, no doubt you're aware of that press conference and the issue?

**TSA:** That's correct.

This warrants a time out (we'll resume with the radio interview shortly). Just two days before this interview, as stated, the FBI chief and our Attorney General held a stunning press conference. They warned Americans of intelligence that indicated the possibility of terrorist attacks within the U.S. in the following months. Ashcroft and Mueller claimed that U.S. intelligence reports, combined with public statements by al Qaeda, suggested that plans for an attack (on the U.S.) were 70 percent complete as of January 1, 2004. By the time of the Madrid bombings on

March 11, 2004, it was believed that the plans were 90 percent complete.[4] John Ashcroft cited possible future targets in the U.S.: The G-8 (group of 8) Economic Summit at Sea Island, Georgia; the Democratic National Convention in Boston; and the Republican National Convention in New York. He said that security would be heightened throughout the summer, especially at the opening of the WWII Memorial and at other major events. Interestingly, Homeland Security Secretary Tom Ridge was not involved in the press conference, and subsequent media reports suggested he was out of the loop on what was said by Mueller and Ashcroft.[5] Moreover, Ridge did not raise the color-coded threat level.

Here is the kicker. Ashcroft called on Americans to be "on the lookout for individuals, and in specific, for each of these seven individuals that are associated with al Qaeda."[6] Photographs of the seven being sought were then released to the media.[7] Ashcroft characterized the seven individuals as "considered armed and dangerous." While one of the seven is an American citizen, the other six fit the very profile we've been discussing. Even the American grew his hair longer and had facial hair, thus appearing like his fellow suspects. Which made me wonder, if the American people can be told to look for this group who share attributes, shouldn't the TSA be seeking out people of similar physical characteristics so as to make sure that no one is missed?

FBI Director Mueller asked three things of the American citizens. First, he wanted cooperation as the FBI launched a series of interviews across the country to gather even more intelligence. Second, he wanted the public, both in the U.S. and abroad, to look for these seven individuals. He asked that anyone who has seen these people in their communities or knows someone who might be hiding them would come forward and alert the authorities. Third, he asked that Americans be aware of their surroundings and remain vigilant.[8] You can't have it both ways. How can Americans be told to be "on the lookout for these seven individuals" without profiling? To be on the lookout, you have to be looking for people who look like these mug shots, no?

So who are the seven?

**Adnan G. El Shukrijumah**. (Not to be confused with Jackie Mason, Samuel Jackson, or Thurston Howell III) He is a Saudi native (surprise, surprise) who lived in South Florida (like many of the 9/11 hijackers) and was nicknamed "Jafar the Pilot" for his ability to fly aircraft. He is believed to be a terror-cell leader similar to Mohammed Atta. His name came to U.S. attention after the interrogation of Khalid Shaikh Mohammed last year, and is of particular interest because of his familiarity with the U.S. and his fluency in English. He left Miami in 2001 for Morocco after spending fifteen years in the U.S. He is thought to be using a Guyanese passport.

**Aafia Siddiqui**. She is a Pakistani national who has studied at MIT and Brandeis University. The U.S. believes that, although she might not belong to al Qaeda, she could help operatives get what they want through her vast knowledge of the U.S. She has spent time in the D.C. area.

**Fazul Abdullah Mohammed**. A native of Comoros (an island nation off the coast of Africa), he is thought to be the ringleader for al Qaeda in Eastern Africa. He was indicted by the U.S. for the embassy bombings in 1998, and is thought to be hiding in Kenya or Somalia.

**Ahmed Khalfan Ghailani**. A Tanzanian who goes by the names Foopie or Fupi or Ahmed the Tanzanian. He is under indictment in the U.S. for the 1998 embassy attacks.

**Amer El-Maati**. Born in Kuwait, he is wanted for possible al Qaeda links. He is a licensed pilot who is believed to have discussed hijacking a plane in Canada and flying it into a building in the U.S.

**Abderraouf Jdey**. A Tunisian who became a Canadian citizen in 1995. He left suicide messages on videos found at the home of Mohammed Atef (bin Laden's military chief killed in U.S. strike in 2001) in Afghanistan. He pledged to die in battle against the infidels. He is reported to have been selected for flight training for a second U.S. attack. **Adam Yahiye Gadahn**. He is a U.S. citizen who goes by the names

Adam Pearlman and Abu Suhayb Al-Amriki. He has attended al Qaeda training camps and has served as a translator for the group. He grew up in California and converted to Islam in his teenage years. An American, yes. But frankly, he looks as shifty as the others.[9]

Now back to my on-air conversation with the TSA:

**MAS:** Well would you agree with me, sir, that the TSA in doing airport screening should be on the lookout for those seven individuals.

**TSA:** I completely agree. We, we, we have made the pictures of these individuals available to our workforce of 45,000 people around the country and they are on the lookout, as all Americans should be.

*(Wait a minute. If we look at the pictures of the seven, aren't we taking appearance into account?)*

**MAS:** Should we not also be on the lookout for individuals who share some of the same characteristics of those individuals—specifically their appearance, the fact that they're from the Middle East, and that they are followers of the Islamic faith.

**TSA:** You know, you're getting into . . . to the profiling issue again and . . .

**MAS:** But see you—you use that word as if it's a dirty word—I'm not convinced that it's a dirty word. It just seems to me like it's common sense that, you know, if . . . if there's a common denominator among the people who are posing a threat to the United States then we should be factoring that in—of all places at the airports.

**TSA:** And we . . . and we have a job . . . and that's why we . . . and we have a job to do and we all . . . we all as Americans have a job to do to try to help the FBI in identifying these individuals. And I just heard this morning that the FBI has already found or already received 2,000 tips on those individuals, so I think we are all doing our jobs trying to identify and help the FBI find these people in the United States.

**MAS**: Yeah, but Mr. Melendez, respectfully, it seems to me like 85-year-old women with aluminum walkers—and I'm quoting now John Lehman, a 9/11 commissioner who posed exactly that comment to Condi Rice—uh, are getting pulled out of line by your employees at the TSA. And instead, individuals who resemble both the 9/11 hijackers and the 7 individuals who were just identified by Bob Mueller and John Ashcroft aren't being treated with a heightened scrutiny when frankly, sir, they should.

**TSA**: Well, you know, that's a . . . that's a good point. And I gotta tell you, you know, when you have a 67-year-old man who has hollowed out his prosthetic leg to get a 10-inch military knife onto a plane, or we find a 7-year-old child with a teddy bear with a gun shoved up inside of it, I think our concern should be every American traveling through those checkpoints. . . .

(*He's a little hot now. And I don't doubt that he was referring to real cases. But they—like Timothy McVeigh—are the aberrations in the war on terrorism. I think we have to play the odds a little. And the odds say, beware of the young, male Arab extremist.*)

**MAS**: I'm not sure. I mean when a seven . . . when a seven. . . .

**TSA**: That they don't get introduced into. . . .

**MAS**: Yeah . . .when a seven . . . when a 7-year-old boy crashes a plane into the Trade Towers, I think we could talk more about the issue, but until that happens I, uh—frankly I just think that the way the TSA is going about this is a waste of resources and is . . . frankly intended so as not to offend individuals who resemble those who pose a security risk to the United States. Fact of the matter is, the 19 hijackers and the 7 folks that were identified two days ago, they look alike. Now if that's . . . if that's somehow offensive for me to say that, I apologize. I think it's good police work to take that into account.

**TSA**: Again, you know, we have a job to do in our security checkpoints and we're doing that job. And that's what this summer travel thing is about to . . . to educate passengers so we don't have to look for that pair of scissors and we don't have to look for that little Swiss army knife coming through the checkpoints. If passengers educate themselves and prepare themselves for coming to the airport and keep that stuff out of the airport, then maybe we could take a little more time to concentrate on the real threats instead of those little pairs of scissors.

*(When he said that, I was thinking of O.J. saying we need to find the real killers.)*

**MAS**: Understood. And my final thought, and I am very respectful of the fact that you offered yourself to the program—we're thrilled to have you. I want to walk through a metal detector. I certainly don't mind taking off my shoes—I curse Osama bin Laden for that, I don't curse the TSA. But on that element as to who's going to be pulled out for an additional level of screening, frankly, we should be profiling. We should be taking into account the physical characteristics of the 9/11 hijackers, the fact that they're all from the Middle East, and that they are followers of the Islamic faith. And for the TSA not to utilize those 3 factors is abhorrent to me as an American.

**TSA**: We . . . we have a job to do, Congress gave us a job to do and we're doing that job the best that we possibly can. And if the American people are supportive of the suggestions that you are making and Congress tells us to do our job differently, then certainly we will take that into consideration.

*(Well, he may have just given me the answer. Perhaps it is the fault of Congress and not the TSA, which, arguably, is carrying out a mission and not setting policy.)*

**MAS**: Okay, alright, we are not going to make headway on this, but I appreciate very much you being in Philly.

**TSA**: Thank you very much.[10]

# 12: CONGRESS AIR

WHEN THE TSA SPOKESMAN TOLD ME THAT ". . . IF THE American people are supportive of the suggestions that you are making and Congress tells us to do our job differently, then certainly we will take that into consideration" I thought he had a pretty good idea. So I decided to take it up with the Congress. My congressman, James Gerlach, is a listener to my radio program and graciously offered to assist in booking onto my show Representative John Mica (R-FL), the Chairman of the House Subcommittee on Aviation. I jumped at the opportunity. Frankly, I was feeling like a one-armed paperhanger (is it still okay to use that expression, or am I offending one-armed paperhangers?) who had pursued my personal inquiry in every conceivable direction, but I had not taken the matter up with anyone in a leadership position in the U.S. House. I figured if the President wouldn't rein in Norman Mineta and the TSA, maybe I could encourage the Congress to do so. I Googled Mica and read where, in July of 2002, he told the Associated Press that "You have to have a broad range of identifying characteristics, I have no problem with the country of origin; that can help sort out some of the bad guys. What we have advocated is using a combination of identifying characteristics. If the administration doesn't act, Congress will," Mica said.[1] Hmmm. This sounded like my kinda guy.

So it was that John Mica and I chatted on June 3, 2004:

**MAS:** [Some of the following is paraphrased, but does not affect original meaning or context.] I'm worried that it's not so much who the people are or for whom they work. I'm worried that the PC movement has intruded in the protection of our airspace and we wonder why 85 year old women are getting pulled out of line for secondary screening.

**MICA:** Well let me say this, um, we tested both systems, well actually I didn't, but we had the inspector general of the Department of Homeland Security test both systems, and we found that in his words both were performing equally poorly. In fact, we have been concentrating on being politically correct. We don't have deployed technology that would give us sort of an instantaneous, uh, look at people who were carrying explosives or dangerous weapons—that's a great concern. The performance of this, uh, TSA operation after spending billions of dollars isn't really much better than what we had pre-September 11th. Now we do have secured cockpit doors, we have, um, air marshals, we have pilots being armed, but we've been concentrating on screening—as you pointed out in those comments of little old ladies—millions of passengers who pose no threat, and not going after bad guys.

MAS: Is there anything wrong with saying that you know good police work demands that we look for folks who resemble the 19 hijackers on September 11th?

MICA: Well absolutely there is no reason we cannot profile, and do it without discrimination. And some of the do-gooders and others who've stopped progress on those projects actually have done us great harm, because we even, as of yesterday, talking with the Secretary, Admiral Lloyd and now Admiral Stone who's in charge of TSA, uh—we're far behind in development at those, uh, at those programs that really will detect bad people. The inability to do that does cause us to harass everyone else.

MAS: Do the folks in Homeland Security look at it the same way you and I look at it?

MICA: Well yesterday even Secretary Ridge expressed frustration at the progress of getting in place the systems that really will help us, and I think they share the same frustrations.

MAS: Is there a legislative change that is necessary so that we can free the hands of law enforcement as they try to protect our airspace?

MICA: I'd be afraid to bring it to the floor. But I'm all for the administrative changes. . . . They're talking about a different direction for TSA, I was very pleased with the results for the meeting. So there's some hope on the horizon.

It's not going to be a legislative fix; I think it will be an administrative reform.

**MAS**: Question over discrimination: And I see it comes down to a definition over the word discrimination. If you factor in any one thing, you are discriminating.

**MICA**: Well if you took just one of those, you know, one of those character-istics, you may be discriminating. If in fact you use a number of those in concert, I don't think you are.

**MAS**: One of the problems is Norman Mineta. I mean the Secretary of Transportation just doesn't get it. He doesn't understand that profiling is not a dirty word.

**MICA**: Well, you know, people are all products of their experiences, and I know Norm well and I respect him. We disagreed, uh, we disagreed I think somewhat on this issue; we disagreed on arming the pilots. It took me awhile but I won on that and I think we're gonna win on this.

**MAS**: I mean he doesn't understand the conversation you and I have just had.

**MICA**: We can devise a system that doesn't discriminate, that doesn't hassle people unfairly, and that's what we want. But also we can develop a system that does target bad people.[2]

Roy Blunt is a Republican from Missouri who serves as the House Majority Whip. He's yet another member of Congress in a high-profile leadership position with whom I have spoken about this subject. And, like John Mica, he seemed to agree with my take on the situation, leaving me to wonder why there is not some legislative effort underway to change the status quo given that so many in powerful positions seem to agree that in a post-9/11 world, we need to fight terrorism by being observant of individuals who resemble the nineteen.

Here is some of what Congressman Blunt said to me: "Well, you know, we got into this whole discussion a few years ago even before 9/11 of pro-filing. I heard what you said earlier" (a reference to me saying we need to consider traits held in common by the nineteen on 9/11) "and I actually agree with that. Whenever you have reason to believe that—matter of fact when you are confident—when you've got eye witnesses at a crime scene that say it was a one armed man that did it . . . you should be looking for a one armed man, not a two armed man. That's a little—not quite that clear always in checking things at an airport, but I do believe there's reasonableness and I believe the American people understand that."[3]

He told me how all profiling—not just that which is ethnically based—should be a factor in airline security and recounted his experience in being singled out for extra screening when he had purchased a one-way ticket. This is exactly what I am talking about. The TSA should at least be paying extra attention to those who share characteristics— either racial or circumstantial—with those who have been known to commit terror acts in the past. Makes sense to me.

There weren't too many places left for me to look for answers. Final destination, the U.S. Senate.

# 13: FINAL DESTINATION: THE U.S. SENATE

I HAVE KNOWN UNITED STATES SENATOR ARLEN SPECTER since 1980, the year he was elected to the U.S. Senate. We're friends. I'm a close friend of his son, Shanin Specter, and daughter-in-law Tracey. The two of them introduced me to my wife. In 1986, while in law school at the University of Pennsylvania, I ran the Philadelphia segment of his reelection. While we don't always agree politically, I have tremendous respect for his ethics and intellect. He's a smart guy and he's tireless, even as he ages. In his very long and distinguished public career, there has never been a whiff of scandal around the man. Sometimes I think Pennsylvanians take him for granted. In the primary election of 2004, for example, Congressman Pat Toomey came close to denying Specter the renomination of the Republican Party to seek a fifth term, even though a Specter defeat would have jeopardized the significant seniority amassed by Specter. He's currently number two on the Appropriations Committee and will probably soon chair the Senate Judiciary Committee.

In the year of my birth, 1962, Richard Nixon wrote a famous book after serving as Vice President called *Six Crises*. The book was a testament to Nixon's having been in the eye of the storm on many occasions before he was President, including the Alger Hiss case, Nixon's famous Fund Speech in the 1952 campaign, and the so-called Kitchen Debate with Khrushchev in 1959. Well, in 2000, Arlen Specter wrote a book that I think of in similar terms. Entitled *Passion for Truth*, Specter's book is a reminder of the role he has played in some of the more significant issues of the modern day: originating the Single-Bullet Theory (he makes me say "Conclusion," not "Theory," when we are together); his handling of Robert Bork's Supreme Court nomination (a subject about which we disagreed); his cross-examination of Anita Hill in the Clarence Thomas Supreme Court confirmation process (perhaps his finest moment, much to the consternation of feminists); and playing a significant role in the Clinton impeachment. While I have considered myself a friend of the Senator for close to two decades, his book gave me an even greater sense of appreciation for the role he has played in shaping the modern debate. He's always in the thick of the action. I remember being with him in the campaign car in 1986 when a worried campaign staffer called to say "don't come to headquarters right now, there is a growing anti-Specter protest unfolding out front." Specter's response? He told the driver to hit the gas, and head straight for the protest. You gotta love that.

I said when this story began that I bumped into Senator Specter at the Phillies 2004 home opener on the very day that my first column on airline security appeared in the *Philadelphia Daily News*. That was my lengthy piece about John Lehman and the 9/11 Commission. At the ballpark, Senator Specter and I talked about John Lehman's questioning of Dr. Condoleezza Rice. Thereafter, I spoke with Senator Specter on a weekly basis, constantly updating him on what I was learning about the role of political correctness in airline security. He expressed great interest. At a certain point, when it became clear that there were conflicting stories being told about airport screening, Senator Specter offered to hold a hearing on the matter in the U.S. Senate. This was an extraordinary offer and one that I immediately welcomed. It was one thing for me to try to get answers by booking guests with knowledge for my radio show, but something altogether different to rely on the U.S. Senate to get to the bottom of things. Senator Specter said he believed the Governmental Affairs Committee would be one possible venue. But this was soon to become a sad story about watching sausage made.

Three weeks before the tentatively scheduled hearing, Senator Specter called my radio program to inform my listeners and me that the hearing had been abruptly cancelled. Not by him, but by Senator Susan Collins, a Republican from Maine who is that Committee's Chairperson. Senator Specter candidly detailed how Senator Collins was angry about a vote he'd just cast on postal reform. Her retribution? Senator Specter's staff received a curt e-mail from her office saying "Chairman Collins is no longer interested in holding this hearing." Unbelievable, I was think-ing, as he explained. We won't have to worry about mailing letters if we don't get ahead of the curve in the war against terrorism.

What I didn't tell my radio listeners when Specter called—because it didn't occur to me until after he'd hung up—was my suspicion as to what had gone on here. Several months prior, in the midst of the Specter/Toomey primary battle, I had attended a Specter fundraiser at the home of some close friends of my wife and me, David and Jamie Field. The Fields are Specter friends who are passionate about the envi-ronment, but not in a whacky sense. (That doesn't stop me from ribbing David that his hybrid car will one day run out of fuel when the world's hash supply is totally smoked.) Well, the guest of honor at the fundraiser was none other than Susan Collins! Now I wonder if maybe she thought Senator Specter owed her support for things like postal reform because she'd come in from Maine to do his event?

In the end, Senator Collins' refusal to hold the hearing was a blessing. We got a major upgrade (my opinion) when Senator Specter approached Senator Richard Shelby of Alabama, and in his role as Chairman of the Appropriations Subcommittee on Transportation, Treasury, and General Government, he agreed to hold a hearing. Given the genesis of this process, Senator Specter very much wanted John Lehman to testify on the issue of political correctness, and his question to Dr. Condoleezza Rice about a quota system in secondary screening ("Were you aware that it was the policy . . . to fine airlines if they have more than two young Arab males in secondary questioning because that's discriminatory?") I suggested, and he agreed, that an invitation also be extended to Edmond Soliday, the former security chief for United Airlines who had testified under oath before the 9/11 Commission as to the instruction he'd been given by the Justice Department not to have too many people at once of one ethnic stripe in a secondary line for questionings (". . . a visitor from the Justice Department told me that if I had more than three people of the same ethnic origin in line for additional screening, our system would be shut down as discriminatory"). As the hearing date drew near, word came from both that they could not appear. In the case of Secretary

Lehman, I was told by a Senate staffer that the Chairman and Vice-Chairman of the 9/11 Commission had requested that such an appearance not occur until the 9/11 Commission final report was issued. With regard to Soliday, it was expressed to me that because of "ongoing litigation" he could not appear either.

Who, then, would offer what I considered to be the critical opinion—that regardless of a quota system per se ever having been used in airport screening, we've clearly allowed political correctness to cloud the airport security issue because we refuse to look for terrorists using factors that the nineteen on 9/11 had in common? Senator Specter told me that he would check with Senator Shelby and see if I could testify. Fine with me. I was more than willing to come to Washington and tell it like it is. That permission was granted. The hearing was set for the afternoon of June 24, 2004.

The evening before the hearing, I was going over my five-minute opening statement when the telephone rang for two back-to-back calls. The first call was from Sil Scaglione, the GM of The Big Talker, who was with Grace Blazer, the program director. It seems that when they circulated a proposed press release about my Senate appearance to a PR flak in-house at Infinity Broadcasting (which owns The Big Talker), some of the suits got a bit nervous at the idea of one of their talk show hosts giving Senate testimony. Keep in mind that this was happening the very week that the Senate passed (by a vote of 99-1) new, huge fines for indecency, so anything having to do with a Senate appearance would be understandably important to Infinity Broadcasting, and its parent, Viacom. Sil wanted me to know that my testifying in the Senate was on the radar screen and that I was to make clear that I was speaking for myself. I told him I would be happy to read to him my proposed remarks. He was thrilled. So to bust his chops, I cleared my throat and said, "Good morning, ladies and gentlemen. Mr. Sumner Redstone has asked me to come here today and express our mutual concerns about the lack of screening of Arabs at airports." (Redstone is the Chairman of Viacom.) "How do you like it so far?" I asked Sil. I'd swear I could hear his heart palpitations over the phone. Then we had a good laugh.

The second call that night was from Senator Specter's office. When I heard he was on the line, I was fearful that the hearing had been postponed or cancelled. Instead, it was the Senator himself, wanting to know from me what I would be saying concerning Secretary Norman Mineta. I told Specter I would echo the comments I'd made in an 18-page written statement I had already submitted to the subcommittee. Specter hadn't yet seen it, but told me that whatever I had circulated was already causing a stir in the Department of Transportation, and that Mineta was not returning his telephone calls. He asked me if I felt it necessary to discuss Secretary Mineta's internment in a camp as a Japanese American during WWII. I explained that my statement did indeed address that fact as a possible explanation for Mineta's views on airport screening. Specter probed a bit, but never told me how to handle my testimony. We were a "go" for the next day.

The combination of the phone calls made me appreciate the significance of what was about to occur. It was exciting. And I was more than a bit proud. All too often I sit behind a microphone and bitch and moan. This was different. This was an opportunity for me to get off the sidelines and get into the game. And I couldn't wait. I was going to Washington to tell a body of the Senate that as an American traveler in a post-9/11 world, I thought we'd compromised safety in the name of civil rights. Quota or no quota for Arabs, the fact remained that we had a conscious policy in this country to turn a blind eye toward appearance, race, religion, and ethnicity despite the fact that the nineteen hijackers had all of those things in common on 9/11. That didn't seem to me like an effective way of winning the way on terrorism and I was going to say so.

To the contrary, we were fining airlines that were believed to be taking these things into account. (The DOT loathes the use of the word "fine" in this context, but in my opinion, that's what it is.) I have already written about the DOT's enforcement actions against Continental, American, and United. Well, check this out. A few days before my trip to Washington, there was news of yet another action initiated by DOT. This time it was Delta that was accused of discrimination post-9/11, and to make the litigation go away, there was an agreement between Delta and the DOT whereby Delta would pay $900,000.00 for kumbaya training. (Delta denied any wrongdoing.) Here's why that is stunning. Remember, it was Delta that sent out a company-wide bulletin the very week that 9/11 occurred, under the signature of Fred Reid, President and COO, telling employees ". . . across the airline industry, we've heard stories of passengers being deplaned because of their skin color or the sound of their accents. We cannot afford to allow this tragic behavior. It is exactly what our enemies are striving for: The end of our open, diverse, and tolerant way of life."[1] The DOT was so impressed with the bulletin when written that they attached it to a memo which the DOT sent to the airline industry on nondiscrimination concerning religion and national origin as a model for behavior.[2] Now, two years later, the DOT was punishing Delta for allegedly removing from a flight or failing to board a passenger on the basis of race, color, national origin, sex, ancestry, or religion. I very much wanted the Senate to ask the DOT about these cases.

The morning of the hearing, June 24, 2004, I did my normal radio show from 5:30–9 AM, and gave the audience a preview of what I intended to say. There was great interest and encouragement from my callers, who had supplied me with tons of e-mailed anecdotes about their own flying experiences in the prior weeks. This was going to be a long day for me. I get up daily at 3 AM to do my show and usually take an hour nap in the afternoon at about 2 PM so I'm not wiped out when the kids come home from school. Lights are out at about 9 or 10 PM at the latest. On this day, naptime would be the hour of the testimony. That day's radio show was significant for another reason. I had scheduled a chat with Alice Hoglan, the mother of Mark Bingham, one of the heroic passengers aboard Flight 93. She had been a radio guest of mine in the past, and I was enthused to have her back. As I was literally headed toward the door to go to Washington to testify, I was curious to learn whether she—one of the more high-profile victims of 9/11 because of her widely publicized cell-phone call with her son from that doomed flight—was aware of the fact that our DOT had gone after airlines in such fashion. Including the airline on which her son was traveling when he died—United.

Here is part of the transcript from my conversation with Mrs. Hoglan on the morning of the hearing:

> **MAS**: Mrs. Hoglan, Mark, your son, was on a United Airlines flight. Are you aware of the fact—and I tell this to radio listeners and I tell to this people in my travels; they are blown away they have no idea of this information—are you aware of the fact that in the aftermath of 9/11, United Airlines and American Airlines, each of which lost 2 planes that day and a total of 33 of their crew combined—are you aware of the fact that they were each fined 1.5 million dollars by our Department of Transportation because our DOT thought that they were improperly screening Middle Easterners?

> **ALICE HOGLAN**: I'm not surprised; I am frankly horrified at the behavior of the airline industry. I'm a flight attendant for United Airlines myself—recently retired—was an active flight attendant on the morning that my son called me from the aircraft on flight 93 and told me that he was on a flight that had 3 guys on board who had taken over the plane and they said they had a bomb. Since my son's death on September 11th, there have been four or five issues that have sort of crystallized in my life and one of them, one of the most important, is the issue of aviation security and yes, indeed, the airlines have a long way to go.

> **MAS**: But Mrs. Hoglan, the issue that most—and I agree with that—but the issue that I find most troublesome—and I'm going to say that in a Senate hearing today—is the idea that our Department of Transportation would beat up on of all airlines, United and American, because they say, 'Well, United and American, you were improperly keeping people who mirrored the 9/11 hijackers off your planes after 9/11.'

> **ALICE HOGLAN**: The Department of Transportation was fining the airlines for improperly discriminating?

> **MAS**: Screening, yeah. Mrs. Hoglan, is this news to you?

> **ALICE HOGLAN**: Yes.[3]

If Alice Hoglan didn't know that United Airlines had been subjected to a DOT enforcement action post-9/11, I was now convinced that few Americans did, and I wanted to make that a key part of my testimony. And after my intense conversation with Mrs. Hoglan to prime me up, I—along with my support staff—was ready to go to Washington.

I've got a bright and eclectic crew that works with me in support of my radio show and writing. Al Franken writes about "Team Franken" in his goofy books; well, I had part of my posse in tow. First, TC Scornavacchi, whom I first met when she taught my kids in a suburban Montessori school. Her personality and Harvard education used to impress all the parents who, in pick-up line, would talk about her talent and worry whether she'd be there long-term. One day after I switched from afternoon drive to morning drive at The Big Talker, two of Infinity's top executives—Scott Herman and Don Bouloukas—came to Philadelphia to take me to lunch. They asked me whom I wanted as a producer. I immediately thought of TC. She's brilliant, personable, and had just been bitten by the media bug as an on-air guest at QVC. To their credit, the Infinity hotshots said she sounded perfect despite having no radio background. My timing was right and she agreed. Also in tow to Washington was Ben Haney, a Notre Dame student working for me for the summer. Ben reminds me of me twenty-five years ago. When Ronald Reagan passed this summer, Ben put on a suit, drove $3\frac{1}{2}$ hours to Washington, and stood in 90-degree heat to pay his respects at the Capitol Rotunda, even though he wasn't yet born the year Reagan was first sworn in. Elliot Avidan, a Naval Academy grad and current Penn Law student, is another of the crew. While at Penn Law, he, too, was interning for me and, now, while splitting his summer schedule between a Washington law firm and a stint at the Pentagon, he has been heavily involved in my research. Elliot was to cover a different Senate hearing on airport issues for me in the morning and then join us in the afternoon. Back in Philly we had Pete Nelson, another fine producer of my morning show, and the three-some of Dave Skalish, Rich Sacco, and Frank Canale, ensuring that we got an audio feed from the Senate so that I could play the testimony on The Big Talker. Behind the scenes, as always, is "Dr. Bart" Feroe (whose role I would like to discuss, but then I'd have to kill you).

The trip to Washington was a total team effort; the entire radio station was pumped for the activism. The day of the hearing, virtually every member of Mike Baldini's sales force at The Big Talker sent me an e-mail and told me they appreciated the initiative. Finally, also along for the ride was Bob Huber from *Philadelphia* magazine, which had expressed interest on how a talk-show host gets a Senate hearing on a subject that interests him, and wanted to see how it would end. Team Franken? On this day, it was team "Team Smerconish."

On the train to Washington, I was worried about what was going to unfold. Because of Senator Specter's call, I knew that my written statement had been circulated, presumably to the other witnesses. But I hadn't read what anyone else had submitted. And while I knew by now who else was scheduled to testify, I had no idea what they would say. The witness list included: me, identified in the schedule as a talk show host and columnist; Jeff Rosen, General Counsel, Department of Transportation; Tom Blank, Assistant Secretary for Security Policy, Transportation Security Administration; Peggy Sterling, V.P. Safety, Security and Environmental, American Airlines; and Christy Lopez, a civil rights attorney, from Relman & Associates.

I'm a lawyer turned talk show host and columnist. I am not an aviation security expert. I had stumbled into this subject of political correctness in my usual manner—by a combination of happenstance and inquisitiveness. I had engaged in a three-month-long crash course of interviews and research into airline security in a post-9/11 world, but I was still an outsider. Maybe I'd overlooked something? Maybe one of the other witnesses was about to stand up and say hey, this guy from Philly doesn't even know about the "such and such" law. That was a concern. What I was certain about—thinking about my 8-year-old being singled out for secondary screening, and John Lehman's comments about "85-year-old women with aluminum walkers"—is that our airport security made no common sense. And I thought I knew why.

We walked the few blocks from Union Station to Capitol Hill. It was a beautiful summer day and Washington was hot and humid. Entering hearing room SD 138 in the Dirksen Building, I saw everything I'd come to expect from television. An enormous bowed desk sat at the front of the room with more than a dozen seats for Senators, facing two witness desks. Behind the witness desks were about seventy-five seats for members of the audience. I couldn't imagine any of them were about to be filled but I had no barometer on the interest. The room has high ceilings and ornate finishes with lots of wood paneling. An hour ahead of the scheduled start, we were already in place. Like I had often done in court when trying legal cases, I always liked to arrive early and get comfortable in the environment. Thirty minutes before show time, I still didn't think anyone would come to watch. Frankly, I thought the odds of Senator Specter being the lone member of the Senate were pretty strong. But as the clock ticked, the room began to fill. A video operator got into position and so too did a stenographer. The press table suddenly got crowded and the seats were rapidly filling. ("Who the hell are these people?" I whispered to TC. We had no idea.)

At the stroke of two, in walked Senator Specter, followed by Senator Shelby. Senator Specter and I exchanged greetings. Next came Senator Patty Murray, a Democrat from Washington, and finally, Senator Herb Kohl, a Democrat from Wisconsin. A Senate staffer began circulating written statements from Senators and witnesses, and I scrambled to get copies, and quickly digest what was about to be said. I was just now learning the drill. The Senators, and the witnesses, sometimes submit lengthy written statements in lieu of actually testifying in detail. The statements become part of the record. The result is more discussion and less of a staid proceeding. In my case, while I had submitted 18 pages (which by my estimation would have taken me twenty-five minutes to read), I was prepared to speak for five minutes, which I'd been told was the limit for an opening.

It was Senator Shelby who got things moving. I followed along with a written copy of his statement, and I was immediately pleased with what I read and heard:

**SENATOR RICHARD SHELBY:** Good afternoon. The subcommittee will come to order. Today, the subcommittee is holding an oversight hearing to examine whether the Federal government has instituted policies to limit an airline from denying transport or requiring additional security screening to individuals who may be unsafe or dangerous.

The Federal Aviation Act allows air carriers the right of permissive refusal which is defined as the ability to refuse to transport a passenger or property the carrier decides is a potential risk to safety or security. The Federal Aviation Regulations authorize the pilot in command of the aircraft to discharge this right of permissive refusal on behalf of the air carrier in light of his final authority and responsibility for the operation and safety of the flight.

Despite this clear authority, however, there seems to be some question about the ability of any airline to remove passengers based on a perceived threat. At the January 27, 2004 hearing of the National Commission on Terrorist Attacks Upon the United States, a former airline executive testified that, "Most recently after 9/11, 38 of our captains denied boarding to people they thought were a threat. Those people filed complaints with the DOT, we were sued, and we were asked not to do it again.

If this is the case, I am concerned that we may be jeopardizing aviation security by placing unnecessary restrictions on pilots and crew to take actions to protect passengers in the plane. . . .

I want to thank my colleague, Senator Specter, for raising this issue with me. I believe that it is important to hold this hearing today to highlight this issue and provide the clarity on what should be the lines of authority in this matter.[4]

I was thrilled with the way Senator Shelby began. Here's why. I was questioning the way we look for terrorists, prompted by the question put to Dr. Rice by Secretary Lehman. The "quota question." But by the time of this hearing, my interest had become far broader. Instead of the narrow, but important, question of whether we actually impose a ceiling on the number of Arabs who get questioned at once, I was more interested in the big picture. And the big picture included two related, but different, circumstances: 1) the way in which passengers are screened, and 2) the basis for pilot refusal to grant passage. In my opinion, in both of those circumstances it is entirely appropriate for appearance, race, ethnicity, and religion to be weighed as part of the criteria for making such a determination. However, I was fearful that some witnesses at this hearing would try to limit the discussion to a quota conversation—i.e., did we or didn't we—whereas I wanted an airing of the larger two issues. Senator Shelby, in his opening, showed that he was on the same page. His interest in the circumstances that give rise to a pilot exercising his discretion in denying someone passage would, I hoped, give me the opportunity to raise the issue of the DOT enforcement actions against Continental, American, United, and now Delta. (Any nervousness I was feeling was now replaced by desire. I couldn't wait to speak.)

Senator Specter then made an opening statement. He acknowledged my role in bringing the matter to his attention.

**SPECTER**: . . . This issue was of sufficient importance to take a little time of our subcommittee. Michael Smerconish, who is a lawyer and a talk show host in Philadelphia, and in the interest of full disclosure a long-term friend of mine, had noted Commissioner Lehman's statement and commented on it publicly. And there is an enormous amount of interest in the Philadelphia region on this subject as illustrated by a great many comments, which he has had to, uh—a very widely heard program.

And as the chairman has noted, we have very heavy responsibilities on national security. And we also have responsibilities not to engage in ethnic, racial profiling. And there needs to be an element of cause no matter what a person looks like before they are detained. But this is a matter of critical importance daily. Tens of thousands of people are boarding airlines every day where this is a keen security interest. And our nation prides itself on elevating civil rights. I'm sorry Commissioner Lehman could not be here, but the leaders of the Commission have urged the commissioners not to appear on hearings—frankly a little surprising since they were on the Sunday talk shows. I tried to reach chairman Kean to try to get a clarification of it but haven't been able to do so yet.

The issue really is whether political correctness has gone too far in the case of aviation security or are we correctly avoiding the pitfalls of unfairly profiling individuals based partly on their ethnicity. So that, these senate hearings have great affect on sensitizing people on all sense. A lot of people pay attention to what we do here even though we don't have absolute answers. The hearing will make everyone more sensitive, which I think will help security and everyone will be more sensitive which will help civil rights.[5]

That is correct. The issue is whether political correctness has gone too far in the case of aviation security, and the answer is yes. Next, there was a brief exchange between Senators Shelby and Specter on the quota issue.

**SHELBY:** In other words, they have a numerical number and you can't look at a group? I hope that's not what the policy is.

**SPECTER:** Well that's what Mr. Soliday said. If "I had more than three people of the same ethnic origin in line our system would be shut down as discriminatory." Now I . . .

**SHELBY:** Crazy.

**SPECTER:** . . . Hasten to add that the federal authorities who are responsible here have said that is not the case, and . . .

**SHELBY:** We'll find out.

**SPECTER:** . . . That's why we have hearings.[6]

Crazy indeed, if true. Jeffrey Rosen, the top lawyer for the DOT, was quick to try to put that issue to bed.

**ROSEN:** I would first like to go directly to the question of whether the Department of Transportation has had a policy to 'fine airlines if they have more than two young Arab males in questioning because that's discriminatory' as some have claimed. And the answer is that the Department has never had any such policy.[7]

Mr. Rosen's written statement has noted that Secretary Lehman's statement about quotas "was repeated in certain media articles in the *Philadelphia Daily News* and elsewhere." That's, of course, a reference to yours truly. But, when questioned by Senator Murray, Mr. Rosen (and Mr. Blank from the TSA) both had to acknowledge that nobody had ever spoken to Edmond Soliday, the former security chief for United, to learn the basis for his having told the 9/11 Commission that there was a quota.

**MURRAY:** To either of your knowledge, has anyone followed up with Mr. Soliday to find out precisely what the Justice Department official was doing under what authority?

**ROSEN:** Not to my knowledge, Senator.

**BLANK:** Not to my knowledge.[8]

As of this writing, I am still wondering about the basis for Mr. Soliday's comments, and my efforts to speak to him have been unsuccessful.

There was then plenty of testimony about the role of pilots as captains of the ship, charged with responsibility for refusing to transport a passenger or property that the airline thinks is inimical to safety. It is this discretion in the hands of the airlines that the DOT thinks was abused by Continental, American, United, and now Delta in a post-9/11 world. Senator Shelby asked Mr. Rosen from the DOT when a pilot would be justified in exercising that discretion.

**SHELBY:** Under what circumstances would a pilot in command of an aircraft be justified in refusing to transport a passenger he or she decides is or might be detrimental to the security of the aircraft and his passengers, while at the same time assuring the airline that it will not be subject from punitive action from the DOT or whomever?

**ROSEN:** There are a wide variety of circumstances. If a passenger behaves in a suspicious manner that is individualized to the passenger—for example, is overheard making cell phone calls and making comments—that would be troublesome. If a passenger has in fact brought something on board, that would be inappropriate. If there is specific intelligence that's been conveyed for which there are then matching identifying characteristics . . . are some of the examples. I think it's difficult in the abstract to identify all of the circumstances, but certainly the pilots have the discretion where if there's a threat to safety or security then they can do that.

**SHELBY**: Do you believe that the pilot has to have that discretion?

**ROSEN**: I think it's important that we have multiple layers in the system and that the law is set up that the pilot has that discretion, and so I'm in favor of adhering to the law.

Quite frankly, it hadn't occurred to me before the hearing that anyone would quibble with having pilots play this role. But indeed there is controversy on this issue. Senator Murray questioned the role giving pilots such power:

**MURRAY**: Does empowering pilots to exclude certain passengers make us any safer? Well, I think we have to look at the facts. Are passengers being excluded because they have ties to terrorist organizations? To my knowledge, we know of no cases where a pilot has excluded an individual with ties to any known terrorist organization.[9]

Senator Specter zeroed in on the enforcement actions and wanted to know the underlying facts that caused the DOT to go after the four airlines. The DOT's top lawyer had trouble giving him what he wanted.

**SPECTER**: Take one of the investigations and tell us what the underlying facts were.

**ROSEN**: Well, Senator, um . . . um . . . I don't mean to be evasive about this, but because these resulted in mutually agreed upon settlements, what the facts were was not resolved through an administrative law judge or ultimately by the Department or by the reviewing courts. The aviation enforcement office presented the facts in one instance in a complaint and in the other instances in discussions with the carriers. And the carriers in some instances did not agree with those facts, but ultimately there was agreement as to a resolution. In terms of the individual facts . . . um, I'm not sure that it . . . um, that it's easy in a forum like this to try to re-litigate or re-go through all of them, nor have I prepared at the level of being able to present this is what our case was or this is what. . . .

**SPECTER**: Mr. Rosen, I don't understand your response. We want to know what kind of a situation led to an investigation and an assertion by the Department that there was inappropriate conduct. . . . Did any of those cases involve a situation where there was someone of a . . . with a Muslim or Arab appearance?

ROSEN: Well, uh, yes. And they also involved complaints in some instances with individuals who had been denied boarding um, who were, um, um, actually individuals who were Hispanic or Indian, or in one instance I think they were Italian.

SPECTER: Well were there factors which led the airlines to exclude the individual beyond their ethnic appearance?

ROSEN: Well, the. . . .

SPECTER: Mr. Rosen, could you provide the details for us in writing. It seems to me that this is a pretty fundamental question when you have only a few cases where you would be prepared to answer specifically. And I don't want to take any more of the subcommittee's time here. But I'd like to know what the facts were which led you to an investigation and assert that there was inappropriate conduct which required some settlement, albeit with a denial of liability.

ROSEN: Alright, Senator, I mean, as I think would be implicit, the aviation enforcement office believed that there was credible evidence of discrimination in some number of the incidents. . . .

SPECTER: Well, Mr. Rosen, it is not implicit, and credible is a matter of evaluation, and we like to know what the facts were. What were the facts as you saw them. That way we can come to a determination as to whether there was the appearance of racial profiling.[10]

The questioning of Mr. Rosen by Senator Specter was something I desperately wanted to address. First, however, I was afforded the chance to make a five-minute opening statement. Here is how I began:

Thank you for this privilege. I have already submitted an 18-page statement to Senator Shelby's offices. At this time, I will offer a 5-minute summary of my thoughts.

Unlike the other witnesses, I come without portfolio. To the extent I represent anyone or anything, I guess you could say I represent the American traveling public in a post-9/11 world.

I have come to Washington to say that I am concerned about the role of political correctness when it comes to airline security.

Three months ago, my wife and I flew with our four children from Atlantic City to Ft. Myers, Florida. We had E-tickets. At the counter, a pleasant woman asked for our identification, and then wanted to know 'Which one is Michael, Jr.?' I pointed to my 8-year-old. 'Oh, that won't work,' she said. She then explained that he'd been designated for secondary screening, meaning he would be subjected to more of a search than just taking off his shoes and walking through the metal detector. I told her I would gladly take his place and she obliged.

The fact that I could so easily negotiate someone else out of secondary screening was itself insightful.

I didn't complain about the inconvenience. Instead, I cursed bin Laden under my breath, and considered this to be my small part to play in the post-9/11 world. Well, I no longer believe that to be the case.

*(I then got to deliver the real thrust of what I'd come to Washington to say.)*

To this day, I don't know if there has ever been a quota system, *per se*, but I do believe that John Lehman and Herb Kelleher are accurate in saying that the PC movement has intruded on safety concerns.

Frankly, I can't understand how we can purposely ignore the race, ethnicity, appearance, and religion of travelers whom we are screening, when in fact, all 19 hijackers on 9/11 had those characteristics in common. Let me be clear, I am not saying that all individuals of Arab descent should be singled out, however, I do believe that a combination of similarities with those who wreaked havoc on this country, and continue to try wreak havoc on this country, needs to be given ample consideration. . . .

I find it troublesome that, not only will the DOT and TSA not look at those factors that I have enumerated, but they fine airlines that they believe do give such consideration. In the aftermath of 9/11, the DOT pursued enforcement actions against American and United Airlines—who lost a combined 33 employees on four planes on 9/11—for their alleged noncompliance with federal statutes prohibiting air carriers from subjecting any air traveler to discrimination. This overlooked the airlines' mandated responsibility to refuse to transport a passenger or property which the carrier decides is, or might be, inimical to safety. It is mind-boggling to me that our government, in the aftermath of 9/11, forced American and United to each pay $1.5 million toward civil rights training.

Just this week, it was announced that now Delta has been on the receiving end of a similar enforcement action, and will be paying $900,000.00.[11]

I continued by stating that it was the type of logic on which I was relying that arguably prevented Flight 93 from hitting Washington because a street-smart customs inspector named Jose Melendez-Perez had prevented a Saudi national named Mohammed Kahtani from ever making it into our country when Mohammed Atta came to pick him up at the Orlando International Airport.

The vice president from American Airlines, Peggy Sterling, spoke next. She made the point that ten of the eleven alleged incidents for which the DOT had initiated an enforcement action against American occurred in the fall of 2001. "In today's climate, it would be unthinkable for the captain of a commercial airline flight to ignore a pre-takeoff report of suspicious or threatening behavior by a passenger." But she did not go as far as I was prepared to say, i.e., that appearance, race, ethnicity, and religion need to be a part of that evaluation. Said Ms. Sterling: "Our policies of non-discrimination and respect for cultural differences have been reiterated to our employees since September 11. These efforts have been particularly directed to ensure that American Airlines' Middle Eastern and Muslim passengers and employees are treated with respect and dignity."[12] I agree with that, it's just that I would like the airlines to say what I suspect they are all thinking—you need to give us the ability to look for terrorists by taking into account the personal characteristics of the nineteen men on 9/11.

Christy Lopez spoke next. She was introduced as a Yale-educated lawyer who has represented a number of individuals who had been denied passage based on discriminatory reasons post-9/11. She was an articulate spokeswoman for a point of view far different from my own. She told the subcommittee that there were indeed "very objective guidelines" for pilots to determine when passengers should be denied passage.

"Currently, too many refusals to transport are based on irrational discriminatory bias rather than legitimate security reasons. Pilots have ordered Arab American passengers deplaned because of crew discomfort while letting the deplaned person's checked luggage remain on flight." She also said, "Air security experts will tell you that ethnic profiling is insane."

Insane? Not in my view. To disregard ethnicity strikes me as insane.

Ms. Lopez also said that "while profiling may be a critical component of airline security, ethnic profiling is not necessary; it is illegal and destructive to us as a nation. It is time to move beyond questions born of fear and misinformation and begin properly preparing airline employees to make decisions based on legitimate security criteria rather than upon ethnic bias. Once we do this, we will make our airlines safer and we will decrease incidents of discrimination."[13]

I didn't agree with her, but there you have the debate, crystallized at last in front of a Senate body. I welcomed the discourse.

I then took the opportunity to return to Senator Specter's questioning of Mr. Rosen about what caused our DOT to go after American and the other airlines post-9/11 for alleged discrimination. Now, keep in mind, I was making this case sitting next to another witness who was a vice president from American Airlines. You would think she—AA's VP—would want to make these points. But I wasn't leaving that to chance. She had identified herself as a non-lawyer and I didn't know if she knew the facts. Her statement was silent on the circumstances that gave rise to American Airlines paying $1.5 million for civil rights training, with the exception of the line: "With all due respect to the DOT, we think its decision to pursue an enforcement action against American exemplified the exact type of second-guessing that should be avoided."[14] Well, I agreed, but we needed some facts poured into the Senate hearing to drive this point. So this was my shot to back up my general thoughts with some specifics.

I addressed Senator Specter: "You had asked earlier, [of] Mr. Rosen, to speak with specificity about any one of the cases. I've read the litigation files to the extent that they're publicly available, and I've read those 11 different complaints, and I can tell you about one of them, and I think that it displays some of the problems, and I've detailed this in my statement. It's the case of Jehad Alshrafi, a self-described 32-year-old Arab American, a naturalized American citizen of Jordanian birth."[15]

I proceeded to tell the hearing what I'd read in the litigation files on this case. I explained how, according to Mr. Alshrafi's declaration, his statement, which accompanied the DOT's complaint, he was working for a defense contractor and claimed to have a secret-level security clearance. I explained that the flight in question occurred on November 3, 2001, two months post-9/11, when he was refused passage on an American Airlines flight from Boston to Los Angeles. That, I pointed out, was the exact same point of origin for two of the flights on 9/11. I told the Senate subcommittee that in the complaint against American Airlines, it stated that the passenger was denied boarding after responding to a page and then reporting to an American Airlines counter. There, he was greeted by an American employee and U.S. Marshal. He said he was told that the pilot had denied him boarding on that flight. At that time the passenger informed the American employee that he had a "secret level" security clearance from the U.S. Department of Defense. He was nevertheless told he was being denied passage. (Explained the passenger: "I was calmly contesting the pilot's decision when a state trooper arrived and asked me to move along and to deal with him. I was humiliated to be confronted by a state trooper in full view of the crowded boarding area.") The passenger missed his flight, but was upgraded to first class on a later flight that day.

I thought that it was only fair to present that information at the hearing. So far, it sounds like denying him passage was a bad call. But here comes the flip side. And this, too, I detailed.

I reported what American Airlines had said: "At least one other passenger had reported what appeared to be his suspicious behavior to an American gate agent. . . . The Federal Air Marshal advised the pilot-in-command that the passenger had been acting suspiciously and had created some kind of disturbance, and that his name was similar to a name on the federal watch list."

I then told Senator Specter that the following information is that which would have been known to the pilot at the time when he was scheduled to depart and had to make the call about what to do with this passenger. To clarify, I enumerated nine factors:

1) just two months prior, the country was victim to the worst terror attack in our history;

2) that terrorism began with airplanes and victimized his employer—men doing exactly what he was now doing lost their lives when their airplanes were used as weapons;

3) the point of origin of two of those flights was Boston's Logan Airport, where he now sat;

4) the destination for those flights on 9/11 was Los Angeles, which is exactly where this plane was headed;

5) the hijackers on 9/11 were, to a person, young Arab males;

6) there is at least one passenger who is ill-at-ease with another passenger who is acting in what passenger No. 1 believes to be a suspicious manner;

7) the Federal Air Marshal had advised that the passenger at issue has been acting suspiciously and has created some kind of disturbance;

8) this passenger has a name similar to one on the federal watch list; and

9) yes, let's not be afraid to say it, he probably resembled the 9/11 hijackers in his appearance.

Now the question becomes one of whether it was arbitrary and capricious for the pilot to say that this guy should stay in Boston for a while longer. To quote Senator Shelby, "Crazy!"

Ms. Lopez was then asked by Senator Specter whether the American pilot acted appropriately assuming the circumstances were as I had described. She said that if American were "acting upon the first 8 factors, then yes, but if he included the 9th, then no."

She then made reference to the DOT's "but/for test" as a justification for her position.

A buzzer sounded and interrupted the solemn tone of the hearing. Senators Shelby, Murray, and Kohl were long gone, and it was Senator Specter, alone, presiding. He told us he too had to go and vote. He asked if anyone had a final thought.

Ms. Lopez said, in part, "It's important not only to hear from security experts and airline CEOs, but also from the people who are affected by this. We didn't have any of those people here today. This sort of inconvenience should not be disregarded. Sitting at the back of the bus is not an inconvenience. Being asked to move to the back of the plane, which people have been, is not an inconvenience. Being told you have a different set of rights because of the color of your skin is not an inconvenience. This has a devastating effect on a large community that is a vibrant part of our country and we need to make sure that we fully consider that when we are considering these issues of airline security."[16]

When it was my turn, I made it short and sweet. I said, "Thank you for the privilege of being here. It's time for us to all acknowledge the fact that the 19 hijackers on 9/11 had many commonalities. The world will be a safer place when we face those facts.[17]

And so it ended.

That night, after a very long day that had begun at 3 AM, I checked my e-mail and saw a note from Michael Klein, who writes for the *Philadelphia Inquirer*.

He wrote, "Whew. You sure impressed one of our national correspondents, who caught you in action and sent me an item for Sunday."

A day later, he sent me a short mention for the Sunday early edition of the *Philadelphia Inquirer* which was cleansed of any compliment, but it did include at least one interesting opinion: "James Zogby, president of the Arab American Institute, said Specter had held the hearing to pay a political debt to Smerconish."[18]

Political debt? One day after the hearing, I ran much of the audio of the proceedings for my radio audience in Philadelphia. They had an incredible response, as evidenced by encouraging telephone calls and e-mails. Later that day, I saw Senator Specter at the swearing-in ceremony for a new federal judge, Paul S. Diamond. He thanked me for being so forceful about the issue and promised to pursue it further. While there is no doubt that my relationship with Senator Specter opened the door for me to get an airing of the issue, it's condescending to say that a Senate hearing on the matter was to satisfy a political debt. And the fact that many high-level individuals, as well as everyday people, had commented over the course of several months, rendered that accusation moot.

The type of dialogue that the Senate hosted the afternoon of June 24 is the first step toward turning around a misguided policy that I believe ties our hands in the war on terrorism. And I think all Americans should be grateful to Senator Specter for having had the courage to raise the question of, as he put it, "whether political correctness has gone too far in the case of aviation security."

When the dust settled from the hearing, I gave thought to the solution to the problem that I hope I have shed light upon. It seems to me that Congress needs to clarify the law that applies to airline security and give some clear direction to those involved in all facets of airport screening. Federal law allows a carrier to refuse to transport a passenger who presents a safety risk.[19] Federal law also says that an "air carrier or foreign air carrier may not subject a person in air transportation to discrimination on the basis of race, color, national origin, religion, sex, or ancestry."[20] Still another part of the federal law prohibits "an air carrier or foreign air carrier" from subjecting anyone to "unreasonable discrimination" on flights between the U.S. and foreign points.[21] Yet another statute requires that U.S. carriers provide "adequate interstate air transportation" which the DOT interprets as prohibiting invidiously discriminatory practices on the part of U.S. carriers generally in their interstate operations.[22]

Sound confusing? Sound at odds? That's a large part of the problem. And in the context of some gray areas, the Norman Mineta view is permitted to control the process. The issue becomes one of setting policy and then communicating the same to those front-line workers and pilots who have to make quick decisions. At present, those decisions are made with the guidance of the "but/for" test that Ms. Lopez referred to, and which I have mentioned previously.

As articulated in a DOT memo dated November 19, 2001, titled: "Answers to Frequently Asked Questions Concerning the Air Travel of People Who Are or May Appear to Be of Arab, Middle Eastern or South Asian Descent and/or Muslim or Sikh":

"Airline and airport personnel must use the 'but/for' test to help determine the justification for their actions. *But for this person's perceived race, ethnic heritage or religious orientation, would I have subjected this individual to additional safety or security scrutiny?* If the answer is 'no,' then the action may violate civil rights laws."[23]

On its surface, it may sound reasonable, but I would argue that the test is actually illogical and needs to be scrapped. Think about it. Consider this hypothetical:

Passenger A is a Saudi national flying from Logan to LAX. He's a thirty-ish man with olive complexion and with Mohammed as a part of his name. He appears to be traveling alone. He paid cash for his one-way ticket.

Passenger B has a home address in Detroit. She's on the same flight with Passenger A. She is an African-American woman traveling with an infant. Her skin is black, her name is Delores Washington, and she too paid cash for her one-way ticket.

Do you want the same level of scrutiny for both passengers? I say no. Why not? Because while both Passenger A and Passenger B have several suspicious things in common with the 9/11 hijackers—one-way ticket and cash payment, for instance—Passenger A has several further commonalities with the 9/11 hijackers that make him more suspicious. But hold on. Those commonalities involve matters of race, ethnicity, and gender! "But for" the race, ethnicity, and gender of Passenger B, I do not see the need for her to be subject to heightened scrutiny. Do they both get screened? For sure. But should Passenger A receive an additional level of scrutiny? Absolutely.

My analysis violates the "but for" test, or rather, infuses it with better logic in our post-9/11 world. And that is why the test is clearly illogical. Because, in certain circumstances, it will be the appearance of the individual that is a determining factor in singling them out, and to do otherwise is to ignore critical, valuable information about that which can be said about our enemy. Does that mean every Mohammed is pulled aside? Heck no. But it does mean that we need to acknowledge the limitations imposed by the present system.

In a word, we need clarity. And that clarity must come from Congress. Congress needs to tell the aviation industry—meaning the DOT, the TSA, and the airlines—that on a list of factors that will be considered in airport screening and decisions by pilots regarding denial of passage, will be the race, ethnicity, appearance, gender, and religion of the passenger in question. No one of those factors alone should subject an individual to greater scrutiny, but taken in tandem with additional information, yes, indeed, those items will be given weight.

✈

# EPILOGUE

I HAVE WRITTEN THIS BOOK TO TELL A STORY THAT I believe America needs to hear. It is a story about a dramatic failure to learn a lesson. I firmly believe what I have written in these pages. The war against terrorism is being compromised by political correctness and that can be seen clearly in, of all places, precisely where terrorism struck on 9/11. I think the implications extend beyond airports. If political correctness is affecting the scene of the crime on 9/11, it stands to reason that it does likewise elsewhere. How about our borders? Nuclear power plant safety and access? Stadiums?

Pulling this project together has required a tremendous amount of my time and effort. It has taken much of my time away from my four children for six months, but I write in large part because I am deeply concerned about them, and their ability to enjoy the quality of life that I have enjoyed, should the message of this book not be grasped and acted upon. I would find it uncomfortable and disingenuous to profit from this manuscript. Money was never my motivation in tracking this subject. It's all about the message and need for change. Therefore, I shall accept no payment for my work in this regard. Any money paid to me in the form of either an advance or royalty will be donated by me to a 9/11 charity. My personal favorite is a Garden of Reflection being constructed in the county of my birth, Bucks County, Pennsylvania. The terror attacks of 9/11 killed nearly 3,000 innocent Americans. Bucks County—due to its proximity to New York City—lost seventeen of its citizens in these attacks. In Lower Makefield Township, a memorial will be constructed in their honor. It will be called the Garden of Reflection. While the site for the memorial has been chosen, the project has yet to be started, as more funding is necessary. The project is a collaborative effort between 9/11-victim family members and local business leaders, and all donations are tax deductible due to the committee's 501c3 status.

You can take a look at it at: www.9-11MemorialGarden.org.

One final note. On July 23, 2004, the 9/11 Commission released its much-awaited report. If I were writing the news headline, it would look like this:

## MISSED OPPORTUNITY

That's my take on the final product of the 9/11 Commission.

I say that because, having scanned the 567 pages of the 9/11 Commission Report, a serious treatment of "terrorist profiling" is nowhere to be found. At least, not the type of treatment that I think is necessary in the war on terrorism.

Call me crazy. I was optimistic that the 9/11 Commission would have had the guts to say that the war on terror against young Arab males who are religious fanatics demands that we be on guard against young Arab males who are religious fanatics. No dice. Nowhere does this report embrace that kind of thinking; not even close. John Lehman must not have been able to get the votes within the Commission.

Instead, there is this Norman Minetaspeak on page 394: "The terrorists have used our open society against us. In wartime, government calls for greater powers, and then the need for those powers recedes after the war ends. This struggle will go on. Therefore, while protecting our homeland, Americans should be mindful of threats to vital personal and civil liberties. This balancing is no easy task, but we must constantly strive to keep it right."

Sounds like the same old, same old. Instead, I wish it would say that in attempting to balance civil liberties and the protection of our nation, we are going to err on the side of protecting the country. It pains me to be critical of the 9/11 Commission because I think it generally did a fabulous job. I was never part of the conservative crowd that questioned the Commission's right to exist. I repeatedly said on the radio that I wanted to know everything about the underlying events of 9/11, even if "knowing all" threatened the reelection of the Bush Administration that I support. While the finished product is a phenomenal body of investigative work that answers many of my questions about the facts that gave rise to 9/11, the analysis in the document appears to have come up short in one area of most importance to me. Nowhere in close to seventy pages of recommendations does the report say we need to take into account race, religion, ethnicity, and appearance—among other factors—when we are looking for terrorists!

The closest the report comes to doing so is to recognize the need to trust "subjective judgment." The report then cites the case of a potential hijacker who "was turned back by an immigration inspector as he tried to enter the United States." That, of course, is a reference to the case of terrorist profiling that presumably saved either the White House or Capitol. Yes, Jose Melendez-Perez, to whom I have referred at length within these pages, is the individual to whom the 9/11 Commission report refers on page 387. Melendez-Perez performed beyond the call of duty at Orlando Airport on August 4, 2001, when he screened a man named Mohammed Kahtani, who was being met at the airport by eventual 9/11 murderer Mohamed Atta.

Jose Melendez-Perez took into account Kahtani's nationality (Saudi), his grooming, dress, height, and shape. He figured the man to be military. And he noted the man's brash attitude. In short, Melendez-Perez engaged in criminal profiling. I only wish the 9/11 Commission had flat out said so, instead of offering the more politically correct recognition of the need for "subjective judgment."

Remember, even Richard Ben-Veniste, a 9/11 Commissioner, told Melendez Perez:

" . . . taking into account that the only plane commandeered by four hijackers, rather than five, crashed before reaching its target, it is entirely plausible to suggest that your actions in doing your job efficiently and competently may well have contributed to saving the Capitol or the White House, and all the people who were in those buildings, those monuments to our democracy, from being included in the catastrophe of 9/11, and for that we all owe you a debt of thanks and gratitude."

Here's the bottom line: even if all the recommendations of the 9/11 Commission are put into place, we will come up short in the war against terror unless we emulate Mr. Melendez-Perez. We need to profile. We still have work to do.

And so I end on the same note with which I began: In the immortal words of Todd Beamer, "Let's roll!"

—Michael A. Smerconish
July 23, 2004
Philadelphia

# APPENDIX

Here is a list of the items appearing in this appendix. Much of this material is quoted in part within the body of this book, but in the interest of complete disclosure, the texts of various official government and airline documents—as well as transcripts from speeches and official statements—are printed here. Also, you'll find the FBI's current (at press time) list of Most Wanted Terrorists with photos, and a Track List for the accompanying audio CD.

Department of Transportation e-mail dated September 21, 2001 to the major airlines and aviation associations concerning the aftermath of the attcks of 9/11

**UNITED STATES OF AMERICA
DEPARTMENT OF TRANSPORTATION
OFFICE OF AVIATION ENFORCEMENT AND PROCEEDINGS
WASHINGTON, DC**

**This message was e-mailed to major airlines and aviation associations on September 21, 2001. It concerns the aftermath of the attacks on the World Trade Center and the Pentagon on September 11, 2001.**

Since the terrorist hijackings and events of September 11, we have seen several reports of airlines apparently removing passengers from flights because the passengers appeared to be Middle Eastern and/or Muslim. We caution airlines not to target or otherwise discriminate against passengers based on their race, color, national or ethnic origin, religion, or based on passengers' names or modes of dress that could be indicative of such classification. Various Federal statutes prohibit air carriers from subjecting a person in air transportation to discrimination on the basis of race, color, national origin, religion, sex, or ancestry. At DOT, we are and will continue to be vigilant in ensuring that the airport security procedures, mandated by FAA and implemented by the airlines, are not unlawfully discriminatory.

We strongly encourage each airline to take steps to ensure that its employees understand that, not only is it wrong, but it is also illegal to discriminate against people based on their race, ethnicity, or religion. Recently, the President and Chief Operating Officer of Delta Airlines sent a letter to all of the airline's employees worldwide requesting tolerance of all people and cultures, and explaining that its employees must comply fully with civil rights laws. A copy of this letter is attached.

Norman Strickman
Assistant Director for Aviation Consumer Protection
Office of Aviation Enforcement and Proceedings
Office of the General Counsel
U.S. Department of Transportation
Delta letter
Sent to:

| | |
|---|---|
| Alaska Airlines | Northwest Airlines |
| America West Airlines | Southwest Airlines |
| American Airlines | Trans World Airlines |
| American Trans Air | United Airlines |
| Continental Airlines | US Airways |
| Delta Air Lines | |
| | |
| Air Transport Association | Regional Airline Association |
| International Air Transport Association | Air Carrier Association of America |

## Delta Airlines Memo to all employees worldwide dated September 21, 2001

Date:     September 21, 2001
To:       All Delta Employees Worldwide
From:     Fred Reid, President and Chief Operating Officer
Subject: Toleranceide

Dear Colleagues,

Last Tuesday's tragedy has affected us in ways that would have seemed inconceivable as little as two weeks ago. Unfortunately, we've seen some Americans become suspicious of people of other cultures – especially those of Mideast descent. And across the airline industry, we've heard stories of passengers being deplaned because of their skin color or the sound of their accents.

We cannot afford to follow this tragic behavior. It is exactly what our enemies are striving for: the end of our open, diverse, and tolerant way of life.

Delta's *Code of Ethics and Business Conduct* states that, "Delta has an uncompromising policy never to discriminate against customers on the basis of race, gender, age, national origin, disability, sexual orientation or similar classifications. The law mandates this policy – discrimination is not only illegal, it is wrong and will not be tolerated."

Safety is our first priority at Delta, and we will not compromise that. If a passenger behaves suspiciously or in a manner that suggests a possible security concern while in the airport or on board our aircraft, we should always take action to investigate the behavior. But our response must be based on the passenger's conduct, not on race or national origin.

Last Tuesday's events changed the way airlines do business from now on, not only in America, but throughout the world. Already, Delta has instituted strict security measures designed to make certain those intent on evil do not reach our airplanes. And our security measures continue to evolve and tighten.

Please continue to be observant and vigilant when enforcing security that protects our passengers and our people. But don't let last Tuesday's events change you into someone suspicious of people just because of the way they look – if you do that, then the terrorists will have won.

Thank you for the strength of character you've shown since the sad events last week. You make me proud to work with you.

## Statement of Secretary Norman Mineta to the U.S. Commission on Civil Rights dated October 12, 2001

STATEMENT OF NORMAN Y. MINETA

SECRETARY OF THE DEPARTMENT OF TRANSPORTATION

BEFORE THE U.S. COMMISSION ON CIVIL RIGHTS

OCTOBER 12, 2001

Chairperson Berry, Vice Chairperson Reynoso, Members of the Commission, and Staff Director Jin, I appreciate the opportunity to submit this statement on the Department of Transportation's (DOT's) work to strengthen transportation security in the aftermath of the horrific attacks that occurred on September 11, and our efforts to ensure that those new security requirements preserve and respect the civil rights of individuals to be protected from unlawful discrimination.

DOT and the agencies under our jurisdiction are working to prevent intentional harm to our critical air, surface, and water transportation systems, as well as to support national security and counter-terrorism policy. In securing our national air transportation systems, where much of our efforts have been directed to date, we have taken specific steps to ensure that persons do not face discrimination on the basis of race, color, national or ethnic origin, religion, sex, ancestry, or disability.

I understand that of particular concern to the Commission is the potential racial, ethnic, or religious profiling of individuals as a result of revised or proposed procedures to strengthen security measures at airline checkpoints and passenger screening locations in response to the terrorist hijackings and tragic events of September 11. As a result, this statement, while describing actions taken throughout the Department, will focus primarily on steps taken to ensure that DOT's efforts to secure our air transportation system do not unlawfully discriminate.

While safety and security are of the highest order of concern to DOT, we also understand the nature of the Nation our efforts are designed to protect: a society that respects civil and constitutional rights and cherishes the values of equal justice and equal opportunity.

As one of the 120,000 Americans of Japanese ancestry interned by the United States government during World War II, I know firsthand the dangers with which we are presented in the current crisis. All of us will face heightened security in the aftermath of September 11, but the security and scrutiny must never become pretexts for unlawful discrimination.

**SECURITY PROCEDURES AT AIRPORTS**
The Department of Transportation's authority in connection with discrimination in airline security and related issues is carried out through two departmental organizations: the Office of the General Counsel in the Office of the Secretary, which is responsible for investigating security related discrimination complaints, and the Federal Aviation Administration (FAA), which is tasked with developing and implementing airline security requirements, as well as monitoring airline compliance. In carrying out those responsibilities, the FAA is careful to ensure that the security requirements comply with the civil rights laws. The FAA, which has the authority to require modification of airline security programs that violate the law, will not tolerate airline security procedures that are unlawfully discriminatory.

Much of the aviation security selection procedures for enhanced checked baggage screening in the United States is now conducted by computer, thus avoiding human error and subjectivity. For screening of passengers, all major U.S. airlines and over 40 U.S. regional carriers are now using the Computer-Assisted Passenger Prescreening System (CAPPS). In late 1997, the Department of Justice found that the CAPPS criteria, as mandated by the FAA and used by U.S. airlines to select persons for additional checked baggage security procedures, are non-discriminatory on their face.

In light of the terrorist hijackings and tragic events of September 11, security measures at airports and airlines have been greatly heightened. The additional security measures include more thorough carry-on baggage screening and allowing only ticketed passengers beyond security checkpoints, except for those with specific medical or parental needs. We are confident that these new security procedures are nondiscriminatory and do not abridge the rights of citizens to be free of discrimination on the basis of race, color, nationality, ethnicity, or religion. We will continue to do everything in our power to ensure that remains the case.

## HANDLING OF DISCRIMINATION COMPLAINTS IN AIR TRAVEL

The Department has an effective system to deal with security related discrimination complaints when they arise. In this regard, our Office of Aviation Enforcement and Proceedings (Enforcement Office) is tasked with ensuring that the civil rights of air travelers are respected by the airlines we regulate.

Over the past four years a primary focus of the office has been on the investigation of security-related discrimination complaints. Of all the civil rights complaints the Enforcement Office receives, those alleging security-related discrimination cause it special concern. This is so because the Federal government establishes the underlying security requirements. We know that if they are not being applied in a nondiscriminatory manner, they will eventually lose their acceptance, to the serious detriment of the public.

The Enforcement Office thoroughly investigates each security-related discrimination complaint it receives and the Department continues to take other actions to perfect our authority to pursue these cases, to change airline procedures that lead to these complaints, to increase our resources to pursue these cases more effectively and to determine if the security procedures have a disparate impact on any minority group.

Members of the public who feel they have been the subject of discriminatory actions or treatment by air carriers may file a complaint by sending an email, a letter, or a completed complaint form to the Department of Transportation's Aviation Consumer Protection Division (ACPD), part of DOT's Enforcement Office. The Department's website provides detailed information on filing complaints, and complaint forms that consumers may download are also available on the website.

Since September 11, the Department has received seven complaints from persons alleging that that they were removed from flights or denied permission to board because they are, or were perceived to be, of Arab, Middle Eastern, or South Asian descent and/or Muslim. The Department has also received three complaints alleging discrimination prior to boarding at security check points. Each of these complaints have been reviewed, are being acknowledged, and will be investigated. We take all these cases very seriously.

## ACTIONS TAKEN SINCE SEPTEMBER 11

Since September 11, the Department has taken or will be taking several proactive steps regarding security-related discrimination issues. For instance, our Rapid Response Team on Airport Security, composed of representatives from airlines, airports, airline manufacturers, labor, and government agencies emphasized that its recommendations for strengthened security measures, released on October 5, 2001, must be implemented in a way that is wholly consistent with America's commitment to the protection of civil rights.

Earlier, on September 21, 2001, the Department of Transportation reminded the eleven major airlines and several airline associations that Federal law prohibits air carriers from discriminating against passengers on the basis of race, color, national origin, religion, sex or ancestry. The Department also strongly encouraged air carriers to take steps to ensure that their employees understand that it is illegal to discriminate against people based on their race, color, national origin, religion, sex, or ancestry. A copy of the "Tolerance" memo that we e-mailed to the airlines has been placed on our website at http://www.dot.gov/airconsumer/01-index.htm and a copy of it is appended to this statement.

On October 1, 2001, as follow-up to the September 21 notice, the Department requested information on actions each airline has taken to make certain that its employees understand their responsibility to treat passengers in a fair and nondiscriminatory manner. So far, seventeen airlines, including the largest U.S. carriers, have contacted us to let us know that they have taken specific steps such as sending a letter to all of their employees worldwide requesting tolerance of all people and cultures, and explaining that their employees must comply fully with this Nation's civil rights laws.

Further, since the September 11, 2001, attacks, I, as well as Administrators of various DOT operating administrations, and other senior-level officials in the Department, have continuously spoken out against discrimination, scapegoating, and incivility. Officials from the Department are committed to working with the public, particularly the Arab-American, South Asian American and Muslim communities, to ensure that heightened security measures do not violate the civil rights of any American. For example, on October 9, 2001, the Assistant General Counsel for Aviation Enforcement and Proceedings met, in Chicago, with representatives of the local Arab-American community, the Sikh community, and other similarly affected groups for an informational session on what to do if confronted with discrimination as a result of the tragic events of September 11. The information session was hosted by the Department of Justice and Illinois State officials, and included representatives from various Federal agencies.

In addition, I am delivering remarks today at the public forum at the University of Rochester on this very subject. In those remarks, I will stress that we must be vigilant against bigotry, intolerance, and discrimination as we heighten security in America's transportation systems..

Finally, because of concerns about intimidation and harassment directed at certain individuals as a result of the terrorist attacks of September 11, 2001, I will soon issue a policy statement reminding the Department's employees carrying out transportation inspection and compliance responsibilities of longstanding DOT policy prohibiting unlawful discrimination against individuals because of their race, color, religion, ethnicity, or national origin.

**CONCLUSION**
At the Department of Transportation, we have been, and will continue to be, vigilant in ensuring that our transportation system is safe, secure, and not unlawfully discriminatory. Protecting the civil rights of passengers is essential to maintaining the security of our Nation, because those civil rights are essential to our most fundamental values. There have been times in our history as a Nation when that has been forgotten. I am committed, and the Administration is committed, to ensuring that it is never forgotten again.

Once again, I am sorry I could not be with you today for this important hearing. I look forward to continuing the work we have done together over the years in building a fair society with equal justice for all.

Thank you again for the opportunity to submit this statement today.

DOT Memo "Carrying Out Transportation, Inspection, and Safety Responsibilities in aNon-Discriminatory Manner," dated October 12, 2001

**UNITED STATES OF AMERICA
DEPARTMENT OF TRANSPORTATION
OFFICE OF AVIATION ENFORCEMENT AND PROCEEDINGS
WASHINGTON, DC**

**October 12, 2001**

*Carrying Out Transportation Inspection and Safety Responsibilities
In A Nondiscriminatory Manner*

This DOT policy statement was e-mailed to major U.S. airlines and aviation associations on October 17, 2001. The Department believes that this guidance could be of benefit to pilots, flight attendants and other customer contact personnel who may have a role in safety or security determinations.

This is a reminder to Department of Transportation (DOT) employees and those carrying out transportation inspection and enforcement responsibilities with DOT financial support of longstanding DOT policy prohibiting unlawful discrimination against individuals because of their race, color, religion, ethnicity, or national origin. The terrorist attacks of September 11, 2001, have raised concerns about intimidation and harassment directed at individuals who are, or are perceived to be, of Arab, Middle Eastern, or South Asian descent and/or Muslim. Federal civil rights laws prohibit discrimination on the basis of a person's race, color, national or ethnic origin, religion, sex, ancestry, or disability. DOT applauds the professionalism and dedication of its safety inspectors and law enforcement investigators and recognizes the enormous challenges we face in ensuring the security of our Nation's transportation system. However, it is important to reemphasize that in performing our critical duties, we may not rely on generalized stereotypes or attitudes or beliefs about the propensity of members of any racial, ethnic, religious, or national origin group to engage in unlawful activity. Protecting the constitutional and civil rights of our constituents/ stakeholders remains one of our highest priorities. This policy is not intended to forbid conduct that is considered legal under U.S. law such as considering citizenship in carrying out port security activities, border control and interdiction missions , and apprehension and detention of illegal drug smugglers. Consistent with DOT's policy, here are several points to keep in mind while doing your important jobs:

- Treat people who may appear to be of Arab, Middle Eastern or South Asian descent and/or Muslim with the same respect you would treat people of other ethnicities and religions, and treat all people in a polite, respectful and friendly manner. To the extent possible and permitted by law, answer questions from persons in a forthright manner.
- Do not subject persons or their property to inspection, search and/or detention solely because they appear to be Arab, Middle Eastern, Asian, and/or Muslim; or solely because they speak Arabic, Farsi, or another foreign language; or solely because they speak with an accent that may lead you to believe they are Arab, Middle Eastern, Asian, and/or Muslim.
- If a search or inspection is necessary for safety or security reasons, whenever possible, provide the person involved a choice of a public or private inspection. Public searches may be viewed as humiliating while private searches may be perceived to be overly intimidating.

- Discriminating on the basis of national origin or religion includes discriminating against someone based solely on an appearance or dress that is associated with a particular national origin or religion. For example, selecting a woman for an inspection solely because her hair is covered or she is wearing a veil, as some Muslim women do, is illegal discrimination. Selecting a man for an inspection solely because he is wearing a long beard or hair covering, as some Muslim men do, is unlawful discrimination. Likewise, selecting a man for an inspection solely because he is wearing a turban, as some Sikh men do, is unlawful discrimination.

- Be aware of inspection/search practices that might be offensive: during an inspection, asking a woman to remove her veil or hair covering may be offensive and could violate her religious tenets and asking a Sikh man to remove his turban could violate his religious tenets.

- Take all available facts and circumstances into account in identifying persons or property that may be a safety or security risk. Although your actions may, at times, offend the person involved, you would continue to be justified in conducting additional questioning, inspections or searches, for safety or security reasons, in certain situations; for example: the driver of a truck containing hazardous material has identification or documentation showing that he or she was born in the United States but the driver does not speak English and appears to only speak Arabic, Farsi, or another foreign language; a person wearing a turban or head dress, while being searched at an airport security checkpoint, triggers the handheld metal detector when it is near his or her head; or a veiled woman shows photo identification to prove her identity but it is difficult to conclude that this woman is the same person as the woman in the photo without checking her face. When it is necessary to verify the identity of a veiled woman, whenever possible, her face should be checked by female safety or security personnel in private or only in the presence of other women so as not to violate her religious tenets.

- Use the "but/for" test to help determine the justification for your actions. Ask yourself, *But for this person's perceived race, ethnic heritage or religious orientation, would I have subjected this individual to additional safety or security scrutiny?* If the answer is "no," then the action may violate civil rights laws.

We hope this information is helpful to you. If you are unsure about what constitutes inappropriate behavior, or if you have any other questions, do not hesitate to contact the Department's Office of Civil Rights or the operating administrations' civil rights offices. The telephone numbers of DOT's headquarters civil rights offices are listed below.

# Statement of Jose Melendez-Perez before the 9/11 Commission on January 26, 2004

**Seventh public hearing of the National Commission on Terrorist Attacks Upon the United States**

**Statement of Jose E. Melendez-Perez to the National Commission on Terrorist Attacks Upon The United States**
**January 26, 2004**

## Background

I am a 26 year honorable veteran of the U.S. Army and am currently on my 12th year as an immigration inspector, now working for Customs and Border Protection under the Department of Homeland Security. I began my career with the Immigration and Naturalization Service in 1992 where I was first assigned to Miami International Airport and subsequently transferred to Orlando International Airport, where I currently work.

My job requires me to know the difference between legitimate travelers to the U.S., and those who are not. This includes potential terrorists. We received terrorist and other types of alerts, such as on document fraud and stolen passports, prior to September 11, but we all consider these alerts in a different light now.

The national security element of my job means that training and experience is important. In my case, training for my job as inspector has been threefold. The first was my 26 years in military service, where I learned effective listening skills, observation of body language, and determination of motives. Second, when I joined the INS, I was required to attend training at the Law Enforcement Training Center where I received approximately (16) hours of training in interview skills, sworn statements, and document fraud. Third, my experience on the job as Immigration Inspector for the past eleven years has greatly improved my skills in detecting document fraud, observing body language and understanding different cultures, including Saudi nationals, many of whom come with their families via the Orlando International Airport on their way to Disney World. Saudi nationals were held to the same legal standards as everyone else. However, service wide they were treated with more "tact". For example, in order to accommodate the Saudi culture, female Saudis unwilling to unveil were inspected by female inspectors, if available. This remains the case today.

In Orlando, as in any other port, an immigration inspector can only return someone foreign back home, for whatever reason under the Expedited Removal law, if the inspector is to be able to substantiate the recommendation. Supervisors for the most part support inspectors who have enough proof to substantiate removing someone. It is my belief that some supervisors in Orlando and nationwide remain intimidated by complaints from the public, and particularly by Congressional letters, about refusing admission to certain aliens. Because of these complaints, supervisors tend to be wary of supporting the inspector who recommends an adverse action against an alien.

I do not know how often people are removed from the United States, nor can I tell you before 9/11 how many Saudis entered the country or how many were refused. However, I can tell you that according to the records we have in Orlando, approximately ten Saudi nationals have been turned around for various reasons. In regard to the incident on August 4, 2001 which I am about to talk about, I note that another inspector on duty that day made a comment that I was going to get into trouble for refusing a Saudi national. I replied that I have to do my job, and I cannot do my work with dignity if I base my recommendations on refusals/admissions on someone's nationality.

The primary inspection officer is the first official that an international traveler comes in contact with. The officer's responsibility is to verify the passenger's travel documents for validity, the purpose of their trip, and check entry/exit stamps for past travel history. In addition, inspectors query databases for passengers who maybe on a lookout list for various reasons, (i.e., terrorism, criminal records, outstanding arrest warrants, etc.). Before 9/11, some of the databases available in 2001 were: (a) TECS-Treasury Enforcement Communication System, (b) CIS-INS Central Index System, (c) NAILS-National Automated Index Lookout System.

### The Encounter on August 4, 2001

On August 4, 2001, I was assigned as a secondary inspection officer at the Orlando International Airport. My supervisor alternates inspectors between primary and secondary inspection, and on this day I was assigned to secondary inspection. At approximately 1735 hours, I was assigned the case of a Saudi national who had arrived on Virgin Atlantic #15 from London, Gatwick Airport. As Saudis coming through Orlando to travel to Disney World are common, I had plenty of line experience with Saudis. In this particular case, the subject was referred to secondary inspection because the primary inspector could not communicate with him and his arrival/departure form (I-94) and Customs Declaration (C-6059B) were not properly completed.

I first queried the subject's name, date of birth, and passport number through the above systems with negative results. Subject's documents appeared to be genuine. A search of subject and his personal belongings were also negative. Subject was enrolled in IDENT and photographed. In addition, a complete set of fingerprints was taken on form FD-249 (red).

Through my INS training and military experience, my first impression of the subject was that he was a young male, well groomed, with short hair, trimmed mustache, black long sleeve shirt, black trousers, black shoes. He was about 5'6", and in impeccable shape, with large shoulders and a thin waist. He had a military appearance. Upon establishing eye contact, he exhibited body language and facial gestures that appeared arrogant. In fact, when I first called his name in the secondary room and matched him with papers, he had a deep staring look.

I had the impression of the subject that he had knowledge of interview techniques and had military training. Upon my initial review of the subject's paperwork and documents, I noticed that he did not have a return airline ticket or hotel reservations. Upon learning that the we had provided no specific grounds for removal, higher up confirmation was needed. My supervisor then proceeded to call the AAPD at home to explain the case and get concurrence for removal. After my supervisor presented the facts to AAPD , he then asked to speak directly with me.

The AAPD asked numerous questions concerning the case. I explained that apart from not having a return ticket and possibly not having sufficient funds, the subject appeared to be malafide. I further explained to the AAPD that when the subject looked at me, I felt a bone chilling cold effect. The bottom line is, "He gave me the creeps". You just had to be present to understand what I am trying to explain. The AAPD then asked if I had tried to place him under oath. I replied that I had tried to place the subject under oath, but the subject refused to answer my questions. The AAPD then stated that under Section 235.1 (a) (5) of the Immigration Nationality Act an applicant could be required to state, under oath, any information sought by an Immigration Officer regarding the purpose and intentions of the applicant in seeking admission to the United States. The AAPD further stated that he was convinced from what I had stated and my beliefs about the subject that the individual was malafide and should be allowed to withdraw his application or be set up for Expedited Removal.

I then proceeded to advise the subject that he did not appear to be admissible to the United States. He was offered the opportunity to voluntarily withdraw his application for admission. Subject chose to withdraw and signed the I-275. Along with another immigration inspector, I escorted subject to his departing gate for his removal. Before boarding the aircraft, the subject turned to other inspector and myself and said, in English, something to the effect of, "I'll be back". On August 4, 2001, subject departed foreign via Virgin Atlantic flight 16 to London with connecting flight to Dubai.

On September 11, 2001 while attending a meeting with the Warden at the Central Florida Processing Center (Department of Corrections) concerning the use of their range, a corrections officer came in and advised the Warden of the incident that had just occurred in New York City. As I watched the television, I could not help but think of the two cases I had processed in August concerning Saudi Nationals. I immediately contacted the Orlando Airport (I do not remember which officer I spoke with) but I asked them to look up the cases and contact the FBI agent assigned to the airport.

To the best of my knowledge, immigration officers made copies of this August 4, 2001 incident and provided that paperwork to the FBI. The FBI has never interviewed me. I do not recall ever speaking with GITMO officials. INS headquarters contacted me once. I have had no other contact with intelligence or law enforcement officials. Outside of legacy INS, the only government contact I have had about this incident came from the September 11 Commission this past fall, from your border team investigating the incident.

*Mr. Melendez-Perez is currently a U.S. Customs and Border Protection Inspector at Orlando International Airport, Orlando, Florida. Prior to the formation of DHS, he was employed by the U.S. Immigration and Naturalization Service (INS) from November 15, 1992 to April 30, 2003.*

*He is a retired member of the United States Army where he served honorably for over 26 years. He served 2 tours of duty in Vietnam, 1965-1966 and 1969-1970. He was later assigned as a first sergeant to the U.S. Army Recruiting Command for approximately 15 years.*

subject did not speak English (or at least that is what he wanted us to believe), I contacted an Arabic interpreter from the Department of Justice's interpreter's list.

My first question to the subject (through the interpreter) was why he was not in possession of a return airline ticket. The subject became visibly upset and in an arrogant and threatening manner, which included pointing his finger at my face, stated that he did not know where he was going when he departed the United States. What first came to mind at this point was that this subject was a "hit man". When I was in the Recruiting Command, we received extensive training in questioning techniques. A "hit man" doesn't know where he is going because if he is caught, that way he doesn't have any information to bargain with.

The subject then continued, stating that a friend of his was to arrive in the United States at a later date and that his friend knew where he was going. He also stated that his friend would make all the arrangements for the subject's departure. I asked him if he knew when his friend was to arrive in the United States and he responded that he was to arrive in three or four days. I asked him what the purpose of this trip was and how long he wanted to stay. He responded that he would be vacationing and traveling through the United States for six days. At this point, I realized that his story did not seem plausible. Why would he be vacationing for only six days and spend half of his time waiting for his friend? It became apparent that the subject was being less than truthful concerning his true intentions.

At this time, I again asked him where he was going to stay. He said, "A hotel". I then told him that without knowledge of the English language or a hotel reservation he would have difficulty getting around Orlando. He answered that there was someone waiting for him upstairs. When asked the person's name, he changed his story and said no one was meeting him. He said he was to call someone from his residence that would then contact someone locally to pick him up. I then asked the subject for the person's phone number and he refused to provide it stating that it was, "...none of my business". He stated that it was a personal matter and that he did not see any reason for me to contact that person. The subject was very hostile throughout the entire interview that took approximately 1-½ hours.

Subject was in possession of $2,800.00 United States dollars and no credit cards. This amount did not appear sufficient for a six-day vacation plus a hotel room and return ticket since a one-way ticket to Dubai, where he originated from, would cost approximately $2,200.00 USD. When confronted with this fact, he responded that his friend was going to bring him some money. I then asked, "Why would he bring you some money"? He replied, "Because he is a friend". I then asked, "How long have you known this person"? He answered, "Not too long".

I said to myself, I'd like to place him under oath. I wanted him to understand the consequences of making a false statement. He agreed to be placed under oath, but when I asked the first question, he said, "I won't answer." The Arabic interpreter said to me that something was not right here.

At this point, I gave my supervisor a synopsis of the case and explained my suspicions that this individual was malafide, (i.e., that his true intent in coming to the United States was not clear and he appeared very evasive). After presenting the case to my supervisor, he felt that Assistant Area Port Director (AAPD) should be contacted for further instructions. Normally, second line supervisors such as AAPD are not contacted in such matters, but because of the facts that

## Excerpt of Testimony from Edward Soliday before the 9/11 Commission on January 27, 2004

MR. LEHMAN: Thank you and I too applaud your willingness to come up here and be beat up a little bit and also to really give us your recommendations for the future. And again I would echo Senator Kerrey that we would very much like your continuing participation and recommendations. The record that has emerged from our staff's research is one in which the weight of the industry has been continuously against tightening up restrictions.

Now, you've articulated well the reasons why you didn't expect the threat that came, but it's like so many of the arguments we've heard earlier. It's not very persuasive that nobody told us, it's not our job to decide what the threat is. And, of course, quite apart from what the regulation that was cited stipulates, of course it's your job. I mean, I would be willing to bet, if I could overhear some of your conversations in a bar somewhere, that you're not full of praise and confidence for the government's brilliance in handling all of your tax issues and your inspection issues and what possible reason would you have to think that you don't have to participate in intelligence assessment, threat assessment?

The FAA was saying that it was perfectly all right for young Arabs to come on to your airplanes with 4-inch knives and, you know, the industry's attitude was, "Hey, it's not our business. The FAA says it's okay, it's got to be okay." What's been missing from a lot of the witnesses that we've had these last two days is an application at the leadership level of the common sense test to some of these things. The record that our staff has produced is one of the industry continuously eroding and blocking and defunding initiatives like the first air marshal initiative, the locked cockpit door initiative, the single key

initiative and one of the things that we've heard constant complaints about from the immigration people is the industry's successful thwarting of their efforts to fix the "transit without waiver" loophole, which the industry has known has been used by terrorists, has been used heavily by smugglers and could be relatively easily fixed with the building of secure transit lounges and the kind of measures that most large countries in the world, if not all of them, have.

Yet, as I understand it, even today, the industry is whinging and whining because the President suspended this huge loophole. I would like to hear how you, without, you don't necessarily have to respond to my indictment of the pre-9/11 era, but how do you see your roles going forward as an active challenger of the bureaucratic inertia that's inevitably part of many of these government regulatory initiatives? Why do we not have a single instance in our research of the industry saying, "We've got to tighten up in screening. We're only paying minimum wage and we have a 100 percent turnover of our people. We should be hiring higher quality people. Why are you letting 4-inch blades aboard our airplanes?"

206 I FLYING BLIND

We don't have any record of that and somehow, you guys have
to change the whole paradigm of the way you approach these safety
issues.  You've got to be proactive and not a drag on the system
which, historically, you have been, unless you can provide us
evidence that challenges the overwhelming weight of evidence that
we have so far.

    MR. SOLIDAY:  Commissioner Lehman, if I could begin the
response and then maybe others would like to join me.  I
understand your frustration and I understand your comments.  As
you know, by my biography, I hold several major trophies for
development of enhanced ground proximity warnings, FOQA systems,
so forth, all of which happen to be on the aviation side.  We are
not mandated by the government.

    Quite frankly, if you look at the record, we tested numerous
things long before they were mandated.  Immediately after TWA
800, we, as a company, talked with the FAA and said we are
prepared to move forward with some security measures to ramp up
because we don't know what caused this.  The problem is -- and
you can make light of it, if you like -- a citizen does not have
the right to search and seize.  There are privacy issues and, for
example, as a company who was prepared to roll CAPPS out and did
roll it out long before any other company, a visitor from the
Justice Department who told me that if I had more than three
people of the same ethnic origin in line for additional
screening, our system would be shut down as discriminatory.

# Consent Order issued by the DOT to American Airlines dated February 27, 2004

**UNITED STATES OF AMERICA
DEPARTMENT OF TRANSPORTATION
OFFICE OF HEARINGS
WASHINGTON, D.C.**

Issued by the Department of Transportation
on the 27th day of February, 2004

| | |
|---|---|
| **American Airlines, Inc.**<br>**Violations of 49 U.S.C. §§40127, 41310, 41702 and**<br>**41712** | **Served: February 27, 2004,**<br><br>**Docket OST 2003-15046** |

## CONSENT ORDER

This order closes an enforcement proceeding involving American Airlines, Inc.'s (American)[1] compliance with Federal statutes prohibiting air carriers from subjecting any air traveler to discrimination on the basis of race, color, national origin, religion, sex or ancestry. The consent order directs American to cease and desist from future violations and to provide civil rights training to its flight and cabin crews and customer service representatives.

Shortly after the terrorist attacks of September 11, 2001, the Office of Aviation Enforcement and Proceedings (Enforcement Office) began to receive complaints against American (and other carriers) from individuals removed from flights or denied boarding on flights allegedly because those persons were, or were perceived to be, of Arab, Middle Eastern or Southeast Asian descent and/or Muslim. Because of concerns about these complaints, the Enforcement Office requested information from American regarding incidents occurring between September 11, 2001, and December 31, 2001, involving the removal or denied boarding of a passenger for safety/security reasons.

Federal law is clear. An airline cannot refuse passage to an individual because of that person's race, color, national origin, religion, sex, or ancestry. 49 U.S.C. § 40127(a). Similarly, 49 U.S.C. § 41310 prohibits air carriers and foreign air carriers from engaging in unreasonable discrimination against individuals on flights between the U.S. and foreign points, 49 U.S.C. § 41702 requires that U.S. carriers provide safe and adequate transportation, and 49 U.S.C. § 41712 prohibits unfair and deceptive practices and, therefore, prohibits invidiously discriminatory practices on the part of U.S. carriers. This proceeding was instituted on April 25, 2003, with the filing of a Notice of Enforcement Proceeding and Assessment of Civil Penalties and related Complaint based on the Enforcement Office's investigation of American's compliance with the aforementioned statutes.

---

[1] In each instance in this consent order in which the name American Airlines or American appears, it shall refer to and be binding upon American Airlines, Inc., American Eagle, Inc., and all their subsidiary or wholly-owned air carriers.

violations of section 40127; and sections 41310 and 41702 do not create an administrative remedy for discrimination on the basis of protected status.[4]

American further emphasizes that all of the alleged incidents occurred shortly after September 11, 2001 a period of unprecedented security concerns and tension for all participants in the nation's air transportation system, especially American one of the two carriers that lost employees, passengers and aircraft in the attacks. During the period following September 11, American states that it was scrupulous in exercising its authority and responsibility under section 44902(b), and remains so today. As one of two carriers that were direct victims of the attack, American points out that it is particularly sensitive to claims that its employees acted in disregard of the law regarding aircraft security following September 11. American, having thoroughly investigated the complaints in question, remains resolute in its conviction that none of its employees, in conducting themselves as they did under extremely difficult and historically unprecedented, circumstances, acted wrongly or with intent to violate any law.

American states that, even though it continues to deny strenuously that any violation of Federal law occurred, it made more sense to settle this matter with the Enforcement Office than to continue with costly and protracted litigation to vindicate the actions of its employees. This is especially the case as the Enforcement Office is willing to settle the matter without the assessment of civil penalties, but rather a commitment by American to incorporate civil rights training into existing training programs for pilots, flight attendants, and customer service representatives. According to American, since it is already fully committed to vigorous compliance with the country's civil rights laws, this training will serve simply to reinforce the company's commitment to these core civil rights protections, an objective to which American is fully committed in any event.

The Enforcement Office recognizes that the September 11 terrorist attacks were unprecedented and clearly created a difficult situation for the airline industry, acting pursuant to FAA-approved security programs, in trying to protect passengers and crew from further attacks. Nonetheless, based on its review of the post-September 11 incidents in which American removed or failed to board passengers purportedly for safety/security reasons, the Enforcement Office believes that some passengers were denied boarding because, or principally because, of the passenger's ethnic background. Even though the Enforcement Office does not dispute that the American employees involved believed they were acting to ensure the safety and security of passengers and crew, the Enforcement Office believes some passengers were denied boarding or removed from flights in a manner inconsistent with the carrier's non-discrimination obligations under Federal law.

The Enforcement Office has carefully considered all the information provided by American, but continues to believe that enforcement action is warranted. In order to end the litigation, the Enforcement Office and American have reached a settlement of this matter. Without admitting

---

[4] American raised these arguments in a motion to dismiss in this proceeding which was denied by the Administrative Law Judge in an order issued on August 21, 2003. See American Airlines Inc., OST-2003-15046-18.

any violations of the law occurred, and without waiving its legal arguments as set forth above, American consents to the issuance of this order to cease and desist from future violations of 49 U.S.C. §§ 40127, 41310, 41702, and 41712 and to provide civil rights training to its flight and cabin crewmembers, as well as its customer service representatives. The Deputy General Counsel and the Enforcement Office believe that this settlement is appropriate and serves the public interest and creates an incentive for all carriers to comply fully with the civil rights laws enforced by the Department of Transportation.[5]

ACCORDINGLY,

1. Based on the above discussion, we approve this settlement and the provisions of this order as being in the public interest;

2. We find that American Airlines, Inc., acted in a manner inconsistent with the requirements of 49 U.S.C. §§ 40127, 41310, 41702 and 41712 when it removed from or refused to board on its flights certain individuals as discussed above;

3. We order American Airlines, Inc., and all other entities owned and controlled by it or under common ownership and control with it, and their successors and assigns to cease and desist from future violations of 49 U.S.C. §§ 40127, 41310, 41702 and 41712, as described above;

4. We order American Airlines, Inc., and its successors and assigns to provide civil rights training to its flight and cabin crewmembers and passenger service representatives. The total cost of the training shall be no less than $1.5 million and shall be expended by a date three years after the service date of the order.[6] Upon the completion of that training, and in no event later than the 14 months after the service date of this order and every 12 months thereafter for two subsequent years, American shall submit a sworn statement from an appropriate company official certifying that all flight and cabin crewmembers and passenger service agents have received the civil rights training required under this order.

5. Any failure by American Airlines, Inc., to conduct the training in accordance with ordering paragraph 4 or to document it adequately to the Enforcement Office shall

---

[5] Additionally, this consent order will settle any and all complaints that could be asserted against American alleging violations of 49 U.S.C. §§ 41310, 41702, 41705 or 41712 arising out of or relating to incidents where American removed from a flight or failed to board a passenger on the basis of the passenger's assumed ethnic background or national origin occurring on or after September 11, 2001, and through the service date of this order.

[6] The Department has contracted with a company to develop an easy to understand technical assistance manual that details the responsibilities of air carriers under Federal nondiscrimination statutes and to develop a model training program, which will include, at a minimum, an overview of the applicable laws and regulations, a cultural awareness component and a job-specific training segment. To support the Department in its mission of ensuring nondiscrimination in air transportation, American has agreed to share with the Department's contractors its civil rights training materials for possible inclusion in the Department's technical assistance manual and model training program.

constitute a continuing violation of this consent order and subject American to enforcement action; and

6. This order makes no findings of violations with respect to any individual incident of alleged civil rights violations and the findings herein shall have no effect in any proceeding not before the Department of Transportation.

This order is issued under authority assigned in 14 CFR 385.11(d) and shall become a final order of the Department 30 days after its service unless a timely petition for review is filed or the Department takes review on its motion.

By:

                                        BURTON S. KOLKO
                                        Administrative Law Judge

(SEAL)

*An electronic version of this document is available on the World Wide Web at*
*http://dms.dot.gov/reports/reports_aviation.asp*

"The Big Question" from 9/11 Commissioner John Lehman to Dr. Condoleezza Rice during the 9/11 Commission Hearings on April 8, 2004

---

**MR. LEHMAN:** . . . Were you aware—it disturbs me a bit—and again let me shift to the continuity issues here. Were you aware that it was the policy of the Justice Department—and I'd like you to comment as to whether these continuities are still in place. For instance, before I go to Justice, were you aware that it was the policy and, I believe, remains the policy today to fine airlines if they have more than two young Arab males in secondary questioning, because that's discriminatory?

**MS. RICE:** No. I have to say that the kind of inside arrangements for the FAA are not really in my purview. . . .

**MR. LEHMAN:** Well, these are not so inside. . . .

Witness list, United States Senate Appropriations Subcommittee on Transportation, Treasury, and General Government dated June 23, 2004

---

 U.S. Senate Committee on Appropriations
*PRESS RELEASE*

June 23, 2004                    Press Contact: Melanie Alvord (202) 224-0992

FOR IMMEDIATE RELEASE

---

**Transportation Subcommittee to Hold Hearing on Thursday, June 24 on Passenger Screening and Airline Authority to Deny Boarding**

The Senate Appropriations Committee's **Subcommittee on Transportation, Treasury and General Government** will hold an oversight hearing on Passenger Screening and Airline Authority to Deny Boarding at 2:00 p.m. on Thursday, June 24th, 2004 in Room 138 of the Dirksen Building.

The scheduled witnesses are:

Panel I

The Honorable Jeff Rosen, General Counsel, Department of Transportation

Mr. Tom Blank, Assistant Administrator, Office of Transportation Security Policy, Transportation Security Administration

Panel II

Mr. Michael Smerconish, Esq., Talk show host and columnist

Ms. Peggy Sterling, Vice President, American Airlines

Ms. Christy E. Lopez, Esq., Relman and Associates

## Statement of Senator Richard Shelby (R-AL) dated June 24, 2004

## Press Release

**SHELBY CHAIRS HEARING ON AIRLINE SECURITY**

**Contact:** Virginia Davis (202)224-6518
Thursday, June 24, 2004

WASHINGTON, DC - U.S. Senator Richard C. Shelby (R-Ala),
Chairman of the Appropriations Subcommittee on Transportation,
Treasury, and General Government, chaired an oversight hearing today
on passenger screening and airline authority to deny boarding. The
following is Senator Shelby's opening statement:

"Good afternoon. The subcommittee will come to order. Today, the
subcommittee is holding an oversight hearing to examine whether the
Federal government has instituted policies to limit an airline from
denying transport or requiring additional security screening to
individuals who may be unsafe or dangerous."

"The Federal Aviation Act allows air carriers the right of permissive
refusal which is defined as the ability to refuse to transport a passenger
or property the carrier decides is a potential risk to safety or security.
The Federal Aviation Regulations authorize the pilot in command of the
aircraft to discharge this right of permissive refusal on behalf of the air
carrier in light of his final authority and responsibility for the operation
and safety of the flight."

"Despite this clear authority, however, there seems to be some
question about the ability of an airline to remove passengers based on
a perceived threat. At the January 27, 2004, hearing of the National
Commission on Terrorist Attacks Upon the United States, a former
airline executive testified that, "Most recently after 9/11, 38 of our
captains denied boarding to people they thought were a threat. Those
people filed complaints with the DOT, we were sued, and we were
asked not to do it again.""

"If this is the case, I am concerned that we may be jeopardizing aviation
security by placing unnecessary restrictions on pilots and crew to take
actions to protect passengers and the plane."

"If this nation has learned anything since terrorists set their sights on
destroying this nation, it is this: terrorists will learn a system, identify the
weaknesses of that system, and then exploit those weaknesses to

inflict harm."

"I believe that we must balance an individual's civil liberties with an
airline pilot's right to ensure the safety and security of the flight. But in
trying to reach that balance, I want to ensure that we have not
established policies or practices that will have a chilling effect on the
willingness of the pilot in command to exercise his authority to
safeguard the crew and all passengers."

"The Transportation Security Administration check point is not, and
should not be, considered the last line of defense to assure the security
of a flight by clearing passengers for boarding. The pilot and the crew of
an aircraft - and even the passengers - are an important layer in
keeping our aviation system secure."

"We should not forget that Richard Reid, the would-be shoe bomber,
was thwarted by other passengers and crew during the flight. Removal
of a passenger must be the final decision of the pilot. The last thing we
should do is undermine the authority of the pilot to deny boarding or
require additional screening to any passenger or group of passengers
when has a reasonable suspicion of a threat to a safe flight."

"I want to thank my colleague, Senator Specter, for raising this issue
with me. I believe that it is important to hold this hearing today to
highlight this issue and provide clarity on what should be the lines of
authority in this matter."

## FBI Most Wanted Terrorist List as of publication date

The alleged terrorists on this list have been indicted by sitting Federal Grand Juries in various jurisdictions in the United States for the crimes reflected on their wanted posters. Evidence was gathered and presented to the Grand Juries, which led to their being charged. The indictments currently listed on the posters allow them to be arrested and brought to justice. Future indictments may be handed down as various investigations proceed in connection to other terrorist incidents, for example, the terrorist attacks on September 11, 2001.

Usama Bin Laden

Ayman Al-Zawahiri

Abdelkarim Hussein Mohamed Al-Nasser

Abdullah Ahmed Abdullah

Muhsin Musa Matwalli Atwah

Ali Atwa

Anas Al-Liby

Ahmed Khalfan Ghailani

Hasan Izz-Al-Din

Ahmed Mohammed Hamed Ali

Fazul Abdullah Mohammed

Imad Fayez Mugniyah

Mustafa Mohamed Fadhil

Sheikh Ahmed Salim Swedan

Abdul Rahman Yasin

Fahid Mohammed Ally Msalam

Ahmad Ibrahim Al-Mughassil

Khalid Shaikh Mohammed

Muhammad Atef

Ali Saed Bin Ali El-Hoorie

Saif Al-Adel

Ibrahim Salih Mohammed Al-Yacoub

## *FLYING BLIND* AUDIO CD TRACK LIST

1. Series of Questions by 9/11 Commissioner John Lehman to Dr. Condoleezza Rice from the 9/11 Commission Hearings . . . 5:10

2. Quota Question by 9/11 Commissioner John Lehman to Dr. Condoleezza Rice from the 9/11 Commission Hearings . . . 0:36

*3. MAS Interview with Commissioner John Lehman from The Big Talker 1210AM . . . 4:03

*4. MAS Interview with Southwest Airlines CEO Herb Kelleher from The Big Talker 1210AM . . . 2:58

*5. MAS Interview with U.S. Senator John McCain from The Big Talker 1210AM . . . 0:51

*6. MAS Interview with U.S. Senator Arlen Specter from The Big Talker 1210AM . . . 1:06

*7. MAS Interview with Former Mayor Rudy Giuliani from The Big Talker 1210AM . . . 2:58

*8. MAS Interview with Former Mayor Ed Koch from The Big Talker 1210AM . . . 2:39

*9. MAS Interview with Former Pentagon Spokeswoman Torie Clarke from The Big Talker 1210AM . . . 3:56

*10. MAS Interview with Transportation Security Administration Spokesman Nico Melendez from The Big Talker 1210AM . . . 11:53

*11. MAS Interview with U.S. Representative John Mica from The Big Talker 1210AM . . . 4:20

*12. MAS Interview with U.S. Representative Roy Blount from The Big Talker 1210AM . . . 3:04

13. Testimony from the U.S. Senate Hearing on Airline Security . . . 28:38

* Denotes material used by permission from The Big Talker 1210AM, WPHT, Philadelphia

# NOTES

## INTRODUCTION

1. Susan Schmidt, "Ashcroft Refuses to Release '02 Memo: Document Details Suffering Allowed in Interrogations." *Washington Post*, June 9, 2004, p. A01.

2. Final vote results for Roll Call 398: HR 3162 (USA PATRIOT ACT). October 24, 2001, at http://clerk.house.gov/evs/2001/roll398.xml, and Senate vote summary for HR 3162 (USA PATRIOT ACT), October 25, 2001, at http://www.senate.gov/legislative/LIS/roll_call_lists/roll_call_vote_cfm.cfm?congress=107&session=1&vote=00313

3. Carl Hulse, "THREATS AND RESPONSES: PLANS AND CRITICISMS; Pentagon Prepares a Futures Market on Terror Attacks." *The New York Times*, July 29, 2003, p. A01.

4. Remarks of Dr. John Poindexter, Director, Information Awareness Office of (Defense Advanced Research Projects Agency) DARPA, DARPA Tech 2002 Conference, August 2, 2002.

## CHAPTER 1: BOARDING

1. Opening Statement of Richard A. Clarke, Former National Coordinator for Counterterrorism, Eighth Public Hearing of the National Commission on Terrorist Attacks upon the United States, March 24, 2004, at http://www.9-11commission.gov/archive/hearing8/9-11Commission_Hearing_2004-03-24.pdf

2. Questioning of Dr. Condoleezza Rice by Richard Ben-Veniste, Ninth Public Hearing of the National Commission on Terrorist Attacks Upon the United States, April 8, 2004, at http://www.9-11commission.gov/archive/hearing9/9-11Commission_Hearing_2004-04-08.pdf

3. Questioning of Dr. Condoleezza Rice by The Honorable John F. Lehman, Ninth Public Hearing of the National Commission on Terrorist Attacks Upon the United States, April 8, 2004, at http://www.9-11commission.gov/archive/hearing9/9-11Commission_Hearing_2004-04-08.pdf
4. Ibid.

5. Ibid.

# CHAPTER 2: READY FOR DEPARTURE

1. MAS Interview with The Honorable John F. Lehman, April 10, 2004, on The Big Talker 1210AM, Philadelphia.

2. Ibid.

3. Ibid.

4. Elisabeth Bumiller and Philip Shenon, "Panel Hasn't Heard from Official It Wants Most." *The New York Times*, March 26, 2004.

5. MAS Interview with The Honorable John F. Lehman on The Big Talker 1210AM, Philadelphia, April 10, 2004.

6. Ibid.

7. Ibid.

8. Ibid.

9. Ibid.

10. Ibid.

11. Ibid.

12. Ibid.

13. Ibid.

14. Ibid.

15. Michael Smerconish, "Tough questions from tough guy on 9/11 commission." *Philadelphia Daily News*, April 12, 2004.

16. MAS Interview with Southwest Airlines CEO Herb Kelleher on The Big Talker 1210AM, Philadelphia, April 14, 2004.

17. Ibid.

18. Michael Smerconish, "Listen to Lehman: The press attention is on the wrong commissioners." *National Review Online*, April 15, 2004.

19. Ann Coulter, "Clinton's Policies Invited 9/11." *Front Page Magazine*.com, April 15, 2004.

## CHAPTER 3: TURBULENCE

1. Statement by Department of Transportation Office of Public Affairs Rep. Brian Turmail to the *Philadelphia Daily News*, e-mail from Brian Turmail to MAS, April 23, 2004.

2. David Isaac, "Death by PC." *Investors, Business Daily*, April 28, 2004.

3. Transcript from *Kudlow & Cramer*, live TV show on CNBC, April 26, 2004.

4. E-mail exchange between MAS and U.S. Department of Transportation Office of Public Affairs Rep. Brian Turmail, April 28, 2001. http://www.mastalk.com/articlefull.asp?ID=17

5. Transcript from *Kudlow & Cramer*, live TV show on CNBC, April 27, 2004.

6. Statement by Department of Transportation regarding Michael Smerconish appearance on *Kudlow & Cramer* to CNBC, April 27, 2004.

## CHAPTER 5: REACHING MACH SPEED

1. Comments of Thomas H. Kean, Chairman, National Commission on Terrorist Attacks upon the United States, January 27, 2004.

2. Testimony of Nydia Gonzalez, American Airlines Operations Specialist, regarding American Airlines Sp. 11, 2001, flight attendant Betty Ong from Flight 11, to the National Commission on Terrorist Attacks upon the United States, January 27, 2004.http://www.9-11commission.gov/hearings/hearing7/witness_gonzalez.pdf

3. Transcript of taped exchange between AA flight attendant Betty Ong and AA Operations Specialist Nydia Gonzalez, played during hearing of the National Commission on Terrorist Attacks upon the United States, January 27, 2004. http://www.9-11commission.gov/archive/hearing7/9-11Commission_Hearing_2004-01-27.pdf

4. Testimony of Edmond Soliday, United Airlines, to National Commission on Terrorist Attacks Upon the United States, January 27, 2004. http://www.9-11commission.gov/archive/hearing7/9-11Commission_Hearing_2004-01-27.pdf

5. Testimony of Gerard Arpey, CEO American Airlines, to National Commission on Terrorist Attacks Upon the United States, January 27, 2004. http://www.9-11commission.gov/archive/hearing7/9-11Commission_Hearing_2004-01-27.pdf

6. Testimony of Andrew Studdert, former CEO United Airlines, to National Commission on Terrorist Attacks upon the United States, January 27, 2004. http://www.9-11commission.gov/archive/hearing7/9 11Commission_Hearing_2004-01-27.pdf

7. Comment from National Commission on Terrorist Attacks upon the United States commissioner, Bob Kerrey during hearing on January 27, 2004. http://www.9-11commission.gov/archive/hearing7/9-11Commission_Hearing_2004-01-27.pdf

8. Testimony of James M. Loy, Deputy Secretary of the Department of Homeland Security to the National Commission on Terrorist Attacks upon the United States, January 27, 2004. http://www.9-11commission.gov/archive/hearing7/9-11Commission_Hearing_2004-01-27.pdf

9. MAS Interview with Arizona Senator John McCain on The Big Talker 1210AM, Philadelphia, April 19, 2004.

## CHAPTER 6: LIFT YOUR TRAY TABLES AND FASTEN YOUR SEATBELTS

1. Williams v. Trans World Airlines, 509 F.2d 942 (2d Cir. 1975).

2. Ibid at 946.

3. Al-Qudhai'een v. America West Airlines, 267 F.Supp.2d 841 (S.D. Ohio, 2003).

4. Ibid at 845.

5. Dasrath v. Continental Airlines, 228 F.Supp. 2d 531 (D.N.J. 2002).

6. North Jersey Media Group, Inc. v. Ashcroft, 308 F.3d 198 (3rd Cir. 2002) *cited* in Dasrath v. Continental Airlines, 228 F.Supp.2d 531, 538 (N.J. 2002).

7. Ibid at 538.

8. 49 U.S.C.S. §40127, 49 U.S.C.S. §41310, 49 U.S.C.S. §§41702, 41712.

9. 49 U.S.C. 44902(b), 14 CFR 91.3 and 49 CFR 1544.2 15(c).

10. Natural Resources Defense Council v. U.S. Environmental Protection Agency, 725 F.2d 761, 767 (D.C. Ct. App. 1984).

11. Continental Airlines, 2004 DOT.

12. United Air Lines, 2003 DOT.

13. Ibid at 4.

14. Ibid.

15. Answer of American Airlines, OST-2003-15046 (Jun. 13, 2003), 1 n.1.

16. Notice of Enforcement Action, OST-2003-15046 (Apr. 25, 2003), exhibit. 1.

17. Answer of American Airlines, 7.

18. 49 U.S.C.S. §44902.

19. Answer of American Airlines, 9.

20. Notice of Enforcement Action, exhibit 2.

21. Answer of American Airlines, 10.

22. 49 U.S.C.S. §§41702, 41712(a) (2004).

23. Answer of the Office of Aviation Enforcement, OST 2003-15046 (Jul. 22, 2003), 17.

24. Order Denying Motion to Dismiss, OST 2003-15046 (Aug. 21, 2003).

25. Consent Order, OST 2003-15046 (Feb. 27, 2004), 1-2.

26. Ibid.

## CHAPTER 7: THE REAL STORY OF FLIGHT 93

1. Submitted statement of Melendez Perez to the Seventh public hearing of the National Commission on Terrorist Attacks Upon the United States, January 26, 2004.
http://www.9-11commission.gov/hearings/hearing7/witness_melendez.htm

2. Ibid.

3. Ibid.

4. Comment by National Commission on Terrorist Attacks upon the United States commissioner Richard Ben-Veniste to Melendez-Perez, January 26, 2004. http://www.9-11commission.gov/archive/hearing7/9-11Commission_Hearing_2004-01-26.pdf

5. Submitted statement of Melendez-Perez to the Seventh Public Hearing of the National Commission on Terrorist Attacks upon the United States, January 26, 2004. http://www.9-11commission.gov/hearings/hearing7/witness_melendez.htm

6. Ibid.

7. Comment by National Commission on Terrorist Attacks upon the United States commissioner Richard Ben-Veniste to Melendez-Perez, January 26, 2004. http://www.9-11commission.gov/archive/hearing7/9-11Commission_Hearing_2004-01-26.pdf

8. Joint Inquiry into Intelligence Community Activities before and after the Terrorist Attacks of September 11, 2001, released December 2002, p. 143. http://a257.g.akamaitech.net/7/257/2422/24jul20031400/www.gpoaccess.gov/serialset/creports/pdf/fullreport_errata.pdf

9. Ted Bridis, "Investigators: Hijackers, not passengers, deliberately crashed Flight 93." Associated Press, August 7, 2003.

10. "Gov't: Hijacker Crashed Flight 93 on 9/11." Associated Press, August 7, 2003. http://tv.ksl.com/index.php?nid=85&sid=41904

11. MAS Interview with Alice Hoglan on The Big Talker 1210AM, Philadelphia, August, 2003.

12. Ibid.

13. Ibid.

14. Ibid.

15. Ibid.

16. The Honorable John F. Lehman speaking at the U.S. Naval Institute 130th Annual Meeting and Annapolis Naval History Symposium, March 31, 2004. http://www.usni.org/seminars/annualmeeting/04/annualmeeting04Lehman.htm

## CHAPTER 8: CAPTAIN GIULIANI

1. MAS interview with Mayor Ed Koch on The Big Talker 1210AM, Philadelphia, May 4, 2004.

2. Rudolph W. Giuliani, *Leadership*. Miramax Books. New York. P. 182, Copyright 2002.

3. Excerpts from articles quoting John F. Lehman and Thomas Von Essen at hearing for the National Commission on Terrorist Attacks upon the United States, May 18, 2004: Corky Siemaszko, "Probers Put all Rudy's Men on Hot Seat." *New York Daily News*, May 19, 2004, and Associated Press, "Quotes from 9/11 Commission Hearings." *Phillyburbs*.com, May 18, 2004.

4. Ibid.

5. Excerpts from testimony of New York City Mayor Rudy Giuliani to the National Commission on Terrorist Attacks upon the United States, May 19, 2004. Devlin Barrett, "Giuliani: N.Y. Never Warned About Attack." Associated Press, May 19, 2004.

6. John F. Lehman, "Missing a Chance to Learn from 9/11." *The New York Times*, May 26, 2004.

7. MAS Interview with Mayor Rudy Giuliani on The Big Talker 1210AM, Philadelphia, May 21, 2004.

## CHAPTER 9: AIRPORT
## (NOT JUST THE MOVIE, I'M AFRAID)

1. Transcript *60 Minutes* Interview on CBS of Secretary Norman Mineta by Steve Kroft, December 2, 2001.

2. Ibid.

3. Ibid.

4. Statement of Norman Y. Mineta, Secretary of the Department of Transportation, Before the U.S. Commission on Civil Rights, October 12, 2001. http://www.usccr.gov/pubs/tragedy/imm1012/mineta2.htm

5. Remarks by Norman Y. Mineta, Secretary of the Department of Transportation, at the University of Rochester Annual Meliora Weekend, October 12, 2001. http://usinfo.state.gov/usa/civilrights/mineta.htm

6. Ibid.

7. Curt Anderson, "FBI Urges Increased Vigilance for July 4" Associated Press. July 1, 2004. http://story.news.yahoo.com/news?tmpl=story2&u=/ap/20040702/ap_on_go_ca_st_pe/terror_threat

8. Amy Kaplan, "Police Seek 3 Who Photographed Ben Franklin Bridge." KYW Newsradio 1060. Philadelphia. July 2, 2004.

9. E-mail from U.S. Department of Transportation to major airlines, September 21, 2001. http://airconsumer.ost.dot.gov/rules/20010921.htm

10. Memo sent from Delta CEO to Delta Airlines employees, September 21, 2001. http://airconsumer.ost.dot.gov/rules/FWRethics.htm

11. Department of Justice press release, October 11, 2001. http://www.fbi.gov/pressrel/pressrel01/101101.htm

12. E-mail from Department of Transportation to major U.S. airlines, October 12, 2001. http://airconsumer.ost.dot.gov/rules/20011012.htm

13. U.S. Government warning regarding possible terrorist attacks, October 29, 2001, "Ashcroft: New terror attack possible." Cnn.com. http://www.cnn.com/2001/US/10/29/gen.attack.on.terror/

14. Department of Transportation document on guidance for screeners and other security personel, November 16, 2001. http://airconsumer.ost.dot.gov/rules/20011116.htm

15. Ibid.

16. Answers to Frequently Asked Questions Concerning the Air Travel of People Who Are or Appear to Be of Arab, Middle Eastern or South Asian Descent and/or Muslim or Sikh by the Department of Transportation, November 19, 2001. http://airconsumer.ost.dot.gov/rules/20011119.htm

17. Ibid.

18. Briefing on homeland security held by Secretary Ridge, December 3, 2001. http://www.whitehouse.gov/news/releases/2001/12/20011203-5.html

19. Howard Chua-Eoan, "Terror on Flight 800," *Time*, July 29, 1996, p. 29.

20. White House Commission on Aviation Safety and Security, Final Report (February 12, 1997).

21. Ibid.
22. Ibid. at Appendix A.

23. Ibid.

24. General Accounting Office, *Terrorism and Drug Trafficking: Threats and Roles of Explosives and Narcotics Detection Technology*, GAO/NSIAD/RCED-96-76BR, March 1996, at 11.

25. Ibid.

26. Richard Lowry, "*Profiles in Cowardice*," *National Review*, January 28, 2002.

27. Michael Higgins, "*Looking the Part: With Criminal Profiles Being Used More Widely to Spot Possible Terrorists and Drug Couriers, Claims of Bias Are Also on the Rise*," *ABA Journal*, November 1997.

28. Teresa Anderson, "*All Systems Go? Airlines and Airports' Protection from Terrorism*," *Security Management*, July 1998.

29. "*Profiles in Cowardice*."

30. General Accounting Office, *Computer Assisted Passenger Screening System Faces Significant Implementation Challenges*, GAO-04-385, February 2004, at 2.

31. Department of Homeland Security, Notice of Status of System of Records. 68 F.R. 45265, 45266 (August 1, 2003).

32. Transportation Security Administration, *CAPPS II Myths and Facts*, at http://www.tsa.gov/public/display?content=0900051980089895, accessed on June 21, 2004.

33. Bartholomew Elias, Congressional Research Service, *Aviation Security: Issues Before Congress Since September 11th*, 2001, RL31969, February 6, 2004, at 9.

34. GAO-04-385, at Highlights.

35. Jon Hilkevitch, "*Registered Flier Program to Be Tested, O'Hare Not Among Five Airports Chosen for TSA Experiment*," *Chicago Tribune*, June 17, 2004, at 14.

## CHAPTER 10: NORMAN AND ME

1. Frederick Schauer, *Profiles, Probabilities and Stereotypes*. The Belknap Press of Harvard University Press, Cambridge, Massachusetts, 2003, p. 5, p. 216.

2. MAS interview with Frederick Schauer, on The Big Talker 1210AM, Philadelphia, June 16, 2004.

3. MAS Interview with Torie Clarke, former Assistant Secretary of Defense for Public Affairs, on The Big Talker 1210AM, Philadelphia, May 27, 2004.

4. Statement of Norman Y. Mineta, Secretary of the Department of Transportation, Before the U.S. Commission on Civil Rights, October 12, 2001. http://www.usccr.gov/pubs/tragedy/imm1012/mineta2.htm

## CHAPTER 11: TSA: TROUBLE SECURING AIRLINES

1. Staff Statement Number Three, National Commission on Terrorist Attacks Upon the United States, January 27, 2004.http://www.9-11commission.gov/hearings/hearing7/staff_statement_3.pdf

2. Ibid.

3. E-mail from TSA to The Big Talker 1210AM, Philadelphia, offering Nico Melendez to come on Michael Smerconish morning show, May 28, 2004.

4. From Shannon McCaffrey, "U.S. Seeks 7 in Terror Alert: Al-Qaeda Attack Plot Is Alleged." *The Philadelphia Inquirer*, May 27, 2004, Associated Press, "FBI Asks Help on Terrorists." *Philadelphia Daily News*, May 27, 2004, and Susan Schmidt and John Mintz, "FBI Seeks Tips on 7 Linked to Al Qaeda Officials Convinced Attack on U.S. Is Being Planned." *Washington Post*, May 27, 2004, and CNN.com, "Transcript: Ashcroft, Mueller news conference." May 26, 2004. http://www.cnn.com/2004/US/05/26/terror.threat.transcript/

5. Ibid.

6. Ibid.

7. Pictures of 7 terror suspects from May 26, 2004, press conference by John Ashcroft and Robert Mueller, CBSnews.com, May 27, 2004. http://www.cbsnews.com/stories/2004/05/27/terror/main619874.shtml

8. From Shannon McCaffrey, "U.S. Seeks 7 in Terror Alert: Al-Qaeda Attack Plot Is Alleged." *The Philadelphia Inquirer*, May 27, 2004, Associated Press, "FBI Asks Help on Terrorists." *Philadelphia Daily News*, May 27, 2004, and Susan Schmidt and John Mintz, "FBI Seeks Tips on 7 Linked to Al Qaeda Officials Convinced Attack on U.S. Is Being Planned." *Washington Post*, May 27, 2004.

9. Associated Press, "Profiles of 7 Suspected al Qaeda Operatives." May 26, 2004.

10. MAS Interview with TSA Rep. Nico Melendez, on The Big Talker 1210AM, Philadelphia, May 28, 2004.

## CHAPTER 12: CONGRESS AIR

1. Associated Press, "Passenger Profiling Scrutinized," July 4, 2004. http://archives.californiaaviation.org/airport/msg21986.html

2. MAS Interview with Congressman John Mica, on The Big Talker 1210AM, Philadelphia, June 3, 2004.

3. MAS interview with Congressman Roy Blunt, on the Big Talker 1210AM, Philadelphia, June 21, 2004.

## CHAPTER 13: FINAL DESTINATION: THE U.S. SENATE

1. Fred Reid, Memo to "All Delta Employees Worldwide," September 21, 2001. http://airconsumer.ost.dot.gov/rules/FWRethics.htm

2. Norman Strickman, DOT e-mail to all major airlines regarding nondiscrimination concerning religion and national origin, September 21, 2001 http://airconsumer.ost.dot.gov/rules/20010921.htm

3. MAS Interview with Alice Hoglan, The Big Talker 1210AM, Philadelphia, June 24, 2004.

4. Opening Statement of U.S. Senator Richard Shelby, Alabama, Chairman, Senate Appropriations Subcommittee on Transportation, Treasury and General Government Hearing: Passenger Screening and Airline Authority to Deny Boarding, June 24, 2004. http://shelby.senate.gov/news/record.cfm?id=223113

5. Opening Statement of U.S. Senator Arlen Specter, Pennsylvania, Senate Appropriations Subcommittee on Transportation, Treasury and General Government Hearing: Passenger Screening and Airline Authority to Deny Boarding, June 24, 2004.

6. Senate Appropriations Subcommittee on Transportation, Treasury and General Government Hearing: Passenger Screening and Airline Authority to Deny Boarding, June 24, 2004.

7. Ibid.

8. Ibid.

9. Ibid.

10. Ibid.

11. Ibid.

12. Ibid.

13. Ibid.

14. Ibid.

15. Ibid.

16. Ibid.

17. Ibid.

18. Email from Michael Klein to MAS, 6/24/04

19. 49 USCS § 44902

20. 49 USCS § 40127 (a)

21. 49 USCS § 41310

22. 49 USCS § 41702

23. "Answers to Frequently Asked Questions Concerning the Air Travel of People Who Are or May Appear to Be of Arab, Middle Eastern or South Asian Descent and/or Muslim or Sikh." Department of Transportation, November 19, 2001.

# INDEX